Essential

MUSIC

DEFINITIONS • COMPOSERS • THEORY
• INSTRUMENT & VOCAL RANGES •

◆

The most practical and useful music dictionary
for students and professionals

LINDSEY C. HARNSBERGER

Alfred Publishing Co., Inc.
Los Angeles

Library of Congress Cataloging-in-Publication Data

Harnsberger, Lindsey, date.

Alfred's essential dictionary of music: definitions, composers, theory, instrumental & vocal ranges / Lindsey Harnsberger.

p. cm.

ISBN 0-88284-728-7 (alk. paper)

1. Music—Dictionaries. I. Title.

ML 100.H33 1966

780'.3—dc20

Special thanks to:

Jennifer Balue, Kyleen Denney, Joe Stoebenau, Patrick Wilson, Tom Gerou,
Ted Engelbart, Judy Teele, Mark and Jodi Malone, Gwen Bailey-Harbour,
Mary Kate Karr, the estate of George Gershwin, Fred and Therese Harnsberger
Morty and Iris Manus, and especially Ron Manus.

Cover design: Carol Kascsak / Ted Engelbart
Interior design & production: Tom Gerou

Cover artwork:

Fender Stratocaster—courtesy Fender Musical Instruments, Inc.;
Egyptian lyre—Pictoral History Research; Portraits of J. S. Bach,
Beethoven, Gershwin and Paganini—Archive für Kunst und
Geschichte, London; Woody Guthrie—Culver Pictures, PNI;
Ma Rainey and Musicians—Archive Photos, PNI

Interior instrument illustrations:

From MUSICAL INSTRUMENTS OF THE WORLD.
Copyright © 1976 by the Diagram Visual Group Ltd.
Reprinted with permission of Diagram Visual Information Ltd,
London.

Second Edition

Table of Contents

Abbreviations

Ban.	Bantu (*an African language*)
c.	circa (*approximately*)
Eng.	English
Fr.	French
Ger.	German
Gr.	Greek
Heb.	Hebrew
Hin.	Hindi
It.	Italian
Jap.	Japanese
Lat.	Latin
Pol.	Polish
Por.	Portuguese
Ru.	Russian
Sp.	Spanish

Words in *italics* are cross-references.

Pronunciations

Syllables in capital letters are accented.

LONG VOWELS

ay	long "a" as in da~
ee	long "e" as in kee
ei	long "i" as in ligh
oh	long "o" as in go

SHORT VOWELS

a	short "a" as in c~
e or *eh*	short "e" as in te
i	short "i" as in sh
o or *ah*	short "o" as in h~
u	short "u" as in cu
uh	as in look

CONSONANTS

zh	as in vision

All other consonants keep their standard pronunciations.

DEFINITIONS

A

A: Abbreviation for *alto*.

a, à (It., Fr., *ah*): At, by, for, in, to, with.

a2: See *a deux*.

ab (Ger., *ahp*): Off.

abandon, abbandono (Fr., *ah-bawn-DOHN*; It., *ahb-BAHN-doh noh*): Abandon, free, passionate.

a battuta (It., *ah baht-TOO-tah*): With the beat.

abbellire (It., *ahb-bel-LEE-reh*): To ornament.

abellimenti (It., *ah-bel-lee-MEN-tee*): Ornaments or *embellishments*.

absolute music: Instrumental music without extramusical associations, as opposed to *program music*.

absolute pitch: The ability to recognize the actual pitch of any note heard.

a cappella (It., *ah kahp-PEL-lah*): Without accompaniment.

accelerando (It., *aht-chel-le-RAHN-doh*): Becoming gradually faster. Abbreviated accel.

accent, accénto (Eng.; It., *aht-CHEN-toh*): To emphasize a note. Indicated by the symbol >.

accented passing tone: See *passing tone*.

accessory notes: See *auxiliary notes*.

acciaccatura (It., *aht-chahk-kah-TOO-rah*): A *grace note* which is played simultaneously with the principal note and immediately released. See p. 305.

accidentals: *Sharps, double sharps, flats, double flats* or *natural signs* used to raise, lower, or return a note to its normal pitch. Their effect lasts through the remainder of the same measure.

accompaniment: Vocal or instrumental parts that accompany a melody.

accord, accordo (Fr., *ahk*-KOHR; It., *ahk*-KOHR-*doh*): Chord.

accordare, accorder (It., *ahk-kor*-DAH-*ray*; Fr., *ahk-kor*-DAY): To *tune*.

accordion: A portable musical instrument where a keyboard and buttons control air which is drawn and pushed by bellows across reeds that vibrate to produce a sound. See p. 334 for range.

accordion

acoustic: A non-amplified or non-electric instrument.

acoustics: The science of sound.

action: The mechanism of an instrument that is set into motion by the performer's fingers.

adagietto (It., *ah-dah*-JET-*toh*): A tempo slightly faster than *adagio*.

adagio (It., *ah*-DAH-*joh*): A slow tempo which is faster than *largo* and slower than *andante*.

added sixth: A triad including the sixth note above the *root*. For example: C, E, G, A.

addolorato (It., *ahd-doh-loh*-RAH-*toh*): With grief.

à demi-jeu (Fr., *ah* DEH-*mee* ZHUH): With half the power.

à demi-voix (Fr., *ah* DEH-*mee* VWAH): With half the power of the voice.

à deux, a due (Fr., *ah* DUH; It., *ah* DOO-*eh*): For two instruments or voices, abbreviated a2. When two parts are written on one *stave*, it indicates that both are to play in unison.

à deux mains (Fr., *ah* DUH *mah*): With two hands.

a due corde (It., *ah DOO-eh COR-deh*): On two strings.

A dur (Ger., *ah door*): The key of A major.

ad libitum, ad lib. (Lat., *ahd LEE-bee-toom*): Optional, or at will. The performer may omit a section, improvise freely, or alter the tempo.

ADSR: In *synthesis*, the abbreviation for "attack, decay, sustain, release."

Aeolian (*ay-OH-lee-an*): A *mode* that corresponds to the half- and whole-step patterns created when playing A to A on the white keys of the piano. It is the same as the natural minor scale. See p. 296.

aeolian harp: A stringed instrument that sounds when struck by a blowing wind.

aerophones: Instruments that produce sounds through the vibration of air.

affetuoso (It., *ahf-fet-too-OH-soh*): With tender emotion.

afflitto (It., *af-FLEE-toh*): Sad, melancholy.

affrettando (It., *ahf-fret-TAHN-doh*): Hurrying.

aftertouch: The ability of an electronic keyboard to determine how hard a key is being depressed after it has been struck.

agilità, agilité (It., *ah-jee-lee-TAH*; Fr., *ah-zhe-LE-teh*): Light or lively.

agilmente (It., *ah-jeel-MEN-tay*): Lightly.

agitato (It., *ah-jee-TAH-toh*): Agitated.

Agnus Dei (Lat., *AH-nyoos DAY-ee*): The fifth part from the Ordinary of the Mass. Literally means "Lamb of God."

agogic accent: To emphasize a note by giving it a longer duration than normal.

air: A *song, melody* or *tune*.

Ais (*Ger.*, AH-*iss*): The note A-sharp.

al, all', alla, alle (*It.*, *ahl*, *ahll*, AHL-*lah*, AHL-*leh*): In the style of

Alberti bass: An accompaniment derived from broken chords usually found in the left-hand part of keyboard music.

Alberti bass in a sonata by Mozart

album 1: A collection of musical pieces either printed or recorded. **2:** Slang for a 12-inch vinyl recording.

Albumblatt (*Ger.*, AHL-*boom-blot*): A short piece usually for piano.

al coda (*It.*, *ahl* KOH-*dah*): To the coda.

aleatory music (*al-ee-ah-*TOR-*ree*): When elements of a piec of music are determined by chance.

al fine (*It.*, *ahl* FEE-*nay*): To the end.

algorithm: The process of how a *synthesizer* solves a problem.

alla breve (*It.*, AHL-*lah* BREH-*veh*): A tempo indication ¢ where the half note recieves the beat rather than th quarter note. $\frac{2}{2}$ as opposed to $\frac{4}{4}$. Also called *cut time*

allargando (*It.*, *ahl-lahr-*GAHN-*doh*): Becoming slower and broader.

allegretto (*It.*, *ahl-leh-*GRET-*toh*): A lively, quick tempo that slightly slower than *allegro*.

allegro (*It.*, *ahl-*LAY-*groh*): Cheerful, quick or fast.

allemande (*Fr.*, *ahl-le-*MAWND) **1:** A German dance usually in *duple meter*, commonly found in a *suite*. **2:** A German dance in $\frac{3}{4}$ time.

allentando (It., *ahl-len-TAHN-doh*): Slowing.

All'ottava (It., *ahl oht-TAH-vah*): At the octave. Play the passage one octave higher than written. Abbreviated $8 - - - - \urcorner$ or $8va - - - - \urcorner$

alphorn: A large Alpine horn from Switzerland which is made of wood and can vary in length anywhere from 7-12 feet.

al segno (It., *ahl SAY-nyoh*): Go to the sign.

alteration: The raising or lowering of a note with an *accidental*.

altered chord: A chord in which one or more notes have been raised or lowered chromatically.

alto (It., *AHL-toh*) **1:** The lowest female singing voice sometimes called a *contralto*. See p. 336 for range. **2:** A high, falsetto male singing voice. **3:** *Viola*. **4:** High.

alto clarinet: See *clarinet*.

alto clef: The C clef usually used by the *viola*, where middle C is found on the third line of the staff. 𝄡

alto flute: See *flute*.

alto saxophone: See *saxophone*.

alto trombone: See *trombone*.

altra, altro (It., *AHL-trah, AHL-troh*): Another.

altra volta (It., *AHL-trah VOHL-tah*): Encore.

AM: Abbreviation for *amplitude modulation*.

amabile (It., *ah-MAH-bee-leh*): Tender, gentle.

A moll (Ger., *ah mohl*): The key of A minor.

amore (It., *ah-MOH-reh*): Love.

amp: Abbreviation for *amplifier*.

amplifier: A device used to strengthen the power of the

sound of an electronic instrument.

amplitude 1: The volume of a sound. **2:** In electronic music, the height of a *waveform* which determines the volume of a sound.

amplitude modulation: To alter the *amplitude* of an electronic instrument or device.

am Steg (Ger., *ahm* SHTEK): On the bridge.

anacrusis (Gr., *ah-nah-*CROO-*sis*): Upbeat or *pickup*.

analog: When voltage is used to control a sound in *synthesis*. As opposed to *digital*.

analysis: The study of form and structure in music.

ancòra (It., *ahn-*KOH-*rah*) **1:** Still, again. **2:** Repeat, *encore*.

andante (It., *ahn-*DAHN-*teh*): A moderate, graceful tempo, slower than *allegretto* and faster than *adagio*.

andantino (It., *ahn-dahn-*TEE-*noh*) **1:** A tempo slightly faster than *andante*. **2:** A tempo slightly slower than *andante*.

anglaise (Fr., *awn-*GLEZ): English.

anima (It., AH-*nee-mah*): Spirit, life.

animato, animoso (It., *ah-nee-*MAH-*toh, ah-nee-*MOH-*zoh*): Animated, spirited.

answer: In a *fugue*, the second entry of the *subject* which is at a different pitch than the first entry.

antecedent 1: The first phrase of a musical *period*. **2:** The *theme* or *subject* of a *canon* or *fugue*. Also see *consequent*.

anthem: A Protestant choral composition, with religious text.

anticipation: One or more nonharmonic tones played before the chord in which it belongs.

antiphon: A short *chant* sung before and after a *psalm* or *canticle* during the Roman Catholic Mass.

antiphonal: When separate groups of performers alternate or respond to each other. Also see *responsoral*.

appassionato (It., *ahp-pahs-syoh-NAH-toh*): Passionately.

appoggiando (It., *ahp-pohd-JAHN-doh*): Emphasized.

appoggiatura (It., *ahp-pohd-jah-TOO-rah*): A nonharmonic grace note that resolves stepwise to a harmonic note. See p. 305.

arabesque (Fr., *ah-rah-BESK*) **1:** A imaginative piano piece. **2:** An ornamented passage accompanying or varying a *theme*.

arcato (It., *ahr-KAH-toh*): Bowed. To *bow* a stringed instrument.

archet, archetto (Fr., *ar-SHAY*; It., *ahr-KET-toh*): To bow a stringed instrument.

arco (It., *AHR-koh*): To bow a stringed instrument.

ardito (It., *AHR-dee-toh*): Spirited, bold.

aria (It., *AH-ree-ah*): A solo vocal piece usually associated with *opera* and *oratorios*.

aria buffa (It., *AH-ree-ah BOOF-fah*): A comic *aria*.

arioso (It., *ah-ree-OH-zoh*): Lyrically.

arpa (It., *AHR-pah*): *Harp*.

arpeggiato, arpeggiando (It., *ahr-ped-JAH-toh, ahr-ped-JAHN-doh*): Harp-like, arpeggiated.

arpeggiator: A device on a *synthesizer* that automatically plays chords as an *arpeggio*.

arpeggio (It., *ahr-PED-joh*): The notes of a chord played one after another.

arpeggione (It., *ahr-ped-JOH-nee*): A fretted instrument similar to a *guitar* that is played with a *bow*.

arraché (Fr., *ahr-rah-SHAY*): Very strong *pizzicato*.

arrangement: An adaptation of a composition for a medium other than that which it was originally written.

ars antiqua (*Lat., ahrs ahn-TEE-kwah*)**:** Literally, "old art." Used to indicate music of the 12th and 13th centuries, especially the music of Leonin and Perotin.

ars nova (*Lat., ahrs NOV-vah*)**:** Literally, "new art." Used to indicate the music of the 14th century, especially the music of Machaut and Landini.

articulation: The manner in which notes are performed, such as *staccato* or *legato*.

artificial harmonic: On stringed instruments, a *harmonic* played on a fingered or fretted string, rather than an open string.

As (*Ger., ahss*)**:** The note A-flat.

ASCAP: Abbreviation for American Society of Composers, Authors and Publishers.

As dur (*Ger., ahss door*)**:** The key of A-flat major.

assai (*It., ahs-SEI*)**:** Very, extremely.

assez (*Fr., ahs-SAY*)**:** Enough, fairly.

assoluto (*It., ahs-soh-LOO-toh*)**:** Absolute.

a tempo (*It., ah TEM-poh*)**:** Return to the original *tempo* or speed.

atonal (*ay-TOH-nul*)**:** Music without a tonal center or key.

attacca (*It., aht-TAHK-kah*)**:** Continue immediately to next section or movement without a break.

attack: The act of beginning a note or phrase.

attendant keys: Those keys relative to a major or minor scale. For example, the attendant keys of C major are D minor, E minor, F major, G major and A minor.

attenuator: A device that adjusts the *amplitude* of a signal in *synthesis*.

audio: The electronic representation of sound.

audition: To perform for a group of judges who evaluate the performer's skill.

Aufschwung (Ger., OWF-*shvoong*)**:** Soaring.

augmentation: Elongating the duration of notes.

augmented: Raised.

augmented triad: A *major triad* with the fifth raised a *half step*. The C augmented triad is C, E and G♯.

augmented interval: An *interval* raised by a *half step*.

augmented sixth chord: A chord that includes the interval of an augmented sixth, that resolves outward to an octave. See *French sixth, German sixth, Italian sixth*.

aulos (Gr., OW-*lohs*)**:** An ancient Greek double-reed wind instrument.

authentic cadence: A *cadence* that ends with the dominant (V) chord progressing to the tonic (I) chord. Also see *perfect cadence*.

Authentic mode: A *mode* whose key note is the lowest note. As opposed to a *plagal mode*, whose keynote is a fourth higher than the lowest note.

Autoharp: A kind of *zither* that is strummed and has buttons that allow chords to change by depressing them.

auxiliary notes: A note a *whole step* above or below the main note.

avec (Fr., ah-VEK)**:** With.

axe: Slang for a musical instrument.

B

B

B.: Abbreviation for *bass*.

B (Ger., *beh*): B-flat.

baby grand: The smallest sized grand piano.

back beat: A popular style of drumming where the second and fourth beats of a measure are emphasized.

backup group: Singers that accompany a lead vocalist.

badinage, badinerie (Fr., *bah-dee*-NAHZH, *bah-dee-neh*-REE): A playful dance occasionally found in a *suite*.

bagatelle (Fr., *bah-gah*-TEL): Short instrumental pieces.

bagpipe: An ancient *wind instrument* that consists of several *reed* pipes which are attached to a bag that is filled with air by the player. The bag is held under the arm and squeezed to force air through the pipes. One of the pipes, called a *chanter*, has finger holes to play melodies and the other pipes are called *drones* which play a single low pitch.

balalaika (Ru., *bah-lah*-LEI-*kah*): Three-stringed Russian instrument similar to a *guitar* and triangular in shape.

ballabile (It., *bahl*-LAH-*bee-leh*): In the style of a dance.

ballad 1: A *song* that tells a story. **2:** A slow sentimental *song*. **3:** Originally a *song* accompanying dancing.

ballade (Fr., *bahl*-LAHD) **1:** A dramatic instrumental *composition*. **2:** A medieval poetic French *song*.

Ballade (Ger., *bahl*-LAH-*de*): German vocal or instrumental pieces based on historical or legendary subjects.

ballata (It., *bahl*-LAH-*tah*): A medieval polyphonic Italian *song*.

ballet (Fr., *bal*-LAY): A dance set to music that depicts a story.

ballo (It., BAHL-*loh*): Dance.

band 1: An ensemble consisting of woodwind, brass and percussion instruments. For example, *marching band*, *concert band* or *symphonic band*. **2:** A full symphony orchestra. **3:** Slang for a group of performers of popular music, for example a *rock* band.

bandola (Sp., bahn-DOH-lah): Instruments in the *lute* family that are similar to the *mandolin*.

banjo: A *fretted stringed instrument* with a long neck like a guitar and a circular body in the shape of a small drum covered with parchment. It is available with either four or five strings. See p. 331 for ranges.

banjo

bar: A *measure*.

barbershop quartet: A four-part male vocal quartet that was popular in America at the beginning of the 20th century.

barcarolle (Fr., bahr-kah-RULL): Music in the style of songs sung by Venetian gondoliers, usually in $\frac{6}{8}$ time.

baritone: The male singing voice which is between the *bass* and *tenor*. See p. 336 for range.

baritone clef: The F clef on the third line of the staff.

baritone horn: A brass instrument in the *baritone* range with three *valves* that is used in *orchestras* and *bands*. Also see *euphonium*. See p. 328 for range.

baritone saxophone: See *saxophone*.

baritone horn

bar line: A vertical line that divides *measures* or *bars*.

baroque: The historical period of music roughly from 1600 to 1750.

B

barre (Fr., *bahr*): In guitar or lute playing, the fretting of several strings with one finger. Literally means "bar."

barrel organ: A 19th-century portable organ.

bass 1: The lowest male singing voice. See p. 336 for range. **2:** The lowest sounding part of a musical composition. **3:** The lowest instrument of an instrumental family. **4:** The *double bass*.

bassa (It., BAHS-*sah*): Deep or low. The marking 8*va* bassa (or 8*vb*) means to play the indicated music one octave lower than it is written. See *ottava bassa*.

bass clarinet: See *clarinet*.

bass clef: The F clef on the fourth line of the staff. 𝄢

bass drum: The largest and lowest sounding drum of indefinite pitch.

basset horn: An *alto clarinet* pitched in F.

bass flute: See *flute*.

bass guitar: A fretted instrument with four, five or six strings tuned an *octave* lower than the *guitar*. Also see *electric bass*.

basso (It., BAHS-*soh*): Bass. See *bassa*.

basso buffo (It., BAHS-*soh* BOOF-*foh*): Comical bass voice in an *opera*.

basso continuo (It., BAHS-*soh kohn*-TEE-*noo-oh*): See *figured bass*.

bassoon: The low-pitched *double-reed* bass member of the *oboe family* which has a soft mellow tone. The *contrabassoon* is pitched an *octave* lower than the bassoon. See p. 319 for ranges.

bassoon

basso ostinato: A bass part of a composition that is repeated.

basso profundo (It., BAHS-*soh proh*-FOON-*doh*): The male *bass* voice that extends below the common *bass* range.

bass saxophone: See *saxophone*.

bass viol: See *double bass*.

baton: The stick used by a conductor to lead an ensemble.

batterie, battery (Fr.; Eng., *baht-te*-REE): The *percussion* section.

battuta (It., *baht*-TOO-*tah*): See *a tempo*.

Be (Ger., *beh*): The *flat* sign ♭.

beam: The horizontal line that connects groups of *eighth notes*, *sixteenth notes*, *thirty-second notes*, etc., in place of *flags*.

beat: Unit of measurement of rhythmic time.

beats: The sound caused by two of the same notes played together that are not in tune.

bebop: A style of jazz that originated in the 1940s, characterized by extended harmonies, improvisation, complex rhythms and fast tempos.

bec (Fr., *bek*): The mouthpiece of a wind instrument.

becarre (Fr., *beh*-KAHR): The *natural* sign ♮.

beguine (*beh*-GEEN): A lively, syncopated Latin-American dance.

bel canto (It., *bel* KAHN-*toh*): Vocal style of great Italian singers of the 18th and early 19th centuries, characterized by flawless technique and beautiful tone. Literally means "beautiful singing."

bell 1: The flared end of many wind and brass instruments. **2:** A hollow metal percussion instrument that is sounded when struck by a clapper hanging inside, or an external hammer. Bells are available in various sizes.

bellicoso (It., *bel-lee-KOH-zoh*): Warlike, martial.

bell-lyra (BEL-*lee-rah*): A portable *glockenspiel*.

bells: See *glockenspiel* or *chimes*.

belly: The upper side of the soundbox of stringed instruments. Also, the soundboard of a piano.

bémol (Fr., *bay*-MULL): The *flat* sign ♭.

bend: A smooth change in pitch similar to a *portamento* or *glissando* used on *guitar*, *harmonica* and *synthesizer*, among other instruments.

Benedictus: From the *Mass*, the conclusion of the *Sanctus*. Literally, "blessed."

bequandro (It., *beh*-KWAHN-*droh*): The natural sign ♮.

berceuse (Fr., *behr*-SUHZ): A lullaby.

bergamasca (It., *behr-gah*-MAH-*skah*): An Italian peasant's dance from the 16th and 17th centuries, based on the harmonic progression of I-IV-V-I.

betont (Ger., *be*-TOHNT): Stressed, accented.

bewegt: Animated.

big band: A jazz band usually made up of groups of *woodwind*, *brass*, *percussion* and sometimes stringed instruments that played music for dancing. They were most popular from the 1920s through the 1940s.

binary form: A musical form where one section is followed by a contrasting section: AB.

bind: See *tie*.

bis (It., *bees*) **1:** Encore! **2:** Repeat the notes or section.

bisbigliando (It., *bees-bee*-LYAHN-*doh*): A soft *tremolo* effect on the *harp*. Literally means "whispering."

biscroma (It., *bees-KROH-mah*): Thirty-second note.

bitonality: When two key centers (or tonalities) are used simultaneously.

biwa (Jap., BEE-*wah*): A Japanese *lute*.

Blasinstrumente (Ger., BLAHS-*in-stroo-men-te*): Wind *instruments*.

Blechinstrumente (Ger., BLEKH-*in-stroo-men-te*): Brass *instruments*.

Blockflöte (Ger., BLOK-*fler-te*): A *recorder*.

bluegrass: A musical style from the American south characterized by quick tempos and elaborate vocals. It usually features *fiddle, banjo, mandolin, guitar* and *bass*.

blue notes: The lowered third, seventh and sometimes, fifth degrees of a major scale that create the characteristic sound of the *blues*.

blues: A kind of American music derived from *spirituals* and work songs characterized by *blue notes* and a form that is usually 12 bars long.

blues harp: Slang for a diatonic *harmonica*.

BMI: Abbreviation for Broadcast Music, Inc.

bocal (Fr., BOH-*kul*) **1:** The part of a bassoon that connects the reed to the instrument. **2:** The mouthpiece of a brass instrument.

bocca (It., BOHK-*kah*): Mouth

bocca chiusa (It., BOHK-*kah* KYOO-*sah*): Closed mouth. Singing or humming with the mouth closed.

Boehm system (*berm*): A keying system for *woodwind instruments* invented by Theobald Boehm that allows both ease of playing and correct acoustical position of the holes.

Bogen (Ger., BOH-*gen*) **1**: A *bow*. **2**: A *slur* or *tie*.

bois (Fr., *bwah*): Woodwinds.

bolero (Sp., *boh*-LEH-*roh*): A Spanish dance usually in $\frac{3}{4}$ time.

bombard: Bass *shawm*

bombardon: *Tuba.*

bones: Percussion instrument consisting of two bones or sticks which are clicked together.

bongos: Small Cuban drums where two drums of different sizes are joined together and played with the thumb and fingers of each hand.

boogie woogie: A *jazz* piano style popular in the United States during the 1920s and 1930s characterized by a steady rhythmic *ostinato* bass in the left hand.

bop: See *bebop.*

bore: The diameter of a *woodwind* or *brass* instrument.

bossa nova (Port., BOHS-*sah* NOH-*vah*): A Brazilian dance popular in the late 1950s and 1960s.

bottleneck: Slang for the glass or metal tube that is placed over a finger of the fretting hand of a guitarist playing *slide* guitar.

bouché (Fr., *boo*-SHAY): *Stopped* notes on a horn. Literally means "closed."

bouche fermée (Fr., *boosh* fehr-MAY): See *bocca chiusa.*

bouffe (Fr., *boof*): See *buffo.*

bourdon (Fr., *boor*-DOHN) **1**: A long, low *drone.* **2**: Large pipes of an *organ.* **3**: A large *bell* with a deep pitch.

bourrée (Fr., *boor*-RAY): A 17th-century French dance in a quick $\frac{2}{4}$ or $\frac{4}{4}$ time that usually begins on an *upbeat*.

bouts: The curved sides of *stringed instruments* which form a waist.

bow: The implement used in string playing that vibrates the string and allows a note to be sustained. It is made from a wooden stick that is strung with horse hair. The end held by the hand is called the *frog* and the other end is called the *tip*.

bowing 1: The technique of drawing the bowhairs across the strings of a stringed instrument. **2:** The different styles or techniques of bowing: Plain bowing, *détaché*, *martelé*, *sautillé*, *jeté*, *louré*, *staccatto*, *sul ponticello*, *sul tasto*, *tremolo* and *col legno*.

bpm: Abbreviation for beats per minute.

brace: A bracket connecting two or more *staves*.

branle (Fr., BRAWN-*le*): A 15th-century dance usually in *duple* time.

brass band: An *ensemble* of *brass instruments*.

brass instruments: The family of *wind instruments* with funnel-shaped mouthpieces that includes *trumpet*, *cornet*, *bugle*, *Flügelhorn*, *alto horn*, *French horn*, *trombone*, *baritone horn*, *euphonium* and *tuba*.

brass quintet: An ensemble usually consisting of two *trumpets*, *horn*, *trombone* and *tuba*, or a composition for that ensemble.

brass trio: An ensemble usually consisting of a *trumpet*, *horn* and *trombone*, or a composition for that ensemble.

Bratsche (Ger., BROT-*che*): *Viola*.

bravo (It., BRAH-*voh*): An exclamation of approval.

bravura (It., *brah*-VOO-*rah*, *brah*-VYOO-*rah*): Boldness, virtuosity. A piece requiring technical proficiency.

break 1: The change from the lower register to the higher register of a *clarinet*. **2:** The point a voice passes from the chest register to the head register. **3:** In *jazz*, a solo section inserted into a vocal or instrumental piece. **4:** See *caesura*.

breit (Ger., *breit*): Broad.

breve (BREH-*ve*, *brev*): Originally considered the shortest note value. Since the 16th century it is the longest note value, equaling two whole notes: |o|

bridge 1: A thin piece of wood on stringed instruments that holds the strings away from the *belly* of the instrument. **2:** Slang for *bridge passage*.

bridge passage: Musical material that connects two *themes*. A *transition*.

brillánte (It., *breel*-LAHN-*teh*): Brilliant.

brio (It., BREE-*oh*): Vigor, spirit.

brisé (Fr., *bree*-ZAY) **1:** Arpeggiated playing. **2:** *Détaché*.

broken chord: See *arpeggio*.

bruscamente (It., *broo-skah*-MEN-*teh*): Brusquely, accented.

brushes: Soft wire brushes used in place of drumsticks to strike percussion instruments.

buffo, buffa (It., BOOF-*foh*. BOOF-*fah*): Comical.

bugle 1: A valveless brass instrument that plays the notes of the *overtone* series. It commonly has a range similar to a B-flat *trumpet* and is used for military signaling. **2:** A generic term for *brass instruments*.

burden 1: A *refrain* of a *song*. **2:** The *drone* of a *bagpipe*.

Burgundian school: The group of composers in the early 15th century who bridged the styles of the Ars Nova

C

and the *Flemish schools*. Most notably the music of Guillaume Dufay.

burlesque 1: A musical farce. **2:** A comical stage show composed of various unrelated segments.

burletta (It., *boor-LET-tah*): See *burlesque*.

BWV: Abbreviation for "Bach-Werke Verzeichnis." The thematic catalogue of the works of J.S. Bach. BWV numbers are used in place of *opus* numbers when referring to J.S. Bach's compositions.

Byzantine chant: Christian church chants similar to *Gregorian chant* from the Byzantine Empire (330-1453 A.D.).

C

C: Common $\mathbf{C}$ or $\frac{4}{4}$ time.

cabaletta (It., *kah-bah-LET-tah*) **1:** A short operatic *song* in popular style with uniform *rhythm* in both the vocal and accompanimental parts. **2:** In late 19th-century Italian *opera*, the final section of an elaborate *aria* that ends with a quick uniform *rhythm*.

caccia (It., *KAHT-chah*): Chase or hunt. A two-part *canon* where the voices "chase" each other.

cacophony: A harsh discordant sound. *Dissonance*.

cadence: The *melodic* or *harmonic* ending of a phrase, section, movement or complete composition. See *authentic cadence, deceptive cadence, half cadence, imperfect cadence, perfect cadence* and *plagal cadence*.

cadenza (It., *kah-DEN-zah*): A virtuosic solo section of a piece used to display the performer's technique, either written by the composer or *improvised* by the performer.

cadenzato (It., *kah-den-ZAH-toh*): Rhythmical.

caesura (*cheh-ZOO-rah*): A symbol // indicating a sudden pause in the music.

caisse (Fr., *kess*): A drum.

cakewalk: An American dance popular in the 1890s with *ragtime* rhythms.

calando (It., *kah-LAHN-doh*): Gradually diminishing, becoming softer and sometimes slower.

calcando (It., *kahl-KAHN-doh*): Accelerating the tempo.

call and response: See *antiphonal.*

calliope (*kahl-LEI-oh-pee*): A pipe *organ* that blows steam through the pipes, rather than air.

calma, calmando, calmato (It., *KAHL-mah, kahl-MAHN-doh, kahl-MAH-toh*): Quieting, calming.

calore (It., *kah-LOH-reh*): Passion, warmth.

calypso: A style of *ballad* from Trinidad that was popular in the United States during the late 1950s and early 1960s.

cambiata (It., *kahm-BYAH-tah*): In *counterpoint*, a *dissonant* note followed by the interval of a third. Also called a *change note.*

camera (It., *KAH-meh-rah*): Music to be played outside of the church, as opposed to *chiesa* which is to be played in the church. Literally means "chamber."

camerata (It., *kah-meh-RAH-tah*): Small schools of writers and musicians in the 16th century.

camminando (It., *kahm-mee-NAHN-doh*): Walking, flowing.

campana (It., *kahm-PAH-nah*): Bell.

campanelle (It., *kahm-pah-NEL-leh*) **1:** Small *bells*. **2:** A *glockenspiel*.

cancan (Fr., *kawn-KAWN, KAN-kan*)**:** A French dance in a fast $\frac{2}{4}$ time, popular in the 19th century.

cancel: The *natural* sign.

canción (Sp., *kahn-SYOHN*)**:** *Song*.

cancrizans: See *crab canon*.

C & W: Abbreviation for *country & western*

canon: The strictest form of *counterpoint* where one melody begins, followed at a specific interval of time by the same melody note for note.

cantabile: (It., *kahn-TAH-bee-leh*)**:** Singing.

cantare (It., *kahn-TAH-reh*)**:** To sing.

cantata (It., *kahn-TAH-tah*)**:** A multi-movement vocal work for chorus and/or soloists with orchestral accompaniment that is performed without staging.

canticle: A non-metrical *hymn* used in a church service.

canto (It., *KAHN-toh*) **1:** *Melody*, *song*. **2:** The instrument or voice with the melody.

cantor (It., *KAHN-tohr*)**:** A solo singer who leads musical portions of religious services.

cantus firmus (Lat., *KAHN-toos FEER-moos*)**:** An existing *melody* that is used as the *theme* of a *polyphonic* piece. Literally means "fixed song."

canzona, canzone (It., *kahn-TSOH-nah, kahn-TSOH-neh*)**:** A *song*.

canzonet, canzonetta (It., *kahn-tsoh-NET-tah*)**:** A short instrumental or vocal piece.

Capellmeister (Ger., *kah-PEL-meis-ter*)**:** Old spelling of *Kapellmeister*.

C

capo (It., KAH-*po*, KAY-*po*) **1:** The head or beginning of a piece. **2:** The *nut* of a stringed instrument. **3:** A *capotasto*.

capotasto (It., *kah-poh*-TAH-*stoh*) **1:** A device placed around the *fretboard* or *fingerboard* of a stringed instrument that raises the pitch of the strings. Also see *barre*. **2:** The *nut* of a stringed instrument.

cappella: In the church style. Also see *a cappella*.

capriccio, caprice (It., *kah*-PREET-*choh*; Fr., *kah*-PREES): An instrumental piece in a free form.

capriccioso (It., *kah-preet*-CHOH-*zoh*): Capricious, lively, fanciful.

carillon (Fr., *kah-ree*-YON or KA-*ril-lon*): A set of bells played from a keyboard.

carol: A joyous *song* of praise, usually sung at Christmas time.

cassa (It., KAHS-*sah*): Drum.

castanets (*kas-tah*-NETS): Two small concave pieces of wood or ivory which are struck together to create a clicking sound.

castrato (It., *kah*-STRAH-*toh*): Adult male singers who were castrated as boys in order to keep the same vocal range as their bodies grew. When they had matured, they had the vocal range of a *soprano* or *alto* and the strength and lung capacity of a man. This practice stopped in the 19th century and their parts are now sung by *sopranos*, *countertenors* or *transposed* down to be sung by *tenors* or *baritones*.

catch 1: A humorous *round* or *canon* for three or more voices. **2:** See *Scotch snap*.

cavatina (It., *kah-vah*-TEE-*nah*) **1:** Songlike instrumental piece. **2:** A short solo *aria*.

C clef: A movable *clef* that indicates the placement of *middle* C on the staff. See *soprano clef, alto clef* and *tenor clef.*

C

CD: Abbreviation for Compact Disc—a *digital* recording on a small disk.

C dur (Ger., *tsa door*): The key of C major.

cédez (Fr., *say-*DAY): Slow down.

celere (It., CHEH-*leh-reh*): Quick.

celesta (It., *cheh-*LES-*tah*): A percussion instrument consisting of steel bars which are struck by hammers that are controlled by a *keyboard.* See p. 334 for range.

celesta

cello, 'cello (It., CHEL-*loh*): See *violoncello.*

cembalo (It., CHEM-*bah-loh*): *Harpsichord.*

cent: "Hundreth." A unit of measuring intervals in music. Each *half step (semitone)* is made up of 100 cents.

cesura (It., *cheh-*ZOO-*rah*): See *caesura.*

cha-cha: A Latin American dance with an insistent *rhythm.* Also called the cha-cha-cha.

chaconne (Fr., *shah-*CUNN) **1:** A continuous set of variations based on a repeating harmonic progression. It is very similar to a *passacaglia.* **2:** A sensual Mexican dance that was popular in Spain during the 16th century.

chalumeau (Fr., *shah-loo-*MOH) **1:** The lowest register of the *clarinet.* **2:** The 17th-century name for an early *oboe* or *clarinet.* **3:** The *chanter* of a *bagpipe.*

chamber music: Music for a small ensemble where each part is played by only one performer and suitable for a small room.

chamber orchestra: A small *orchestra.*

chance music: See *aleatory music.*

C

change note: See *cambiata*.

changes: Slang for chord progression.

channel: The different pathways available when transmitting MIDI data.

chanson (Fr., *shawn-SOHN*): Song.

chant: Unaccompanied *monophonic sacred plainsong* in free rhythm. Also see *Gregorian chant*.

chanter: The *pipe* on a *bagpipe* on which the melody is played.

chanterelle (Fr., *shawn-teh-REL*): The highest string on a stringed instrument.

chantey, chanty, shanty (SHAN-*tee*): A work *song* sung by sailors.

character piece: A short instrumental composition that expresses a mood or story.

Charleston: A fast American dance popular in the 1920s.

chart(s): Slang for a musical *score* and/or *parts*.

chest voice: The lower register of a voice.

chiesa (It., KYEH-*sah*): Music to be played in the church as opposed to *camera* which is to be played outside the church. Literally means "church."

chimes: A set of tuned metal tubes which are struck by a hammer. See p. 333 for range.

chitarra (It., *kee-TAR-rah*): Guitar.

chitarrone (It., *kee-tar-ROH-neh*): The largest lute.

chimes

chiusa, chiuso (It., KEW-*sah*, KEW-*soh*): Closed. Also see *stopped*.

choeur (Fr., *kuhr*): Choir, *chorus*.

choir: A group of church singers, or singers of *sacred* music.

choke: To quickly stop the vibrations of a percussion instrument.

chops: Slang for a musician's technique.

choral, chorale 1 (KOR-ul)**:** Vocal music. **2** (koh-RAHL)**:** A group of singers. Also see *choir*.

chorale prelude: *Organ* music based on a *chorale* or *hymn* tune.

chord: Three or more *tones* sounded simultaneously. Two *tones* are usually referred to as an *interval* or a *dyad*.

chordophones: Instruments whose sounds are created by means of strings stretched between two points.

chorister: A singer in a *choir*.

chorus 1: A group of singers not associated with a church. Singers of *secular* music. **2:** Music sung by such a group. **3:** The *refrain* or *burden* of a *song*. **4:** *Bagpipe*.

chromatic 1: Notes foreign to a *key* or *scale*. **2:** A series of notes moving in half steps.

chromaticism: The use of *chromatic chords* and *intervals*.

chromatic scale: A scale composed of all twelve *half steps* of an *octave*.

church modes: *Scales* originally used in medieval church music. These *modes* include the *Dorian, Phrygian, Lydian, Mixolydian, Aeolian, Locrian* and *Ionian modes*.

cimbalom (CHEEM-bah-lohm)**:** A large Hungarian *dulcimer*.

cinelli (It., chee-NEL-lee)**:** *Cymbals*.

circle of fifths: The clockwise arrangement of successive *keys* arranged in order of ascending fifths. See p. 297.

circular breathing: A breathing technique used by *wind instrument* players where air is inhaled through the nose at the same time air is expelled from the mouth. This technique allows for sound to be sustained for an indefinite length of time.

C

Cis (*Ger., tsiss*): The note C-sharp.

Cis dur (*Ger., tsiss door*): The key of C-sharp major.

Cis moll (*Ger., tsiss mohl*): The key of C-sharp minor.

cither, cithern, cittern (SITH-*er*, SITH-*ern*, SIT-*tern*): An instrument similar to a *lute* or *guitar* that was used in the 16th and 17th centuries.

clam: Slang for a wrong note.

clarinet: A group of *single-reed woodwind* instruments which are made of wood or plastic. The different types include, from highest to lowest, the E-flat clarinet, B-flat clarinet (most common), A clarinet, E-flat alto clarinet, B-flat bass clarinet, E-flat contra-alto clarinet, B-flat contrabass clarinet. See pp. 319–321 for ranges.

clarinet

classical 1: The musical period from 1750-1820 where form and structure was stressed over expression. Composers of this period include Haydn, Mozart, and Beethoven. **2:** "Serious" or "art" music as opposed to popular or *folk music*.

classical Viennese school: See *Viennese school*.

clausula (*Lat.*, KLAH-*sool-yaw*) **1:** *Cadence.* **2:** Compositions of the 12th and 13th centuries based on a short fragment of the *Gregorian chant*.

clavecin (*Fr.*, klah-veh-SAN): *Harpsichord.*

claves (KLAH-*ves*, KLAH-*vayz*): Cuban percussion instruments consisting of cylindrical wooden blocks that are struck together.

clavichord: A rectangular keyboard instrument used from the 15th to 18th centuries whose strings, rather than being plucked like a *harpsichord*, are struck by a metal wedge called a *tangent*.

C

clavier (*klah*-VEER): A *keyboard*.

clef: The symbol written at the beginning of a *staff* that indicates which notes are represented by which lines and spaces.

cloches (Fr., *klohsh*): Bells, chimes.

close harmony: When the tones of a chord are as close together as possible, usually within an *octave*. See *open harmony*.

clusters: Groups of notes a major or minor second apart that are played simultaneously.

C moll (Ger., *tsa mohl*): The key of C minor.

coda (It., KOH-*dah*) **1:** An ending section of a movement or piece. **2:** The symbol ⊕.

codetta (It., *koh*-DET-*tah*): A short *coda*.

col (It., *kohl*): With.

col arco (It., *kohl* AHR-*koh*): With the *bow*.

coll', colla (It., *kohl*, KOHL-*lah*): "With the."

col legno (It., *kohl* LEN-*yoh*): In string playing, playing with the wood (bow-stick) part of the *bow*.

coll'ottava (It., *kohl oht*-TAH-*vah*): Play the written notes and those notes one octave higher.

coll'ottava bassa (It., *kohl oht*-TAH-*vah* BAHS-*sah*): Play the written notes and those notes one octave lower.

color: See *isorhythm*.

coloratura (It., *koh-loh-rah*-TOO-*rah*): Fast, ornamented, virtuoso-like vocal music.

combo: Slang for a small group of musicians, usually less than six.

come prima (It., KOH-*meh* PREE-*mah*): As before.

come sopra (It., KOH-*meh* SOH-*prah*): As above.

comic opera: An opera with comical elements and a happy ending.

common chord 1: A major or minor *triad*. **2:** In modulation—see *pivot chord*.

common time: $\frac{4}{4}$ meter. The time signature used is **C**.

common tone: A note that is the same in two consecutive chords.

còmodo (It., KOH-*moh-doh*): Comfortable, leisurely.

comp.: In *jazz*, short for accompany. An improvised chordal accompaniment usually played by a pianist or guitarist.

composer: A person who writes music.

compound interval: An interval greater than an octave.

compound meter: A time signature where each beat is divisible by three. For example, $\frac{6}{8}$, $\frac{6}{4}$, $\frac{9}{8}$, $\frac{9}{4}$, $\frac{12}{8}$, etc. See *simple meter*.

compression: In electronic music, to reduce the extreme louds and softs of the dynamic range.

compressor: A device used for *compression*.

con (It., *kohn*): With.

concert: A public performance of music.

concertante (It., *kohn-chehr*-TAHN-*teh*): A piece for two or more soloists with orchestral accompaniment.

concert band: An ensemble consisting of *woodwind*, *brass* and *percussion* instruments.

concert grand: The largest *grand piano*.

concertina (It., *kon-chehr*-TEE-*nah*): A small instrument similar to an *accordion* but has a hexagonal shape and uses buttons rather than a *keyboard*.

concertino (It., *kohn-chehr*-TEE-*noh*) **1:** A short *concerto* usually in one movement. **2:** The group of soloists in a *concerto grosso*.

concertmaster: The first violinist in an *orchestra*.

concerto (It., *kohn-CHEHR-toh*)**:** A composition for orchestra and soloist.

concerto grosso (It., *kohn-CHEHR-toh GROHS-soh*)**:** A baroque *concerto* that uses a full orchestra (*ripieno*) and a group of soloists (*concertino*).

concert overture: An *overture* written as an independent composition, not as an introduction to a larger work. Frequently used to open a concert.

concert pitch 1: The sounding pitch of an instrument as opposed to a written pitch. For example, the written C on a B-flat clarinet has a concert pitch of B-flat. **2:** The note used as standard tuning for all instrumentalists of an ensemble. The standard tuning is usually A440.

concord: See *consonance*.

conduct: To direct a group of musicians.

conductor: The director of a group of musicians.

conductus: *Sacred* or *secular* Latin songs written in the 12th century.

conga: An African dance in $\frac{2}{4}$ where the dancers form a chain or line that moves in straight lines or circles.

conjunct: Successive notes of a *scale*.

consecutive intervals: See *parallel intervals* and *parallel (consecutive) fifths, octaves*.

consequent 1: The second phrase in a musical *period*. **2:** The *answer* of a *fugue*. Also see *antecedent*.

conservatory: A school specializing in music.

C

console 1: The part of the *organ* operated by the organist. **2:** An *upright piano* slightly taller than a *spinet.*

consonance: Combinations of notes that produce the feeling of rest. When no further harmonic progression is necessary. Consonant intervals are major and minor thirds and sixths, and perfect fourths, fifths and octaves.

con sordino (It., *kohn sohr-DEE-noh*)**:** With *mute.* Abbreviate con sord.

consort: An old English term for chamber group.

contemporary music: See *modern.*

continuo (It., *kohn-TEE-noo-oh*)**:** Abbreviation for *basso continuo.* See *figured bass.*

continuous controllers: In electronic music, adjustments to MIDI codes which are made by moving levers, pedals, sliders or wheels.

contra (It., *KOHN-trah*)**:** An octave below. Literally means "against."

contrabass: The *double bass.*

contrabass clarinet: See *clarinet.*

contrabassoon: See *bassoon.*

contradanza: English country dance.

contrafagotto (It., *kohn-trah-fah-GOHT-toh*)**:** Double bassoon—*contrabassoon.*

contralto: See *alto.*

contrapuntal: In the style of *counterpoint.*

contrary motion: Two lines of music moving in opposite directions.

cor (Fr., *kor*)**:** Horn.

cor anglais (Fr., *kor awn-GLEH*)**:** English horn.

corda, corde (It., *KOHR-dah*; Fr., *kord*)**:** String.

cornet, cornetta: A B-flat brass instrument similar to a  *trumpet* with three *valves* and a conical *bore*. See p. 326 for range.

cornet

cornett: A medieval *wind instrument* made of wood or ivory that has holes like a *woodwind* instrument and a cup-shaped mouthpiece like a *brass* instrument.

cornetto: A *cornet* or *cornett*.

cornett

corno (It., KOHR-*noh*): Horn.

cornopean (*kor*-NOH-*pee-an*): Old name for a *cornet*.

coro (It., KOH-*roh*): *Chorus* or *choir*.

corona (*koh*-ROH-*nah*): *Fermata*.

corrente (It., *kohr*-REN-*teh*): See *courante*.

cotillon (Fr., *koh-tee*-YOHN, *koh*-TIL-*yon*) **1:** A French dance popular during the 18th and 19th centuries that would be the final dance of the evening. **2:** A *quadrille*.

counterpoint: Composing with two or more melodies that are to be played simultaneously. Literally "note against note."

countertenor: The highest male singing voice.

country: An American popular music characterized by dance rhythms, a simple musical structure and down-to-earth lyrics.

country & western: See *country*. Abbreviated C&W.

courante (Fr., *koo*-RAWNT): A 16th-century French dance in *triple meter* that later became a standard *suite* movement.

cowbell: A metal bell, similar in shape to a bell which is

C

hung around a cow's neck, but without a clapper and struck with a *drumstick*.

crab canon: A *canon* in which one part is played backwards—*retrograde*.

crash cymbal 1: A pair of large *cymbals* that are struck together to create a loud crashing sound. **2:** A single large *cymbal* struck with a *mallet* or *drumstick*.

Credo (*Lat.*, KREH-*doh*): The third part of the *Ordinary* of the Mass. It means "I believe."

crescendo (*It.*, kreh-SHEN-*doh*): Gradually becoming louder $<$. Abbreviated cresc.

croche (*Fr.*, *krohsh*): *Eighth note*.

crook: A tube inserted into a *horn* or *trumpet* that changes its pitch. Crooks were used before *valves* were introduced.

cross relation: See *false relation*.

cross rhythm 1: Simultaneous use of conflicting rhythms, for example, two notes against three. **2:** Shifting the beats of a measure, for example, dividing a measure of $\frac{9}{8}$ into 3+2+2+2 eighth notes instead of the usual 3+3+3.

crotales (*kroh*-TAH-*layz*): Small tuned *cymbals*.

crotchet: *Quarter note*.

crumhorn: See *krummhorn*.

csárdás, czardas (CHAR-*dahsh*): A 19th-century Hungarian dance in two parts. The first part is a slow introduction (*lassù*) and the second part is in a quick *duple time* (*friss*).

cue 1: Small notes on an instrumental part that show another instrument's part. **2:** A conductor's gesture to a performer to acknowledge an entrance.

3: A musical piece in a movie.

cut time: $\frac{2}{2}$ meter. Sometimes the time signature ¢ is used.

cycle: A group of complete pieces or songs that are to be performed together.

cyclic, cyclical 1: A musical compositions made up of several complete movements, such as a *sonata*, *suite*, *symphony* or *cantata*. **2:** Compositions that have related thematic material in some or all of the movements.

cymbals: Thin metal disks that are either struck together or suspended and hit with a *drumstick* or *mallet*.

hi-hat cymbals

D

D: Abbreviation for "Deutsch," the cataloguer of Schubert's works. D numbers are used for Schubert's compositions in place of *opus* numbers.

da capo (It., *dah* KAH-*poh*)**:** From the head or from the beginning. Go back to the beginning.

da capo al coda (It., *dah* KAH-*poh ahl* KOH-*dah*)**:** Go back to the beginning of the piece and play to the "To Coda" indication, then skip down to the *Coda*.

da capo al fine (It., *dah* KAH-*poh ahl* FEE-*neh*)**:** Go back to the beginning of the piece and play to the "Fine," which is the end of the piece.

da capo aria (It., *dah* KAH-*poh* AH-*ree-ah*)**:** An opera *aria* in three sections, with the third being a repetition of the first.

dal segno (It., *dahl* SAY-*nyoh*): Go back and play from the sign 𝄋. Abbreviated D.S.

dal segno al coda (It., *dahl* SAY-*nyoh ahl* KOH-*dah*): Go back to the D.S. and play to the "To Coda" indication, then skip down to the *Coda.*

dal segno al fine (It., *dahl* SAY-*nyoh ahl*-FEE-*neh*): Go back to the D.S. and play to the "Fine," which is the end of the piece.

damper 1: On a *piano*, the mechanism that stops the strings from vibrating. **2:** *Mute.*

damper pedal: On a *piano*, the pedal on the right that allows the strings to vibrate.

Dampfer (Ger., DAHM-*pfer*): *Mute.*

dance 1: To rhythmically move to music. **2:** A composition used to accompany those who are dancing.

danse, danza (Fr., *dawns*; It., DAHN-*tsah*): *Dance.*

DAT: Abbreviation for "digital audio tape."

dB: Abbreviation for *decibel.*

D.C.: Abbreviation for *da capo.*

D dur (Ger., *day door*): The key of D major.

decay: The gradual fading out of a sound.

delay: In *electronic music*, a device that produces *effects* such as *echo.*

deceptive cadence: Where the progression moves from the *dominant* (V) chord to a chord other than the *tonic* (I)—usually to the *submediant* (vi).

decibel: A unit for measuring the loudness or intensity of sound. Abbreviated *d*B.

deciso (It., *deh*-CHEE-*zoh*): Decided, bold, with decision.

decrescendo (It., *deh-kreh*-SHEN-*doh*): Gradually becoming softer: ——▷. Abbreviated decresc.

D

degree: One of the notes of a *diatonic* scale which is assigned a number by counting up from the *keynote*.

delicato (It., *deh-lee*-KAH-*toh*): Delicately.

demi- (Fr., DEH-*mee*): Half.

demisemiquaver: *Thirty-second note.*

demo: Slang for a recording that is used to demonstrate a performer's talents or a composer's music. Short for "demonstration."

Des (Ger., *dess*): The note D-flat.

descant 1: The highest part in *polyphonic* music. **2:** A high *obbligato* part above the melody. **3:** The name given to the highest-pitched instrument in an instrumental family.

descriptive music: See *program music.*

desk: A music stand shared by two stringed instrument players.

destra (It., DEH-*strah*): Right.

détaché (Fr., *day-tah*-SHAY): Detached *bowing.*

development: The melodic, harmonic or rhythmic elaboration of a *theme.*

di (It., *dee*): Of, from, with, to.

diapason (Gr., *dei-ah-*PAY-*sun*) **1:** An *octave.* **2:** The range of a voice or instrument. **3:** The principal or main foundation stop of an *organ.* **4:** Standard *pitch,* see *concert pitch.*

diatonic: The notes found within a major or minor scale.

didgeridoo: A wind instrument native to Australia made of wood or bamboo.

die (Ger., *dee*): The.

dièse, diesis (Fr., *dee-*EZ; Gr., *dee-*EH-*sees*): Sharp.

Dies Irae (Lat., DEE-*es* EE-*ray*): The *sequence* for the *Requiem Mass.* Literally means "day of wrath."

digital: When the numerical representation of data is used to record and/or control sounds in *synthesis.*

digital piano: An electronic keyboard instrument whose sounds are *digital samples.*

diluendo (It., *dee-loo-*EN-*doh*): Becoming softer.

diminished: Smaller.

diminished interval: Minor or perfect *intervals* lowered by a *half step.*

diminished seventh chord: A chord consisting of a root, minor third, diminished fifth and diminished seventh. The E diminished seventh chord is E, G, B-flat and D-flat.

diminished triad: A *triad* consisting of a root, minor third and diminished fifth. The C diminished triad is C, E-flat and G-flat.

diminuendo (It., *dee-mee-noo-*EN-*doh*): Gradually becoming softer: $\diagdown$. Abbreviated dim.

diminution: Shortening the duration of notes.

direct: A marking given at the end of a *staff* or page that gives warning of the next note.

D

dirge: A vocal or instrumental piece that is written to be performed at a funeral.

Dis (*Ger., dis*): The note D-sharp.

discant: See *descant*.

disco: Upbeat dance music popular in the 1970s.

discord: See *dissonance*.

discothèque (*Fr., dis-koh-TEK*): A place where people gather to dance.

disjunct motion: Moving by *leaps*.

Dis moll (*Ger., dis mohl*): The key of D-sharp minor.

dissonance, dissonant: Two or more notes that when played together cause tension or require resolution.

distortion: Electronic *effect* that alters the sound of an amplified instrument by making it sound less clear.

divertimento (*It., dee-vehr-tee-MEN-toh*): A light instrumental piece with multiple movements.

div.: Abbreviation of *divisi*.

divertissement (*Fr., dee-vehr-tees-MAHN*) **1:** A *ballet*, dance or *entr'acte* in an opera that is not essential to the plot. **2:** See *divertimento*.

divisi (*It., dee-VEE-see*): Divided. Indicates that when two or more parts are written on one staff, they are to be played by separate performers. Abbreviated *div*.

Dixieland: A style of *jazz* developed in New Orleans during the early 1900s characterized by *syncopated* rhythms and *improvisation*. The standard instrumentation includes *cornet, clarinet, trombone, piano, drums, banjo* (or *guitar*) and *tuba*.

D moll (*Ger., day mohl*): The key of D minor.

do (*It., doh*) **1:** In the *fixed-do* system, the note C. **2:** In the

D

movable-do system, the first note of the scale.

Dobro®: A type of *guitar* with a circular metal *resonator* on its belly.

dodecaphonic (*doh-dek-ah-FON-ic*): Twelve-tone music. See *serial music*.

doh: See *do*.

doit: A technique on *wind instruments* where the main note is sounded, followed by a *glissando* upwards from one to five steps. Notated:

dolce (It., DOHL-*cheh*): Sweet.

dolente (It., *doh*-LEN-*tay*): Sorrowful.

doloroso (It., *doh-loh*-ROH-*zoh*): Sorrowful, grieved.

dominant: The fifth *degree* of a major or minor scale.

dominant seventh chord: A chord consisting of a root, major third, perfect fifth and minor seventh. The C dominant seventh chord is C, E, G and B-flat.

domra (DOHM-*rah*): A Russian stringed instrument similar to a *balalaika* used during the 16th and 17th centuries.

Doppel (Ger., DOHP-*pel*): Double.

doppio (It., DOHP-*pyoh*): Double, twice.

Dorian: A *mode* that corresponds to the whole- and half-step patterns created when playing D to D on the white keys of the piano. See p. 295.

dot 1: A dot over or under a note indicates it is to be played *staccato*. **2:** A dot to the right of a note indicates the note's value is increased by half. A second or third dot to the right of a note indicates the note's value is increased by half of the value of the dot

is increased by half of the value of the dot preceding it.

double **1:** To play or sing in *unison* with another performer. **2:** To play or sing the same part an *octave* above or below another performer. **3:** To play a second instrument.

doublé (Fr., *doo*-BLAY): The *turn*.

double bar: Two vertical lines drawn through the staff that indicate the end of a section, *movement* or *piece*.

double bass: The largest and lowest sounding of the *violin* family. See p. 330 for range.

double bass

double bassoon: See *contrabassoon*.

double concerto: A *concerto* for orchestra and two solo instruments.

double counterpoint: See *invertible counterpoint*.

double croche (Fr., DOO-*ble krohsh*): Sixteenth note.

double dot: See *dot*.

double flat: The symbol ♭♭ that lowers the pitch of a note two *half steps* or one *whole step*.

double fugue: A *fugue* with two *subjects*.

double horn: A French *horn* that has the tubing of both an F and B-flat horn. The different sets of tubing are selected by use of a fourth valve.

double reed: A mouthpiece that consists of two thin pieces of cane that vibrate against each other when air is blown through. Double reeds are used on *wind instruments* such as the *oboe*, *English horn*, *heckelphone*, *bassoon* and *contrabassoon*. Also see *single reed*.

double sharp: The symbol ✕ that raises the pitch of a note two *half steps* or one *whole step*.

D

double stop: Two notes played simultaneously by one player.

double time: Play twice as fast.

double tonguing: On a *flute* or *brass instrument*, the *tonguing* of rapid passages by silently pronouncing ta-ka.

douce, doux (Fr., *doos, doo*): Sweet.

downbeat: Downward motion of a *conductor's* hand that indicates the first beat of a measure.

down bow: To draw a *bow* downward from the *frog* to the tip. A down bow is indicated by the symbol ⊓.

doxology (Gr., *dox-AHL-o-jee*): A *song* of praise and glory to God. In the Protestant church, it refers specifically to the hymn "Praise God From Whom All Blessings Flow."

drag: A drum *rudiment* consisting of two short *grace notes* played before the main note.

droit, droite (Fr., *drawh, drawht*): Right, rights.

drone 1: A long sustained note. **2:** See *bagpipe*.

drum: Percussion instruments consisting of a cylindrical wood or metal body with a membrane *head* stretched over one or both ends which is struck by a *drumstick*, *mallet* or *brushes* to produce sounds. Also see *membranophones*.

drum and bugle corps: An ensemble consisting of *brass* and *percussion instruments* that perform choreographed marching maneuvers as they play.

drumhead: The membrane or plastic that stretches over the top of a drum which is struck by a *mallet*, *brushes* or *drumstick*.

drum kit, drumset: A group of *drums*, *cymbals* and other *percussion* instruments positioned so that one person can easily play them.

drum machine: An electronic device with *analog* or *digital* percussion sounds that organizes those sounds into rhythmic patterns. Also see *sequencer*.

D

drumstick: A cylindrical wooden stick that is used to strike a *drum*. Also see *brushes* and *mallets*.

D.S.: Abbreviation for *dal segno*.

due (It., DOO-*eh*): Two.

duet (*doo*-ET) **1:** A composition for two performers. **2:** A composition for two performers playing on one instrument, usually the *piano*. Also called a *duo*.

dulcimer (DUL-*si-mer*): An ancient *stringed instrument* consisting of wire strings stretched over a *sound box* that are either plucked with a *pick* or struck with small hammers.

dumka (Pol., DOOM-*kah*): A Slavonic folk *ballad*.

dump, domp, dumpe: English instrumental music of the 16th and early 17th centuries.

duo: See *duet*.

duple meter: A *time signature* with two beats to the measure.

duplet: Two notes played in the time of three.

dur (Ger., *door*): Major.

duramente (It., *doo-rah*-MEN-*teh*): Harshly.

duration: Length.

durchführung (Ger., DOORH-*fir-oong*) **1:** The *exposition* of a *fugue*. **2:** The *development* of a *sonata* form.

dyad: A group of two tones.

dynamic markings: The symbols that indicate varying degrees of *volume*. See p. 306.

dynamics: See *dynamic markings*.

E

e (It., *ay*): And.

ear training: The process of learning how to recognize and notate *pitches*, *intervals* and *rhythms*.

ecclesiastical modes: See *church modes*.

ecco, eco (It., EK-*koh*, AY-*koh*): Echo.

échappée (Fr., *ay-shahp*-PAY): See *escape tone*.

échelle (Fr., *ay*-SHEL): The *scale*.

echo, eco (Eng., It., AY-*koh*): Quiet repetition of a previous phrase.

écossaise (Fr., *ay-kohs*-SEZ): An English country dance usually in ${2 \atop 4}$ time, popular in the late 18th and early 19th centuries.

E dur (Ger., *eh door*): The key of E major.

effects: Electronic device that alters the characteristics of an *audio* signal.

eighth note: A note half the length of a *quarter note*. See p. 277.

eighth rest: A rest half the length of a *quarter rest*. See p. 278.

8va, 8va bassa: See *ottava alta, ottava bassa*.

8vb: The incorrect symbol for 8va *bassa* or *ottava bassa*.

Einklang (Ger., EIN-*klahng*): Unison.

Einsatz (Ger., EIN-*zots*) **1:** An entrance. **2:** An attack.

Eis (Ger., EH-*iss*): The note E-sharp.

electric bass: An electric solid-body *guitar* with four strings tuned to the same pitches as the *double bass*.

electric guitar: A *guitar* that is electronically amplified with a *pickup*.

electric piano: An electronic keyboard instrument that creates sounds by striking bars, reeds or strings.

electric guitar

E

electronic instrument: An instrument whose sound is completely or partially created by an electronic device or is electronically amplified.

electronic music: Music partially or completely created, manipulated or reproduced by electronic devices including *electronic instruments*, *synthesizers* and recording equipment.

elegy: A piece in a melancholy mood usually written in honor of someone's death.

eleventh: The diatonic interval from the first to the eleventh notes of a *scale*.

embellishment: Notes which are added to *ornament* a melody.

embouchure (Fr., AHM-*boo-shoor*) **1:** The position and shape of the mouth and lips of a *wind* player. **2:** A mouthpiece of a *wind instrument*.

E moll (Ger., *eh mohl*): The key of E minor.

ému (Fr., *ay*-MUE): With feeling, with emotion.

encore (Fr., ON-*kor*): Again. The adding or repeating of a piece due to overwhelming enthusiasm from the audience; usually occurs at the end of a concert.

end-blown flute: A *recorder*. A *flute* that is played vertically.

English horn: An alto *oboe* in F, that sounds a fifth below its written pitch. See p. 318 for range.

enharmonic: Two notes that sound the same, but are spelled differently. For example, B-flat and A-sharp are enharmonically the same.

ensemble (Fr., *on*-SOM-*ble*): Any group of musicians performing together.

entr'acte (Fr., *ahn*-TRAHKT): An instrumental piece performed between acts of a play, *opera* or *ballet*.

entrada (Sp., *en*-TRAH-*dah*): A *prelude* or *introduction*.

entrée (Fr., *ahn*-TRAY): See *entrada*.

envelope: In *synthesis*, the shape of a sound's *amplitude* over time.

envelope generator: An electronic device that controls the *envelope* of a sound.

episode 1: A section of a *fugue* that does not include the *subject*. **2:** A secondary section of a piece that does not include the main *theme*.

EQ: Abbreviation for *equalizer* or *equalization*.

equalization: The act of accurately balancing the frequencies of recorded or amplified sounds.

equalizer: An electronic device that enables *equalization*.

equal temperament: The tuning of an *octave* into 12 equal *semitones*.

eroica (It., *ay*-ROH-*e*-*kah*): Heroic.

Es (Ger., *ess*): The note E-flat.

escape tone: In harmony, a nonharmonic tone approached by a step and left by a leap in the opposite direction.

Es dur (Ger., *ess door*): The key of E-flat major.

Es moll (Ger., *ess mohl*): The key of E-flat minor.

espressivo (It., *es-pres*-SEE-*voh*): Expressive. Abbreviated espress.

estampie (Fr., *eh-tawm*-PEE): Instrumental or vocal dance music from the 13th and 14th centuries.

estinto (It., *es-TEEN-toh*): Barely audible, as soft as possible.

ethnomusicology: The study of music in relation to its cultural context.

ethos (Gr., *EE-thohs*): The ancient Greek concept that each scale implies a different character or mood.

étouffé (Fr., *ay-toof-FAY*): Muted, damped.

étude (Fr., *ay-TUED, AY-tood*): A study. A piece that emphasizes a specific technique.

etwas (Ger., *ET-vahss*): Somewhat.

euphonium (*yoo-FOH-nee-um*): A *brass instrument* similar to a *baritone horn* but with a larger *bore* and four valves.

eurhythmics (*yoo-RITH-miks*): A system developed by Emile Jaques-Dalcroze that teaches *rhythm* through the movement of the body.

evaded cadence: A *cadence* that does not resolve where it is expected to resolve. Also see *deceptive cadence*.

exercise: A short technical study.

exposition 1: The first section of the *sonata form* that includes the *primary theme*, a *transition*, the *secondary theme* and a *closing theme*. **2:** The first section of a *fugue*, where the *subject* is stated in all of the *voices*.

expressionism: A style of early 20th-century music where composers expressed their innermost feelings as opposed to *impressionism*.

expression marks: Words or symbols that indicate how a piece should be interpreted, i.e., *articulation*, *dynamics*, *tempo*, etc.

extemporization: See *improvisation*.

F

f: The abbreviation for *forte*.

fa, fah 1: In the *fixed-do* system, the note F. **2:** In the *movable-do* system, the fourth note of the scale.

faburden: A 15th-century English compositional technique where parallel thirds and sixths are used.

facile (It., FAH-*chee-leh*): Easy.

fado (Port., FAH-*doh*): A popular Portuguese *song* and dance.

Fagott (Ger., *fah*-GOHT): *Bassoon*.

fake book: A collection of popular *songs* where only the melody lines, lyrics and chord symbols are given.

false cadence: See *deceptive cadence*.

falsetto (It., *fahl*-SET-*toh*): A method used by male singers to extend their vocal range above the normal range.

fandango (Sp., *fahn*-DAHN-*goh*): A lively Spanish dance in *triple meter*.

fanfare: A ceremonial *prelude* or *flourish* commonly played by *brass instruments*.

fantaisie, fantasia, fantasy (Fr., *fawn-teh*-ZEE; It., *fahn-tah-*ZEE-*ah*) **1:** Music with an improvisatory feel. **2:** A piece in free form. **3:** *Improvisation*.

farandola, farandole (It., *fah-rahn-doh-*LAH; Fr., *fah-rawn-*DUL): A quick circle-dance.

fauxbourdon (Fr., *foh-boor*-DUN): See *faburden*.

F clef: The *bass clef*. 𝄢

F dur (Ger., *ef door*): The key of F major.

feedback: A "whining" sound created when sound being output is fed back through the input during amplification. This sound is often used by guitarists as an *effect*.

feminine cadence: When a final chord occurs on a weak beat. Also see *masculine cadence*.

fermata (It., *fehr-MAH-tah*)**:** A hold or pause sign ⌒ that indicates a note should be held longer than its normal duration.

***ff*:** Abbreviation for *fortissimo*

***fff*:** Abbreviation for *fortississimo*.

f-hole: The f-shaped holes found in many stringed instruments. Also see *sound hole*.

fiato (It., *FYAH-toh*)**:** "Stromenti a fiato" are *wind instruments*. Literally means "breath."

fiddle: Slang for *violin*.

fife: A small *flute* with six to eight holes.

15ma: See *fifteenth* and *quindicesima*.

fifteenth: Two octaves above, abbreviated 15*ma*. Also see *quindicesima*.

fifth: The interval of five *diatonic* steps.

figure: See *motif*.

figured bass: A bass part with numbers that indicate the intervals of harmony that are to be played above the bass note. Figured bass was used by keyboard players in the *baroque* period to create accompaniments.

film music: Music composed or adapted for a film.

filter: A device, in *synthesis*, that suppresses or emphasizes certain audio *frequencies*.

fin: (Fr., *fehn*)**:** End.

finale (It., *fee-NAH-leh*) **1:** The last *movement* of a piece in several movements. **2:** The closing section of an *opera*.

fine (It., FEE-*neh*): End.

fingerboard: The part of a *stringed instrument* where the fingers press down on the strings to produce different pitches.

finger cymbals: Small *cymbals* in pairs that are placed on the fingers and struck together.

fingering, finger 1: The placement of fingers on an instrument. **2:** The markings in music that guide a performer's placement of their fingers.

fingerpicking: A style of *guitar* or *banjo* playing where the player uses their fingers or *fingerpicks* to pluck the strings.

fingerpicks: Metal or plastic *picks* that attach to each finger of the picking hand of a *guitar* or *banjo* player. Also see *fingerpicking*.

Fis (*Ger.*, *fiss*): The note F-sharp.

Fis dur (*Ger.*, *fiss door*): The key of F-sharp major.

Fis moll (*Ger.*, *fiss mohl*): The key of F-sharp minor.

Five, the Russian: A group of five Russian composers who, in the late 19th century, wrote in a nationalist style. They were Balakirev, Borodin, Cui, Mussorgsky and Rimsky-Korsakov.

fixed-do: In this system, the note C is always called *do*, as opposed to the system of *movable-do*.

flag: A hook that, when placed on the stem of a note, indicates an *eighth note*. Two flags indicate a *sixteenth note*. Three flags indicate a *thirty-second note*, etc.

flageolet (*fla-joh*-LAY, *fla-joh*-LET): A small 16th-century *end-blown wind instrument* similar to a *recorder*.

flam: A drum *rudiment* consisting of a short *grace note* played before the main note. ♪

flamenco (Sp., *flah-MEN-koh*) **1:** A rhythmic Andalusian (Spanish) dance or *song*. **2:** A rhythmical and improvisatory style of *guitar* playing.

flanging: An electronic *effect* that creates a hollow sound.

flat 1: The symbol ♭ that indicates a note to be lowered one *half step*. Also see *double flat*. **2:** When a pitch is lower than normal, i.e., out of tune.

flauto (It., *FLAHW-toh*): Flute.

flebile (It., *FLEH-bee-leh*): Mournful.

Flemish school: Reniassance composers from the Netherlands and Belgium who developed the *polyphonic* style of that period. Notable composers include Ockeghem and des Pres.

flexatone: A *percussion instrument* consisting of a thin triangular piece of steel and two wooden nobs attached to springs. When shaken, the wooden nobs strike the thin steel creating a sound similar to a *musical saw*.

flip: A technique on *wind instruments* where the main note is played, raised in pitch and then is dropped into the following note. Notated:

flourish 1: A *trumpet fanfare*. **2:** A passage with *ornamentation*.

flue pipes: *Organ* pipes that create sounds without the use of reeds.

flugelhorn (*FLOO-gel-horn*): A *brass instrument* similar to a *cornet*, but with a larger *bore* and a mellow tone. See p. 327 for range.

flute: A group of woodwind instruments made of a hollow wood or metal tube that is closed at one end. Sound is created by blowing into a hole near the closed end. The different types include, from highest to lowest, the *piccolo*, flute, G *alto flute*, bass flute. See pp. 317–318 for ranges.

flutes

flûte à bec (Fr., *fluet ah* BEK): *Recorder*.

flutter tonguing: A *tonguing* technique on *wind instruments* where a *tremolo* effect is created by rapid fluttering of the tongue.

FM: Abbreviation for *frequency modulation*.

F moll (Ger., *ef mohl*): The key of F minor.

FM synthesis: A type of *synthesis* where sounds are created by controlling the frequency modulation of *waveforms*.

folk music, folk song 1: Music passed down orally from generation to generation. **2:** Music of a specific region.

foot: The unit of measurement for the pitch and size of *organ* pipes.

form: The organization and structure of a *composition*.

forte (It., FOHR-*teh*): Loud, abbreviated *f*.

fortepiano (It., FOHR-*teh-pyah-noh*): Early name for the *piano*.

fortissimo (It., *fohr-*TEES-*see-moh*): Very loud, abbreviated *ff*.

fortississimo (It., *fohr-tees-*SEES-*see-moh*): Very, very loud, abbreviated *fff*.

forza (It., FOR-*tsah*): With force.

forzando, forzato (It., *fohr-*TSAHN-*doh, fohr-*TSAH-*toh*):

Accented, abbreviated _fz_.

fourth: The interval of four _diatonic_ steps.

fourth chord: A chord made up of intervals of a _fourth_.

fox trot: A ballroom dance in _duple meter_ that originated in the United States around 1913.

_fp_: Abbreviation for a _dynamic_ symbol meaning loud (_forte_) then soft (_piano_).

française (Fr., _frawn-SEZ_)**:** A French country dance in _triple meter_.

free reed: A thin tongue of metal that is fastened over an opening through which air is forced either by bellows (_harmonium, accordion_) or by the player's lungs (_harmonica_).

French horn: A circular-shaped _brass instrument_ with a conical _bore_ and a mellow tone. See p. 324 for range.

french horn

French overture: A type of _overture_ developed in the 18th century that has three sections: the first is slow, the second is fast and the third is slow.

French sixth: A chord consisting of major third, augmented fourth and augmented sixth above the bass. Sometimes called an "augmented six-four-three." Also see _augmented sixth chord_.

frequency: The _pitch_ of a sound determined by the number of vibrations per second that are created by a given _tone_.

frequency modulation: To alter the _frequency_ of an _electronic instrument_ or device.

fret: Thin wedges of wood, metal or ivory that are placed across the _fingerboard_ of certain _stringed instruments_, primarily the _guitar, banjo_ and _mandolin_.

fretboard: A *fingerboard* with *frets*.

Freude (Ger., FROY-*deh*): Joy.

frisch (Ger., *frish*): Vigorous, lively.

friss: See *csárdás*.

frog: The end of a *bow* that is held in the player's hand.

fuga (Lat., It., FOO-*gah*) **1:** *Fugue.* **2:** In music from the Middle Ages until the 17th century—a *canon*.

fugato (It., foo-GAH-*toh*): A passage in the style of a *fugue*.

fughetta (It., foo-GET-*tah*): A short *fugue*.

fugue: A *contrapuntal* procedure in two or more *parts* that is based on a *subject* which is stated successively in each part. Elements found in fugues are the *subject*, *answer*, *countersubject*, *stretto* and *episode*.

full score: A *score* where every instrumental and/or vocal part appears on its own staff.

fundamental 1: The *root* of a chord. **2:** The lowest note of a *harmonic series*.

funèbre (Fr., foo-NEH-*brh*): Funeral.

funk: A highly-amplified style of *rhythm & blues*.

fuoco: Fire, passion.

furiant: A quick Bohemian dance with frequently changing rhythms and *accents*.

fusion: A style of popular music that combines the styles of *jazz* and *rock*.

fuzz tone: An electronic *effect* used most commonly with *electric guitar* that imitates the sound of an amplifier with its volume turned up to the point of distorting the sound.

***fz*:** Abbreviation for *forzando* and *sforzando*.

G

Gagaku (Jap., *gah-gah-*KOO): Orchestral music of the Japanese court that dates back to the 8th century.

gallant: The light, elegant style of the 18th century.

galliard (*gahl-*LYARD): A spirited dance from the 15th century in *triple meter*.

galop: A quick round dance of the mid-19th century in $\frac{2}{4}$ time.

gamba (GAHM-*bah*): Viola da gamba.

gamelan (GAM-*e-lon*): An Indonesian orchestra consisting of *gongs, drums, cymbals, pitched percussion* and some *stringed* and *woodwind instruments*.

gato: A popular country dance of Argentina in $\frac{3}{4}$ or $\frac{6}{8}$ time.

gavotte (Fr., *gah-*VOT): A French dance of the 17th century in *duple meter* that begins on the *upbeat*.

G clef: The *treble clef*.

G dur (Ger., *gay door*): The key of G major.

Gebrauchsmusik (Ger., *ge-*BROWKHS-*moo-zik*): Utility music. Music intended to be played by amateurs.

gedämpft (Ger., *ge-*DEMPFT): *Muted*.

Gehend (Ger., GAY-*ent*): *Andante*.

Geige (Ger., GEI-*ge*): *Violin*.

gemässigt (Ger., *ge-*MA-*siht*): Moderate.

gemendo (It., *jeh-*MEN-*doh*): Lamenting.

General MIDI: A standardized organization of drum and instrumental sounds for MIDI instruments. Abbreviated GM.

general pause: See *grand pause*.

German sixth: A chord consisting of a major third, perfect fifth and augmented sixth above the bass. Sometimes called an "augmented six-five-three." Also see *augmented sixth chord.*

Ges (*Ger., gess*)**:** The note G-flat.

Gesang (*Ger., ge-ZAHNG*)**:** *Song.*

geschleift (*Ger., ge-SHLEIFT*)**:** *Legato.*

Ges dur (*Ger., ges door*)**:** The key of G-flat major.

Ges moll (*Ger., ges mohl*)**:** The key of G-flat minor.

gestopft (*Ger., ge-SHTOHPFT*)**:** *Stopped.* The *muting* of a *horn* with the hand that produces a "buzzing" sound.

gig: Slang for a musical job.

gigue (*Fr., zheeg*) **1:** A dance, usually in $\frac{6}{8}$, commonly found in a *suite.* **2:** A *jig.*

giocoso (*It., joh-KOH-zoh*)**:** Humorous.

Gis (*Ger., giss*)**:** The note G-sharp.

Gis dur (*Ger., giss door*)**:** The key of G-sharp major.

Gis moll (*Ger., giss mohl*)**:** The key of G-sharp minor.

giusto (*It., jee-U-stoh*)**:** Exact, strict.

glass armonica: An 18th-century instrument developed by Benjamin Franklin that consists of a set of various-sized glasses that are rubbed by a wet finger to produce different pitches. Sometimes referred to as the "glass harmonica."

glee: Unaccompanied English *secular* choral music of the 18th century.

gliss.: Abbreviation for *glissando.*

glissando (*It., glees-SAHN-doh*) **1:** To slide from one note to another. **2:** On a *piano,* a rapid scale produced by sliding fingers over the desired keys. See *portamento* and *gliss.*

Glocke (*Ger.*, GLOH-*ke*): A *bell.*

glockenspiel (*Ger.*, GLOK-*en-shpeel*):
A percussion instrument
made up of tuned metal bars
that are arranged like a
keyboard and played with
mallets. Also see *bells.*
See p. 332 for range.

glockenspiel

Gloria (*Lat.*, GLOH-*ree-ah*): The second part of the *Ordinary*
of the *Mass.* It means Glory [to God in the highest].

GM: Abbreviation for General MIDI.

G moll (*Ger.*, *gay mohl*): The key of G minor.

gong: A suspended circular metal plate that is struck with a
large felt *mallet.* Also known as a *tam-tam.*

gopak: A Ukranian folk dance in a quick $\frac{2}{4}$ time. Sometimes
spelled *hopak.*

gospel song: A Protestant *hymn.*

G.P.: Abbreviation for *grand pause.*

grace note: A small note ♪ played quickly before the beat.
Not to be confused with an *appoggiatura.*

gran, grand', grande (*It.*, *grahn*, *grahnd*, GRAHN-*deh*): Large,
great.

gran cassa (*It.*, *grahn* CAHS-*sah*): Bass drum.

grandioso (*It.*, *grahn-dee-OH-zoh*): Grand, majestic.

grand opera: An *opera*, usually in five acts, that treats a
heroic, historic or mythological subject in a grand
style.

grand pause: A rest for all performers in an ensemble.
Abbreviated G.P. and sometimes referred to as a
general pause.

grand piano: A *piano* with its frame, strings and *soundboard* arranged horizontally.

grand staff: The combination of the bass and treble staves which is commonly used to notate music for the *piano*.

grand piano

grave (It., GRAH-*veh*): Slow, heavy, solemn.

gravicembalo (It., *grah-ve-chem*-BAHL-*oh*): Harpsichord.

grazia, grazioso (It., GRAH-*tsee-ah, grah-tsee*-OH-*zoh*): Grace.

great pause: See *grand pause.*

great staff: See *grand staff.*

Gregorian chant: Roman Catholic liturgical *chants* developed by Pope Gregory I.

grosse caisse (Fr., *grus kes*): Bass drum.

grosso, grosse (It., GROHS-*soh*; Ger., GROHS-*se*): Great, large.

ground bass: See *basso ostinato.*

growl: A harsh sound played on a *wind instrument* that imitates the growl of an animal.

grunge: A style of *rock* similar to *heavy metal*, popular in the 1990s.

gruppetto, groppo, gruppo (It., *groop*-PET-*toh*, GROHP-*poh*, GROOP-*poh*): Ornaments or groups of *grace notes.*

guaracha (*gwah*-RAH-*chah*): A Spanish folk dance in two sections, one in *triple meter*, the other in *duple meter.*

guiro (GWEE-*roh*): A percussion instrument consisting of a notched gourd which is "scraped" by a stick.

guitar: A *stringed instrument* with six strings, a flat back, curved sides and a long narrow fretted neck. The strings are either plucked with the fingers, picked

with a *pick* or strummed. See p. 330 for range.
Also see *electric guitar*.

gusto (It., GOO-*stoh*): Style, zest.

guitar

H

H: (Ger., *hah*) The note B-natural.

H.: Abbreviation for "Hoboken," the cataloger of Haydn's
works. H numbers are used for Haydn's
compositions in place of *opus* numbers.

habanera (Sp., *hah-bah-NEH-rah*): A syncopated Cuban
dance in *duple meter*.

half cadence: See *imperfect cadence*.

half note: A note one half the length of a whole note.
See p. 277.

half rest: A rest one half the length of a whole rest.
See p. 278.

half step: The smallest *interval* commonly used which is
equal to the distance between two adjacent notes
on a *piano* keyboard or the distance of one fret on a
guitar. There are 12 half steps in an *octave*.

hammer: Small felt-covered hammers that strike the
strings of a *piano*. Also see *action*.

Hammerclavier (Ger., HAHM-*mer-klah-veer*): Pianoforte.

hammer-on: A technique on *stringed instruments* where the
first note is played, then a second note is tapped
down with another finger. Both notes are played on
the same string. See p. 313.

handbell: A musically tuned bell with a handle usually
made of leather or plastic. It has a clapper which
travels in one plane and is controlled by springs to

prevent the clapper from resting against the bell when struck.. The bell is used often in group ringing by a handbell ringer who is part of a handbell choir.

hand organ 1: English *barrel organ*. **2:** Italian street *organ* used by organ-grinders.

Harfe (*Ger.*, HAR-*fe*): *Harp*.

harmonic 1: See *harmonics*. **2:** See *overtone series*.

harmonica 1: A small *free reed* instrument with two sets of reeds: half of them fixed to play with an exhale, and the other half with an inhale allowing different pitches for each set. They are available as either *diatonic* or *chromatic*. See p. 335 for ranges.

harmonica

harmonic analysis: The study of harmonies or *chords* within a piece of music.

harmonic minor: A *natural minor scale* with a raised seventh providing a leading tone. See p. 279.

harmonic rhythm: The pattern created by changes of harmony throughout a composition.

harmonics: Notes of the *harmonic series* which are very clear and pure.

harmonic series: A series of notes (*overtones*) that vibrate above a *fundamental* note. The dark notes are out of tune.

harmonium: A *free-reed organ* in which the air is supplied by bellows which are operated by pedals.

harmonizer: In *synthesis*, a device that electronically changes the *pitch* of sounds.

harmony: The result produced when *tones* are sounded simultaneously. Also see *chords*.

harp 1: A stringed instrument with a triangular shape whose strings run vertically and seven pedals that change the pitch of the strings. See p. 335 for range. **2 :** Slang for a *harmonica*.

harp

harpsichord: A keyboard instrument similar to the *piano*, but strings are plucked by a quill rather than struck by a hammer. See p. 335 for range.

hastig (*Ger.*, HAHS-*teesh*): Hurrying.

Hauptstimme (*Ger.*, HOWPT-*shtim-meh*): The principal part. As opposed to *Nebenstimme*.

haut, haute (*Fr.*, *oh, oht*): High.

hautbois, hautboy (*Fr.*, *oh*-BWAH; *Eng.*, HOH-*boy*): Oboe.

Hawaiian guitar: See *steel guitar*.

H dur (*Ger.*, *hah door*): The key of B major.

head 1: The beginning of a piece or movement. **2:** The tip of a *bow*. **3:** A *drumhead*.

head voice: The higher *register* of a voice.

heavy metal: Highly amplified style of *rock* music popular from the late 1960s through the 1980s.

heckelphone (HEK-*el-fohn*): A baritone *oboe* with a range one octave below the oboe.

Heldentenor (*Ger.*, HEL-*den-ten-or*): Heroic tenor. A *tenor* with a robust voice, used for singing highly demanding operatic roles.

helicon: A *tuba* with a circular shape designed to allow the player to carry it over their shoulder while marching. Also see *sousaphone*.

hemidemisemiquaver: Sixty-fourth note: ♪.

hemiola (*hee-mee-OH-lah*): The rhythmic relationship of three notes in the time of two, or two notes in the time of three. It is usually the alteration of $\frac{6}{8}$ and $\frac{3}{4}$ time.

Hertz: A unit of measuring cycles per second of *waveforms*. Abbreviated Hz.

heterophony (Gr., *het-er-AH-foh-nee*): The simultaneous performance of modified or ornamented versions of the same melody performed by two or more singers or instrumentalists.

hexachord: A group of six notes.

hidden fifths, hidden octaves: See *parallel fifths, parallel octaves*.

high fidelity: Sounds reproduced electronically with a very high quality.

hi-hat cymbals: A pair of horizontally mounted cymbals on a stand which are struck together by means of a foot pedal. Usually part of a *drum kit*.

His (Ger., *hiss*): The note B-sharp.

H moll (Ger., *hah mohl*): The key of B minor.

hocket: A medieval polyphonic device where one voice will stop and another will come in, usually for only one note or a short phrase, creating a "hiccuping" effect.

hold: See *fermata*.

homophony: Music with one melodic part that is supported by a chordal accompaniment.

homorhythmic: When all the voices or parts move in the same *rhythm*.

honky-tonk: A loud, tinny style of *ragtime* piano playing from the early 20th century.

hook: A memorable phrase of a *song* repeated several times in order to intrigue or "hook" the listener.

hopak: See *gopak*.

hoquet (Fr., *oh*-KEH): See *hocket*.

horn 1: See *French horn*. **2:** Slang for any *wind instrument*.

hornpipe: A lively English dance popular from the 16th to 19th centuries.

humbucking pickup: A *pickup* on *electric guitars* and *basses* that eliminates noise and hum.

humoresque (Fr., *ue-mor*-ESK): A light, humorous instrumental piece.

hurdy-gurdy: A portable medieval stringed instrument with six strings and a range of two octaves. It is played by cranking a handle that is connected to a resin-coated wheel that vibrates the strings, and notes are changed by use of a keyboard.

hurdy-gurdy

hymn 1: A sacred *song* of praise to God. **2:** A nationalistic *song*.

hyper- 1: A prefix meaning above. **2:** A *mode* that begins and ends a fifth above the initial tone.

hypo- 1: A prefix meaning below. **2:** A *mode* that begins and ends a fifth below the initial tone.

Hz: Abbreviation for *Hertz*.

I

I (*It., ee*): The.

ictus (*Lat.,* IK-*toos*) **1:** A marking used in *Gregorian chant* that indicates groupings of notes. **2:** An *accent*.

idée fixe: A "fixed idea" or recurring *theme* in a piece.

idiomatic style: Music written with a complete understanding of the technical strengths and weaknesses of the instrument(s).

imitation: In *contrapuntal* music, the same *theme, subject, melody* or *motive* repeated in a different part either with or without modification.

imperfect cadence: A *cadence* that ends on a *dominant* chord.

impresario (*im-pre*-SAH-*ree-oh*): The manager or agent of an orchestra or opera company.

impressionism: A late 19th- through early 20th-century French style of composition where subtle impressions are evoked by using colorful *instrumentation* and unusual harmonies.

impromptu (*Fr., im*-PROMP-*too*): A piece in a free form that sounds like an *improvisation*.

improvisation: Music that is created spontaneously.

incidental music: Music written for a play.

incomplete cadence: A *cadence* where the highest note of the *tonic chord* is not the *keynote*.

indeterminacy: See *aleatory music*.

instrument: Devices or objects that produce musical sounds.

instrumentation: The act of *composing, arranging* or

orchestrating music for instruments.

interlude 1: *Organ* music played between *verses* of a *psalm* or *hymn*. 2: An instrumental piece played between the acts of a play.

intermezzo (It., *een-tehr-*MED*-zoh*) 1: A short lyrical instrumental piece either part of a larger work or as an independent composition. 2: Comical musical entertainment played between the acts of an *opera* during the 18th century.

interpretation: Those aspects of a performance that come from a performer rather than the composer.

interrupted cadence: See *deceptive cadence*.

interval: The distance in *pitch* between two notes. See p. 300.

intone, intonation 1: Playing or singing in tune with other performers. 2: The opening phrase of *plainsong* that establishes the *mode*.

intrada (It., *een-*TRAH*-dah*): An *introduction* or opening movement.

introduction: A section at the beginning of a piece or *movement* that is preparatory. It is usually in a slow tempo.

Introit (Lat., EEN*-troh-eet*): The part of the Roman Catholic *Mass* that is sung as the priest approaches the altar. Literally means "entrance."

invention: A short *contrapuntal* composition usually for keyboard.

inversion 1: Harmonic: The transferring of a lower pitch of an interval an octave higher, or a higher pitch an octave lower. 2: Melodic: To change each ascending interval into the corresponding descending interval. 3: Chords: A chord whose lowest tone is other than the root. A first inversion chord has the third in the bass. A second inversion chord has the fifth in the bass. A third inversion chord is a seventh chord with the seventh in the bass.

inverted canon: A *canon* that uses melodic *inversion*.

inverted mordent: A musical *ornament* consisting of the alternation of the written note with the one immediately above it. Also see *mordent*. See p. 304.

invertible counterpoint: *Contrapuntal* music written so that the lowest part can also be played above the upper part.

Ionian (*ei*-OH-*nee-an*): A *mode* that corresponds to the whole- and half-step patterns created when playing C to C on the white keys of the piano. It is the same as a *major scale*. See p. 295.

isometric: When all parts (voices) of a *polyphonic* piece have the same *rhythm*.

isorhythm: A medieval compositional technique that uses a repeated rhythmic pattern (called a talea) and a repeated pitch pattern (called a color) which do not necessarily coincide. An isorhythm was usually the tenor part of a *motet*.

istesso (It., *ee*-STES-*soh*): Same.

Italian sixth: A chord consisting of a major third (doubled) and an augmented sixth above the bass.

J

jack 1: A piece of wood that holds the quill or leather that plucks the string of a *harpsichord*. **2:** A receptacle for an electronic plug.

Jagd- (Ger., *yakt*): Hunt.

jam: An *improvisation* by a jazz or rock group.

Janizary music: Music imitating Turkish military bands. Also spelled Janissary.

jarábe (Sp., *hah-RAH-beh*): A Mexican dance in moderate tempo.

jazz: An American musical style of the 20th century characterized by *syncopated* rhythms and *improvisation*.

jazz-rock: See *fusion*.

jeté (Fr., *zheh-TAY*): The bouncing of the *bow* on the string during a down bow so as to play a series of repeated notes.

jew's harp: A small metal-framed instrument that holds a small metal strip. The frame is held between the teeth and the metal strip is plucked.

jig: A popular 16th-century dance usually in $\frac{6}{8}$ time. Also see *gigue*.

jingle 1: Catchy music used to promote a product on television or radio. **2:** Small metal plates attached to a *tambourine*.

jodel: See *yodel*.

joropo (Sp., *hoh-ROH-poh*): A fast Venezuelan dance and *song* in $\frac{3}{4}$ time.

jota (Sp., *HOH-tah*): A fast Spanish dance in *triple meter*.

jubiloso (It., *yoo-bee-LOH-zoh*): Jubilant.

just intonation: A system of tuning where all intervals are derived from the pure fifth and the pure third, as opposed to *temperament*.

K

K: K numbers are used instead of *opus* numbers for the following two composers **1:** The abbreviation for Köchel, the cataloguer of Mozart's works. **2:** The abbreviation for Kirkpatrick, the cataloguer of Domenico Scarlatti's works.

Kalimba (*kah*-LIM-*bah*): See *m'bira*.

Kammer (*Ger.,* KAHM-*mer*): Chamber.

Kanon (*Ger.,* KAH-*nohn*): See *canon*.

Kapelle (*Ger.,* *kah*-PEL-*le*) **1:** Chapel. **2:** A small private ensemble.

Kapellmeister (*Ger.,* *kah*-PEL-*meis-ter*): *Conductor* or director.

karaoke (*Jap.,* *ka-ray-*OH-*kee*): To sing along with a recorded accompaniment.

kazoo: A small tubular instrument with a vibrating membrane at one end which is played by humming into it.

kettledrum: A tunable orchestral drum that looks like a large brass kettle with a membrane stretched over the top. Usually played in pairs and also called *timpani*.

key 1: The tonal center of a composition. **2:** The part of the *action* of a *keyboard* instrument that is touched by the fingers. **3:** A lever on a *woodwind instrument* that is moved by the fingers.

keyboard: The set of *keys* on a keyboard instrument such as the piano, organ, harpsichord or accordion.

key bugle: A *bugle* that uses *keys* to alter its pitch.

keynote: The first note of a *scale* or *key*. Also see *tonic*.

key signature: The group of sharps or flats that appears at the beginning of a *staff* which indicate the *key*.

kit 1: A small *violin* used in the 17th and 18th centuries. **2:** Slang for a *drum kit*.

kithara (*Gr.*, KITH-*ah-rah*): An ancient Greek stringed instrument similar to a *lyre*.

Klang (*Ger.*, *klang*): Sound.

Klangfarbenmelodie (*Ger.*, *klung-fahr ben*-MEL*,-oh-dee*): A 20th-century compositional style where melodies are created from *tone colors* rather than *pitches*.

Klarinette: German for *clarinet*.

Klavier (*Ger.*, *klah*-VEER) **1:** A *piano*. **2:** Any stringed keyboard instrument. **3:** A keyboard. Also see *clavier*.

kleine (*Ger.*, KLEI-*ne*): Small, little.

Köchel listing: See K.

Konzertstück (*Ger.*, *kohn*-TSART-*shtook*): Concert piece.

koto (*Jap.*, KOH-*toh*): A Japanese stringed instrument similar to a *zither*.

kräftig (*Ger.*, KREFT-*ikh*): Vigorous.

krakowiak (*Pol.*, *kra*-KOH-*vyak*): Brisk Polish dance in $\frac{2}{4}$ time.

Kreuz (*Ger.*, *kroyts*): The *sharp* sign.

Krummhorn (*Ger.*, KROOM-*horn*): A Renaissance *double reed* woodwind instrument.

kujawiak (*Pol.*, *koo*-YAH-*vyak*): A fast Polish dance in *triple meter*.

krummhorn

kurz (*Ger.*, *koorts*): Short.

Kyrie (*Gr.*, KEE-*ree-eh*): The first part of the *Ordinary* of the *Mass*. Literally means "Lord [have mercy]."

K

L

la 1: In the *fixed-do* system, the note A. **2:** In the *movable-do* system, the sixth note of the scale.

Lacrimosa (Lat., *lah-kree-MOH-zah*): A section of the Requiem mass.

lacrimoso (It., *lah-kree-MOH-zoh*): Mournful, tearful.

laisser vibrer (Fr., *les-SAY vee-BRAY*): Let vibrate.

lament: See *elegy*.

lamento, **lamentoso** (It., *lah-MEN-toh, lah-men-TOH-zoh*): Mournful.

lancio: Vigor.

Landini cadence: A *cadence* named after the medieval composer Francesco Landini characterized by the sixth *degree* of the scale inserted between the *leading tone* and the tonic.

Ländler (Ger., *LEND-ler*): A slow Austrian *waltz* popular in the early 19th century.

langsam (Ger., *LAHNG-zahm*): Slow.

lap steel guitar: See *steel guitar*.

largamente (It., *lahr-gah-MEN-teh*): Broadly, largely.

largando (It., *lahr-GAN-doh*): Gradually slowing down.

larghetto (It., *lahr-GET-toh*): A tempo slightly faster than *largo*.

largo (It., *LAHR-goh*): Very slow and broad.

lassù: See *csárdás*.

Latin 1: A style of music that uses rhythms popular in South America. **2:** The ancient language often used for choral music of the Catholic church.

Laute (*Ger.*, LOW-*te*)**:** Lute.

leader 1: A *conductor*. **2:** A *concertmaster*.

leading tone: The seventh degree of a *major* or *harmonic minor scale* that tends to "lead" to the tonic.

lead sheet: A *score* to a *song* including only the melody line, chords and lyrics.

leap: A *skip*.

lebendig (*Ger.*, *leh*-BEN-*dikh*)**:** Lively.

lebhaft (*Ger.*, LEHP-*hahft*)**:** Lively.

ledger lines: Short horizontal lines used to extend a *staff* either higher or lower.

legando: See *legato*.

legato (*It.*, *leh*-GAH-*toh*)**:** To play or sing groups of notes smoothly and without separate attacks.

leger lines: See *ledger lines*.

légèrement, leggeramente: See *leggero*.

leggero, leggiero (*It.*, *led*-JEH-*roh*)**:** Light, delicate.

legno (*It.*, LEN-*yoh*)**:** Wood. See *col legno*.

leicht (*Ger.*, *leisht*)**:** Light, brisk.

leise (*Ger.*, LEI-*ze*)**:** Soft.

leiser: Softer.

leitmotif, Leitmotiv (*Ger.*, LEIT-*moh-teef*)**:** A recurring musical *theme* or motive associated with a specific character. Also see *idée-fixe*.

leno (*It.*, LAY-*noh*)**:** Faint, quiet.

lentamente (*It.*, *len-tah*-MEN-*teh*)**:** Slowly.

lentando (*It.*, *len*-TAHN-*doh*)**:** Becoming slower.

lento (It., LEN-*toh*): Slow.

Les Six: See *Six, Les.*

lesto (It., LEH-*stoh*): Lively, quick.

LFO: Abbreviation for "low-frequency oscillator."

L.H.: Abbreviation for left hand.

liberamente (It., *lee-beh-rah*-MEN-*teh*): Freely.

libretto (It., lee-BRET-*toh*): The words or text of an *opera, oratorio* or *musical.*

licenza (It., *lee*-CHEN-*zah*): License, freedom.

licks: Slang for short melodic phrases.

lieblich (Ger., LEEB-*leesh*): Sweet, lovely.

Lied, Lieder (Ger., *leed,* LEED-*er*): *Song,* songs. Commonly refers to 19th-century German art songs.

lieto (It., *lee*-EH-*toh*): Joyful.

lievo (It., *lee*-EH-*voh*): Light.

ligature 1: A notational sign, from the 13th to 16th centuries, that combines two or more notes into one symbol. **2:** An adjustable band that holds the *reed* to the *mouthpiece* on clarinets and *saxophones.*

light opera: See *operetta.*

limiter: An electronic *signal* processor that reduces peaks in volume.

lip trill: A trill performed on a brass instrument that is made without using valves.

lira (It., LEE-*rah*) **1:** A medieval bowed stringed instrument. **2:** See *lyre.*

liscio (It., LEE-*shoh*): Smooth, even.

l'istesso (It., *lee*-STES-*soh*): The same.

litany (LIT-*en-ee*): A Christian prayer of supplication usually sung by a priest and answered by the congregation.

liturgical drama: Medieval plays representing Biblical stories with *monophonic* music.

liturgy (LIT-*er-jee*): The officially authorized Christian church service.

liuto (It., *lee-oo-toh*): Lute.

loco (It., LOH-*koh*): Play as written. Usually follows a passage marked *8va* or *8vb*. Literally means "place."

Locrian (LOK-*ree-an*): A *mode* that corresponds to the half- and whole-step patterns created when playing B to B on the white keys of the piano. See p. 296.

loudness: The intensity of sound. Also see *volume*.

loud pedal: The right pedal on a *piano* that lifts the dampers.

lourde (Fr., *loord*): Heavy.

loure (Fr., *loor*) **1:** A 17th-century dance in a moderate $\frac{6}{4}$ time. **2:** A *bagpipe*.

louré (Fr., *loo-RAY*): *Legato*. A bowing that gives a slight separation to each note of a slurred passage.

luftig (Ger., LOOF-*tikh*): Light.

Luftpause (Ger., LOOFT-*pow-ze*): A pause to breathe.

lullaby: An instrumental or vocal cradle *song*.

lunga, lungo (It., LOON-*gah*, LOON-*goh*): Long.

lustig (Ger., LOOS-*tikh*): Merry, cheerful.

lute: A plucked *stringed instrument* similar to a *guitar*, but with a bowl-shaped back, and an angled peghead.

lute

luthier (Fr., *lue-TYAY*): A maker of stringed instruments including *guitars*, *lutes* and *violins*. Literally means "lute maker."

l.v.: Abbreviation for *laissez vibrer*.

Lydian (LID-*ee-an*): A *mode* that corresponds to the half- and whole-step patterns created when playing F to F on the white keys of the piano. See p. 296.

lyra, lyre (LEE-*rah*, *leir*) **1:** An ancient Greek stringed instrument similar to a *harp*. **2:** An attachment to an instrument to hold music while marching. **3:** A *glockenspiel*.

lyric 1: The words or text of a popular *song*. **2:** In a singing or expressive style.

M

M.: In organ music, the abbreviation for *manual*.

ma (It., *mah*): But.

madrigal: Italian vocal music through the 14th and 16th centuries, usually unaccompanied. English madrigals were also written during the 16th and 17th centuries.

maestoso (It., *mah-es-TOH-zoh*): Majestic.

maestro (It., *mah-ES-troh*): Master. A title given to respected composers, conductors or teachers.

maggiore (It., *mahd-JOH-reh*): Major.

main (Fr., *mah*): Hand.

majeur (Fr., *mah-ZHER*): Major.

major: A term used to describe *chords*, *intervals* and *scales*.

major chord: See *major triad*.

major scale: A scale made up of two whole steps, one half step, three whole steps and one half step, in that order. See *Ionian mode*. See p. 279.

major triad: A *triad* consisting of a root, major third and perfect fifth.

C major triad

malagueña (*Sp., mal-lah-GEH-nyah*): A type of folk music from southern Spain.

malinconico (It., *mah-leen-KOH-nee-koh*): Melancholy.

mallet: A *drumstick* with a large tip that is either hard (wood, plastic or metal) or soft (felt).

mambo (*MAHM-boh*): A West Indian ballroom dance similar to the *cha-cha* and *rumba*.

mancando (It., *mahn-KAHN-doh*): Dying away.

mandolin (*man-doh-LIN*): A stringed instrument similar to a *lute* with eight strings tuned in pairs.

mandolin

Mannheim school (*MAN-heim*): A group of late 18th-century composers based in Mannheim, Germany who helped develop *orchestration* and the form of the classical symphony.

mano (It., *MAH-noh*): Hand.

manual: An *organ* keyboard.

manuscript 1: An original copy of a piece of music, physically written by the composer. **2:** A type of paper with blank *staves* on which music is written.

maracas (*mah-RAH-cahs*): A Latin American percussion instrument consisting of a pair of gourds filled with seeds which are shaken.

marcato (It., *mar-KAH-toh*): Accented, stressed. Indicated by the symbol ∧.

march: A composition in *duple* or *quadruple meter*, which is used for marching.

marcia (It., MAR-*chah*): March.

mariachi (Sp., *mah-ree-AH-chee*): An ensemble of Mexican folk musicians.

marimba: A tuned percussion instrument, similar to a *xylophone*, with tubular metal *resonators* under each wooden bar.

mark tree: A percussion instrument similar to *wind chimes* but larger and usually made of brass tubes.

marqué (Fr., *mar*-KAY): Accented, stressed.

Marsch (Ger., *marsh*): March.

martelé, martellato (Fr., *mar-teh*-LAY; It., *mar-tel*-LAH-*toh*): A *bowing* technique where short strokes are released suddenly which produces a marked *staccato*.

marziale (It., *mar*-TSYAH-*leh*): Martial.

masculine cadence: When a final chord occurs on a strong beat. Also see *feminine cadence*.

masque, mask: A 16th- and 17th-century stage production that combines acting, dancing, music and poetry, presented lavishly for the nobility.

Mass: The Roman Catholic church service that includes the *Kyrie, Gloria, Credo, Sanctus, Benedictus* and *Agnus Dei*.

Mässig (Ger., MES-*sish*): Moderate.

master 1: An electronic device that controls other devices. See *slave*. **2:** The final version of a recording.

Matins (Fr., *mah*-TAN): Morning prayer.

mazurka (Pol., *mah*-ZOOR-*kah*): A Polish folk dance in *triple meter* characterized by accents on weak beats and dotted rhythms.

m'bira (Ban., *um*-BEE-*rah*): A hand held African instrument consisting of thin metal or cane tongues which are

M

plucked by the thumbs. Sometimes called a *thumb piano*.

m.d.: The abbreviation for *main droite* or *mano destra*, both meaning right hand.

me: See *mi*.

mean-tone temperament: A system of tuning used from the early 1500s until around 1830 which provided pure intonation for the key of C major at the expense of many notes outside of that key being out of tune.

measure: The notes and rests between two bar lines.

medesimo (It., *meh-DEH-see-moh*): The same.

mediant: The third degree of a scale.

medieval: The historical period of music roughly from 500 to 1450. Also known as the *Middle Ages*.

medley: An arrangement that links together two or more popular songs.

mélange (Fr., *may-LAWNZH*): See *medley*.

melisma: More than one note sung to one syllable.

mellophone: A brass instrument similar to a *French horn* but with a forward-facing bell to facilitate marching.

melodia (It., *meh-loh-DEE-ah*): Melody.

melodic minor: A *natural minor scale* with the sixth and seventh degrees raised while ascending, and the sixth and seventh degrees lowered while descending. See p. 279.

melody: A succession of single notes.

melos (Gr., *MEH-lohs*): Song.

membranophones: Instruments that produce sounds through the vibrations of a membrane or *drumhead*.

meno (It., *MEH-noh*): Less.

mensural notation: A system of musical notation used from around 1250 to 1600 that indicates the

M

duration of each note.

menuet, Menuett (Fr., meh-nue-AY; Ger., mey-noo-ET): See *minuet*.

messa di voce (It., MES-*sah dee* VOH-*cheh*): An 18th-century *bel canto* vocal technique where the vocalist will gradually *crescendo* and *decrescendo* on a sustained note.

mesto (It., MES-*toh*): Sad.

metallophone: Percussion instrument with tuned metal bars.

meter, metre: The pattern of beats by which a piece of music is measured. Also see *time signature*.

metronome: An adjustable device that indicates the exact tempo of a piece. See M.M.

mezza, mezzo (It., MED-*zah*, MED-*zoh*): Half, moderately.

mezza voce (It., MED-*zah* VOH-*cheh*): Half voice. Half the volume.

mezzo forte (It., MED-*zoh* FOHR-*teh*): Moderately loud, abbreviated *mf*.

mezzo piano (It., MED-*zoh* PYAH-*noh*): Moderately soft, abbreviated *mp*.

mezzo soprano (It., MED-*zoh* soh-PRAH-*noh*): A female voice with a range between a *soprano* and an *alto*.

mezzo staccato (It., MED-*zoh* stahk-KAH-*toh*): Short, but not as short as *staccato*. Indicated by a dot and a slur or a dot and a *tenuto* mark.

mf: The abbreviation for *mezzo forte*.

m.g.: The abbreviation for *main gauche*, meaning left hand.

M

mi (It., *mee*) **1:** In the *fixed-do* system, the note E. **2:** In the *movable-do* system, the third note of the scale.

microtone: An interval smaller than a *half step*.

Middle Ages: See *medieval*.

middle C: The note C that is near the middle of the piano keyboard. It is notated between the treble and bass staves of the *grand staff*.

MIDI: Abbreviation for "musical instrument digital interface." A *digital* language used to connect computers, *synthesizers* and *sequencers*.

MIDI In, Out, Thru: The cable *ports* that receive (In), transmit (Out) or pass through (Thru) MIDI data.

mineur (Fr., *mee*-NER): Minor.

miniature score: A *full score* that is reduced in size so as to be inexpensive and convenient for study purposes. Also known as a *study score*.

minim: A *half note*.

minimalism: A late 20th century compositional style characterized by short melodic and rhythmic figures, a steady pulsing beat and a large amount of repetition with variations that are barely perceptible. Also called *process music*.

minim rest: A *half rest*.

minor: Smaller. A term used to describe chords, intervals and scales.

minor chord: See *minor triad*.

minor scale: See *natural minor*, *harmonic minor* and *melodic minor*. Also see p. 279.

minor triad: A *triad* consisting of a root, minor third and perfect fifth.

minstrel: A professional musician of the Middle Ages.

minuet: A French country dance in *triple meter*. Frequently used as the third movement of symphonies and other forms of the *classical* period.

mirror canon: A *canon* that sounds the same whether performed backwards or forwards.

missa (Lat., MEES-*sah*): Mass.

misterioso (It., *mees-teh-ree-OH-zoh*): Mysteriously.

misura (It., *mee-ZOO-rah*): Bar, *measure*.

mit (Ger., *mit*): With.

mix: To create the correct balance of recorded *tracks*.

mixer: An electronic device that enables one to *mix*. Also called a *mixing console* or *mixing board*.

mixing console, mixing board: See *mixer*.

Mixolydian (*mix-oh*-LID-*ee-an*): A *mode* that corresponds to the whole- and half-step patterns created when playing G to G on the white keys of the piano. See p. 296.

M.M.: 1: The abbreviation for "Maelzel's metronome." See *metronome*. **2:** Abbreviation for a master's degree in music.

modal: Pertaining to the *modes*.

modality: Harmonies and/or melodies based on the *modes*.

mode: Notes arranged into a specific scale. See *Aeolian, Dorian, Ionian, Locrian, Lydian, Mixolydian, Phrygian*. See p. 295. Also see *authentic mode, plagal mode, hyper-* and *hypo-*.

moderato (It., *moh-deh-RAH-toh*): In a moderate tempo.

modern: Music composed during the 20th century, also known as *contemporary music*.

modulate, modulation: To change *key* within a composition.

moll (Ger., *mohl*): Minor.

molto (It., MOHL-*toh*): Very.

monochord: An ancient instrument with one string stretched over a sound box and a moveable bridge which is adjusted to produce different pitches.

monophonic, monophony: A single melodic line without any additional parts or accompaniment. As opposed to *polyphony*.

monothematic: A composition based on one *theme*.

monotone: Reciting liturgical text on one pitch.

morceau (Fr., *mor-SOH*): Piece, composition.

mordent (Ger., *MOR-dent*): A musical *ornament* consisting of the alternation of the written note with the one immediately below it. Also see *inverted mordent*. See p. 304.

morendo (It., *moh-REN-doh*): Dying away.

mosso (It., *MOHS-soh*): Moved, agitated.

motet (*moh-TET*) **1:** A short unaccompanied contrapuntal choral composition of the 13th through 15th centuries. **2:** A choral piece, usually accompanied, written in the 17th and 18th centuries.

motif, motive (Fr., *moh-TEEF*; Eng., *MOH-tiv*): A short melodic or rhythmic figure that recurs throughout a composition.

moto (It., *MOH-toh*): Motion.

Motown sound: A style of popular music that orginated in the 1960s which combined *gospel*, *rhythm & blues* and pop styles. Its name comes from Motown Records.

mouth organ: Harmonica.

mouthpiece: The part of a *woodwind* or *brass instrument* that is placed on the lips or in the mouth of the performer.

movable-do: A system of assigning syllables to notes where the first note of any diatonic scale is called "do." Also see *fixed-do*, *solfège* and *solmization*.

movement: The complete and independent sections of a larger work such as a *sonata*, *suite* or *symphony*.

M

mp: The abbreviation for *mezzo piano*.

m.s.: The abbreviation for *mano sinistra*, meaning left hand.

multiphonics: The production of two or more notes, simultaneously on a *wind instrument*.

multitimbral: The ability to play more than one sound simultaneously on a *synthesizer*.

multitracking: To record each voice, instrument or sound onto different *tracks* which are to be *mixed* later.

musette (Fr., mue-ZET) **1:** A French *bagpipe* popular in the 17th and 18th centuries. **2:** A dance with a *drone* bas imitating the sound of a *bagpipe*. **3:** A *flageolet*.

music: Organized sound.

musica ficta: Questionable chromatic alterations used in the performance of music from the 10th through the 16th centuries. In modern editions, the are shown as accidentals placed above the notes.

musical: The popular 20th-century American and British development of the *operetta*.

musical saw: A large handsaw that is played with a violin *bow* and bent to change pitch.

music drama: A term used by Richard Wagner to describe *opera*.

musicology: The study of *music*.

musique concrète (Fr., mue-ZEEK kohn-KRET): Music created by preparing recorded natural and man-made sounds.

muta (It., MOO-tah): Change. Indicates to change the note of a *timpani* or the change of the key of a *brass instrument*.

mute: A device added to an instrument to soften or muffle its tone.

muting: To *mute*.

m.v.: The abbreviation for *mezza voce*.

N

N: Abbreviation for *niente*.

nach (*Ger.*, *nahkh*): After, in the manner of.

Nachschlag (*Ger.*, NAHKH-*shlahk*): The notes that end a *trill*.

Nachtmusik (*Ger.*, NAHKHT-*moo-zik*): Night music. A *serenade*.

nach und nach (*Ger.*, NAHKH *oont* NAHKH): Little by little.

naked fifth: See *open fifth*.

NARAS: Abbreviation for the "National Academy of Recording Arts and Sciences." This organization is responsible for the Grammy awards.

natural: The symbol ♮ that indicates a note is neither sharp nor flat.

natural harmonic: A *harmonic* produced on an open string of a stringed instrument. Also called an *open harmonic*.

natural horn

natural horn: A *horn* without valves.

natural minor: A scale made up of one whole step, one half step, two whole steps, one half step and two whole steps, in that order. Also see *Aeolian* mode. See p. 279.

N.C.: The abbreviation for "no chord."

Neapolitan school: A school of composers in the 18th century that originated in Naples.

Neapolitan sixth: A first inversion chord built on the lowered second degree of a scale. A Neapolitan sixth chord in the key of C is F, A-flat, D-flat.

Nebenstimme (*Ger.*, *nay-ben*-SHTIM-*meh*): A secondary part. As opposed to *Hauptstimme*.

neck: The long thin part of some *stringed instruments* to which the *fingerboard* or *fretboard* is attached.

neighboring tone: A nonharmonic tone one scale step above or below another tone that returns to the first tone.

neoclassicism: A 20th-century revival of forms and ideas of the *classical period*.

neoromanticism: A revival in the middle to late 20th century of forms, harmonies and ideas of the music of the 19th-century *romantic* period.

neumes: Notational symbols used during the *Middle Ages*.

New Age: A late 20th-century musical style characterized by repetition, simple harmonies, little structure and soft gentle sounds.

new Viennese school: See *Viennese school*.

niente (It., *nee-EN-teh*): Nothing, silence. Abbreviated *N*.

ninth: The interval of nine steps (an octave plus a second).

ninth chord: A chord consisting of a root, third, fifth, seventh and ninth.

nobile (It., *NOH-bee-lay*): Noble.

nocturne (Fr., *nohk-*TUERN; Eng., NOK-*turn*): A *romantic* piece in a melancholy mood, usually for *piano*.

node: The points of a vibrating object that are at rest.

noël (Fr., *noh-*EL): Christmas *carol* or *song*.

non (It., *nohn*): Not.

nonet 1: A composition for nine performers. **2:** A group of nine performers.

nonharmonic notes: Notes that are not part of the harmony at that moment.

notation: The method of writing down music (*pitch, rhythm, dynamics*, etc.) for performance.

note: The symbols used to notate music:

whole note: o, half note: 𝅗𝅥, quarter note: 𝅘𝅥,

eighth note: 𝅘𝅥𝅮, sixteenth note: 𝅘𝅥𝅯,

thirty-second note: 𝅘𝅥𝅰. See p. 277.

notehead: The head or main round part of a *note*.

note on/note off: MIDI codes that instruct when a note starts and ends.

notturno (It., *noht*-TOOR-*noh*) **1:** A *serenade*. **2:** A *nocturne*.

nowell (Eng., *noh*-EL): See *noël*.

nuance: Subtle changes in musical expression including *dynamics*, *phrasing* and *tempo*.

nut 1: The part of a stringed instrument at the top of the neck that keeps the string raised over the *fingerboard* or *fretboard*. **2:** Part of a *bow*, at the *frog*, that adjusts the tension of the bow-hairs.

O

o 1: The symbol for a *harmonic*. **2:** The symbol for an open string. **3:** The symbol for a *diminished* chord.

O: (It., *oh*) Or.

obbligato, Obligato (It., *ohb-blee*-GAH-*toh*; Ger., *oh-blee*-GAH-*toh*): An essential part that should not be omitted. More recently this term has come to mean a part that can be freely omitted if necessary.

ober (Ger., OH-*ber*): Higher.

oblique motion: When one voice remains stationary and the other moves.

oboe: A *double-reed* woodwind instrument that is the highest member of the *oboe family*. See p. 318 for range.

oboe

oboe da caccia (It., OH-*boh-eh dah* CAH-*tchah*): An early version of the *English horn* used during the *Renaissance*.

oboe d'amore (It., OH-*boh-eh dah*-MOH-*reh*): A mellow-sounding *double-reed* instrument pitched a minor third below an oboe.

oboe family: A family of *double-reed* instruments that includes the *oboe*, *English horn*, *heckelphone*, *bassoon* an *contrabassoon*.

ocarina (It., *oh-kah*-REE-*nah*, *ok-uh*-REE-*nuh*): A bird-shape wind instrument with finger holes and a *whistle mouthpiece*.

octave: The interval of eight diatonic steps or from one note to its nearest note of the same name, 12 half steps away. Also see *all'ottava*.

octet 1: A composition for eight performers. **2:** A group of eight performers.

ode 1: A musical work of praise. **2:** A chorus in ancient Greek plays.

oder (Ger., OH-*der*): Or.

oeuvre (Fr., *erv*): See *opus*.

Offertory: The fourth part of the Roman Catholic *Mass* sur by the choir during the offering.

ohne (Ger., OH-*ne*): Without.

oliphant: An ancient *horn* made from an elephant's tusk (ivory).

Op.: The abbreviation for *opus*.

open 1: On stringed instruments, a string that is not fingered. **2:** On brass instruments, not *muted* or *stopp*

open fifth: A *triad* that does not contain the third.

open fifth

open harmonic: See *natural harmonic*.

open harmony: When the tones of a chord are spaced over more than an octave. Also see *close harmony*.

open triad: See *open fifth*.

opera 1: A drama set to music for voices and orchestra, presented with costumes and sets. **2:** The plural of *opus*.

opéra bouffe, opera buffa (Fr., oh-pay-RAH boof; It., OH-pay-rah BOOF-fah): See *comic opera*.

opéra comique (Fr., oh-pay-RAH kuh-MEEK): See *comic opera*.

opera seria (It., OH-peh-rah SEH-ree-ah): A serious opera.

operetta (It., oh-peh-RET-tah): A short *opera* in a light, popular style.

ophicleide (AW-fi-kleid): The bass *key bugle*. Parts originally written for the ophicleide are now played by the *tuba*.

Opp.: The abbreviation for *opera*, which is the plural of *opus*.

Op. Posth.: Abbreviation for a posthumous *opus*, that is, a work published after the composer's death.

ophicleide

O

opus (Lat., OH-puhs): A number given to chronologically order the works of a composer. Literally means "work."

oratorio (It., oh-rah-TOH-ree-oh): A composition for voices and instrumental accompaniment, usually with a *sacred* text.

orchestra: A large group of instrumentalists usually consisting of *stringed*, *woodwind*, *brass* and *percussion* instruments.

orchestration: To designate which instruments play which parts of a composition.

Ordinary: The parts of the Roman Catholic Mass that remain the same from day to day, as opposed to the *Proper*. The *Ordinary* includes the *Kyrie, Gloria, Credo, Sanctus* and *Agnus Dei*.

organ 1: A keyboard instrument with both manual and pedal keyboards that produces sound by sending air through pipes of various lengths. **2:** An electronic instrument that creates the sounds made by a *pipe organ*.

organum (It., OHR-*gahn-oom*) **1:** An early form of *polyphonic* music from around 900 to 1200 that consists of a *plainchant* melody harmonized with parallel fourths or fifths. **2:** An *organ*.

Orgel (Ger., OR-*gl*): Organ.

ornamentation: To embellish a melody. See p. 304.

ornaments: The notes that embellish a melody. See *acciaccatura, appoggiatura, grace notes, inverted mordent, mordent, trill* and *turn*. See p. 304.

oscillator: An electronic device that generates audio *waveforms*.

ossia (It., *ohs*-SEE-*ah*): An alternate part.

ostinato (It., *ohs-tee*-NAH-*toh*): An accompaniment figure that is repeated. Also see *basso ostinato*.

ottava (It., *oht*-TAH-*vah*): Octave.

ottava alta (It., *oht*-TAH-*vah* AHL-*tah*): Play an octave higher. Abbreviated 8*va*.

ottava bassa (It., *oht*-TAH-*vah* BAHS-*sah*): Play an octave lower. Abbreviated 8*va bassa* or 8*va* placed below the note(s).

ottavino (It., *oht-tah-*VEE-*noh*): A *piccolo*.

overblow: To blow a woodwind instrument so hard that a *harmonic* is sounded.

overdrive: Distortion, which is used as an *effect*, created by overloading an amplifier.

overdub, overdubbing: To record a *track* over a previously used *track*, or to add to a recording by recording onto an unused *track*.

overtone series: The notes of the *harmonic* series except for the *fundamental*.

overture: An instrumental composition used as an introduction to a *ballet*, *opera* or *oratorio*. Also see *concert overture*.

P

P.: The abbreviation for *pedal*. Also see P*ed*.

***p*:** The abbreviation for *piano*.

pacato (It., *pah-*KAH-*toh*): Calm.

palm mute: To *mute* a *guitar* with the palm of the plucking hand. Abbreviated PM. See p. 311.

pandiatonicism: A 20th-century compositional technique using the free harmonization of the *diatonic* scale.

panning: To move an amplified sound between two or more speakers.

panpipes: An ancient wind instrument consisting of a number of tuned pipes of different sizes which are bound together.

pantomime: A dramatic play with musical accompaniment in which the actors do not speak or sing.

pantonality: See *atonal.*

paradiddle: A drum *rudiment* where strokes are alternated as follows:

parallel chords: The successive sounding of the same chord up or down a scale.

parallel (consecutive) fifths, octaves: Two parts moving in parallel motion a fifth or an octave apart

parallel keys: Major and minor keys with the same *keynote.*

parallel motion: The movement of two or more parts, with the interval between the parts remaining the same.

parameter: A variable in *synthesis* that can be changed.

parlando, parlante (It., *par*-LAHN-*doh, par*-LAHN-*teh*) **1:** A singing style that approximates speech. **2:** Clear and crisp.

part 1: A melodic line in *contrapuntal* music. **2:** The music for a particular instrument or voice. **3:** A section of a composition.

partials 1: Notes of the *harmonic series.* **2:** Harmonics.

partita (It., *par*-TEE-*tah*) **1:** A suite. **2:** Variation.

partition, Partitur, partitura (Fr., *par-tee*-SYOHN; Ger., *par*-TEE-*toor*; It., *par-tee*-TOO-*rah*): Score.

part song: An unaccompanied *homophonic* choral composition for three or more voices.

paso doble (Sp., PAH-*soh* DOH-*bleh*): A Spanish dance in a quick $\frac{2}{4}$ or $\frac{6}{8}$ time popular in the 1920s.

passacaglia (It., *pahs-sah*-KAH-*lyah*): A continuous set of variations based on a repeating bass line. Similar to a *chaconne.*

passage: A section of a composition.

passepied (Fr., *pahs-se*-PYAY)**:** A spirited French dance in a fast *triple meter*.

passing tones: A non-chordal tone that is melodically placed between two chord tones and usually occurs on a weak beat. When on a strong beat, it is an *accented passing tone*.

Passion: A musical setting of the suffering and death of Christ.

passionato (It., *pahs-see-oh*-NAH-*toh*)**:** With passion.

passione (It., *pahs-see*-OH-*neh*)**:** *Passion*

pastorale (It., *pahs-toh*-RAH-*leh*)**:** A vocal or instrumental piece imitating the music of shepherds or idyllic scenes.

patch 1: A set of *parameters* stored in the memory of a *synthesizer*. **2:** To connect various electronic devices with *patch cords*.

patch bay: A group of input and output sockets into which *patch cords* are plugged to route *signals* for recording.

patch cords: Cords used in recording to route *signals* to and from recorders, *mixers*, computers and other devices.

pathétique (Fr., *pah-tay*-TEEK)**:** With great emotion.

patter song: A fast, humorous *song*.

Pauken (Ger., POW-*ken*)**:** *Timpani*.

pausa See *pause*.

pause 1: A *rest*. **2:** A *fermata*.

pavane (Fr., *pah*-VAHN)**:** A slow 16th-century Italian court dance usually in $\frac{4}{4}$ or $\frac{4}{2}$ meter.

PCM: Abbreviation, in *synthesis*, for "pulse code modulation," which is a method of storing *samples*.

ped.: The abbreviation for *pedal*.

pedal 1: A mechanism on a musical instrument that is operated with the feet, most frequently found on the *piano*, *organ*, *harp* and *harpsichord*. **2:** The lowest notes available on a brass instrument (*fundamental*). See also *pedal tone*. **3:** Abbreviation for *pedal point*.

pedal board: A *keyboard* played with the feet.

pedal point: A long, sustained note, usually in the bass, that is held while harmonies change in the other parts.

pedal steel guitar: An electronic *steel guitar* mounted on a stand with *pedals* and knee levers that change the tunings of the strings.

pedal tone 1: A sustained or continually repeated note. **2:** The lowest notes available on a brass instrument (*fundamental*). Also see *pedal*.

peg: Device on stringed instruments that is used to adjust the tension of a string.

pentatonic scale: A scale having five tones to the octave. usually avoids any half steps and corresponds to the notes played on the black keys on the piano. See p. 279.

percussion instruments: Instruments whose sounds are created by striking or shaking. They include *drums*, *cymbals*, *tambourine*, *bells*, *triangle*, *piano*, etc. They can create definite pitch (notes) or indefinite pitch (sounds). See *tuned percussion*

perdendosi (It., *per-DEN-doh-see*)**:** Dying away.

perfect cadence: A *cadence* where the progression moves from a root-position dominant chord to the root-position tonic chord (V-I). Also see *authentic cadence*.

perfect interval: An unaltered interval of the unison, fourth, fifth or octave.

perfect pitch: See *absolute pitch*.

period: A group of measures that complete a musical thought, usually consisting of two or more contrasting *phrases* and a *cadence*.

perpetual canon: A *canon* whose ending leads back to the beginning so it can be repeated indefinitely.

pesante (It., *peh-SAHN-teh*): Heavy.

petit (Fr., *puh-TEE*): Little.

peu à peu (Fr., *PUH ah PUH*): Little by little.

pezzi (It., *PET-zee*): Pieces.

pezzo (It., *PET-zoh*): Piece.

pf: Abbreviation for *pianoforte*.

phrase 1: A complete musical idea. **2:** A part of a *period*.

phrasing 1: The shaping of a melodic line. **2:** An *articulation* mark used to imply the phrasing of a line.

Phrygian (*FRIG-ee-an*): A *mode* that corresponds to the whole- and half-step patterns created when playing E to E on the white keys of the piano. See p. 295.

pianissimo (It., *pyah-NEES-see-moh*): Very soft, abbreviated *pp*.

pianississimo (It., *pyah-nees-SEES-see-moh*): Very, very soft, abbreviated *ppp*.

piano (It., *PYAH-noh*) **1:** Soft, abbreviated *p*. **2:** A *pianoforte*. See p. 334 for range.

pianoforte (It., *pyah-noh-FOHR-teh*): The full name of the keyboard percussion instrument commonly known as the *piano*. Sound is produced by hammers that strike strings when keys are depressed on the keyboard. It literally means "soft-loud."

piano quartet: An ensemble consisting of *piano*, *violin*, *viola* and *cello*, or a composition for that ensemble.

piano quintet: An ensemble usually consisting of *piano*, two *violins*, *viola* and *cello*, or a composition for that ensemble. Schubert's "Trout" quintet uses the unusual ensemble of *piano*, *violin*, *viola*, *cello* and *double bass*.

piano score: An arrangement of an orchestral or vocal work for *piano*.

piano trio: An ensemble consisting of *piano*, *violin* and *cello*, or a composition for that ensemble.

piatti (It., PYAHT-*tee*): *Cymbals*.

Picardy third: When a piece in a minor key ends with a major chord.

piccolo (It., PEEK-*koh-loh*): See *flute*.

pick: A device used to pluck or strum the strings of a stringed instrument such as a *guitar*, *bass guitar* or *mandolin*. It is sometimes called a *plectrum*.

pick scrape: A *guitar* technique of sliding a pick sideways down a wound string (usually the lower four).

pickup 1: A *note* (or notes) that occurs before the first complete measure. Also see *anacrusis* and *upbeat*. **2:** An electronic device that converts vibrations of an instrument into electrical impulses.

piece: A musical composition.

pipe 1: Wind instruments in the shape of a tube. **2:** A tube that creates a musical tone when air is forced through, like those in an *organ*.

pipe organ: See *organ*, 1.

piston: A *valve*.

pitch: The location of a note related to its highness or lowness.

pitch bend: A device on a *synthesizer* that allows the pitch of a note to be bent.

pitch class: Those notes with the same letter name, regardless of octave.

pitch pipe: A small wind instrument with one or more pipes with fixed pitch used as a reference to set the pitch for a choir, or tune instruments.

più (It., *pyoo*): More.

pivot chord: In *modulation*, a chord that is common to both the old key and the new key.

pizz.: Abbreviation for *pizzicato*.

pizzicato (It., *peed-zee-KAH-toh*): To pluck a string. Abbreviated *pizz*.

placido (It., *PLAH-see-doh*): Calm, placid, tranquil.

plagal cadence: A *cadence* where the progression moves from a subdominant chord to the tonic chord (IV-I). It is sometimes called an Amen *cadence*.

plagal mode: A *mode* whose *keynote* is a fourth higher than the lowest note. Also see *authentic mode*.

plainchant, plainsong 1: *Gregorian Chant*. **2:** Monophonic, unmeasured *chant*.

player piano: A mechanical piano that plays back music that has been recorded onto a paper roll or, more recently, magnetic tapes or computer disks.

plectrum: See *pick*.

plein-jeu (Fr., *plen-ZHUH*): Full organ.

P

plop: A technique on wind instruments where a rapid chromatic or diatonic scale is played down into the main note.

plop

PM: Abbreviation for *palm mute*.

poco a poco (It., POH-koh ah POH-koh): Little by little.

poi (It., *poy*): Then.

point: The tip of a *bow*.

pointillism: A 20th-century compositional style where emphasis is placed on single notes.

polka: A fast Bohemian dance in *duple time* that originated around 1830.

polonaise (Fr., poh-loh-NEZ): A stately Polish dance in a moderate *triple meter*.

polychoral style: A composition where the ensemble, vocal or instrumental, is divided into separate groups that play individually as well as together.

polychords: Single chords created by combining two or more chords.

polymetric: Using two different *meters* simultaneously.

polyphonic 1: An instrument capable of sounding two or more notes at one time. **2.** *Polyphony*.

polyphony: When two or more melodic lines are combined. As opposed to *monophony*.

polyrhythm: Two or more different rhythms played simultaneously.

polytonality: When two or more keys, or tonal centers, are used simultaneously.

P

pomposo (It., *pohm-POH-zoh*): Majestic, pompous.

ponticello (It., *pohn-tee-CHEL-loh*): The *bridge* of a stringed instrument.

port: A socket or plug on an *electronic instrument*, computer or other device in *synthesis*.

portamento: To slide smoothly from one note to the next.

portative organ: A small portable *organ* of the Middle Ages.

portato (It., *por-TAH-toh*): See *louré*.

pos.: Abbreviation for *position*.

Posaune (Ger., *poh-ZOW-ne*): *Trombone*.

position 1: The arrangement of the notes of a chord. See *inversion*. **2:** The placement of the hand on the *fingerboard* or *fretboard* of a stringed instrument. **3:** The placement of the slide of a *trombone*.

positive organ: A large portable *organ* of the Middle Ages that required an assistant to work the bellows.

posthorn: A *horn* without valves that was originally used to announce post coaches.

postlude 1: An instrumental piece played at the conclusion of a church service, usually for an *organ*. **2:** A *coda*.

potentiometer: In *synthesis*, a nob, fader or other device used to control a *signal*.

poussé, poussez (Fr., *poos-SAY*): Up-bow.

pp: The abbreviation for *pianissimo*.

ppp: The abbreviation for *pianississimo*.

praeludium (Lat., *pray-LOO-dee-oom*): *Prelude*.

Pralltriller (Ger., *PRAHL-tril-ler*): An *inverted mordent*.

prebend: To bend a string on the *guitar* before playing it.

preciso (It., *preh-SEE-zoh*): Precise.

prélude (Fr., *pray-LUED, PRAY-lood*): A musical *introduction*.

première (Fr., *pre-MEER*): The first performance.

preparation: When the *dissonant* note of a chord was a *consonant* note of the previous chord.

prepared piano: Placing foreign objects such as screws, paper, felt, etc. onto the strings of a *piano* in order to alter the sound.

presets: A preprogrammed sound, or *patch*, on a *synthesizer*.

pressure sensitivity: A feature on some *synthesizers* where sounds can be controlled by the amount of pressure placed on a *key*. (See *key*, **2**.)

prestissimo (It., *pres-TEES-see-moh*): The fastest tempo. Extremely fast.

presto (It., *PRES-toh*): Very fast.

prima donna (It., *PREE-mah DOHN-nah*) **1:** The main female singer in an *opera*. **2:** A conceited, jealous performer.

prime 1: The first note of a *scale*. **2:** A *unison*.

primo (It., *PREE-moh*): First. Also see *secondo*.

principal 1: The leader of an orchestral section. **2:** A *diapason* stop on an organ.

processional: A *hymn* sung in church as the clergy enter.

process music: See *minimalism*.

program music: Music inspired by a non-musical idea, as opposed to *absolute music*.

progression: The movement from one note to another note, or one chord to another chord.

progressive jazz: A style of *jazz* of the 1950s with flowing melodies.

pronto (It., PROHN-*toh*): Prompt, swift.

Proper: The parts of the Roman Catholic *Mass* in which the text changes from day to day, as opposed to the *Ordinary*. It includes the *Introit*, Gradual, Alleluia, *Offertory* and Communion.

proportional notation: See *mensural notation*

psalm: Sacred *songs* or *hymns* based on the poems in the Book of Psalms.

psalter (SAHL-*ter*): The Book of Psalms.

psaltery (SAHL-*ter-ee*): An ancient stringed instrument similar to a *zither* that is played by plucking the strings with the fingers or a *pick*.

pull-off: A technique on stringed instruments where two notes are fingered on the same string, the higher note is played, then the finger of the higher note is raised keeping the lower note fingered. See p. 313.

pulse: A *beat*.

pulse wave: A *waveform* common in *synthesis*.

Pult (Ger., *poolt*): A music stand.

punk rock: A style of *rock* music popular in the late 1970s characterized by simple melodies and harmonies, and political lyrics.

punta (It., POON-*tah*): Point.

purfling: Inlaid borders on stringed instruments.

Pythagorean scale (*pi-thag-oh-*REE-*an*): A diatonic scale with all tones derived from the interval of a pure fifth.

P

Q

quadrille (Fr., *kwah-DREEL*): A French, 19th-century square dance in five sections that alternate between $\frac{6}{8}$ and $\frac{2}{4}$ time.

quadruple meter: A *time signature* with four beats to the *measure*.

quadruplet: Four notes played in the time of three notes of the same value.

quality of tone: Those characteristics of an instrument's tone that make it different from another instrument.

quantize: To round off the rhythmic value of a note when using a *sequencer* or *drum machine*.

quartal haromony: Harmony based on the interval of a fourth.

quarter note: A note half the length of a *half note*. See p. 277.

quarter rest: A rest half the length of a *half rest*. See p. 278.

quarter tone: An *interval* equal to one-half of a *half step*.

quartet 1: A composition for four performers. **2:** An ensemble of four performers.

quasi (It., *KWAH-zee*): As if, almost.

quaver: An *eighth note*.

quickstep: A quick *march* at about 108 steps per minute.

quill: The part of a *harpsichord* that plucks the string.

quindicesima (It., *kween-dee-CHEH-zee-mah*): The interval of a 15th (two octaves). Abbreviated 15*ma*.

quintal harmony: Harmony based on the interval of a fifth.

quintet 1: A composition for five performers. **2:** An

ensemble of five performers.

quintuple meter: A time signature with five beats to the measure.

quintuplet: Five notes played in the time of four notes of the same value.

quodlibet (*Lat.*, KWAHD-*li-bet*)**:** A composition that uses well-known tunes played either successively or simultaneously.

R

R: Abbreviation for right.

racket: A *double-reed wind instrument* used during the Renaissance. A forerunner of the *bassoon.*

racket

raga: Scales used in the music of India which are associated with different moods.

ragtime: A style of syncopated American music popular from around 1895 to 1918 that is an early type of *jazz.*

rallentando (*It.*, *rahl-len*-TAHN-*doh*)**:** Becoming gradually slower. Abbreviated *rall.*

R&B: Abbreviation for *rhythm & blues.*

range: The notes that an instrument or voice is capable of creating, from the lowest to the highest.

rap: A style of popular music that originated in the late 1970s characterized by rhyming lyrics that are spoken or half-sung in a *syncopated* style over a rhythmic *accompaniment.*

rasch (*Ger.*, *rahsh*)**:** Fast.

rasgado, rasgueado (*Sp.*, *rahz*-GAH-*doh*, *rahz-geh*-AH-*doh*)**:** A

Flamenco *guitar* technique where the strings are rapidly strummed with the backs of the fingernails.

ratamacue (RAT-*a-mah-kyoo*): A drum *rudiment* with the following pattern:

rattle: A percussion instrument consisting of a notched wooden cogwheel that is rotated against a flexible strip of metal or wood.

re (It., *ray*) **1:** In the *fixed-do* system, the note D. **2:** In the *movable-do* system, the second note of the scale.

real-time mode: To enter data into a computer or *sequencer* in actual time or a speed porportional to actual time. As opposed to *step-time mode*.

rebec (REH-*bek*): A medieval bowed stringed instrument, shaped like a pear, with one to five strings.

rebe

recapitulation: The section of a movement in *sonata form*, when the themes of the *exposition* are repeated. Usually the second *theme* is repeated at a new pitch level, primarily the *tonic* key.

recessional: A *hymn* sung in church as the clergy leave after a service.

recital 1: A performance by one or two performers. **2:** A performance featuring the works of one composer.

recitative (It., *re-chi-tah*-TEEV; Eng., *re-si-ta*-TEEV)**:** A style of singing that imitates speech, usually found between *arias* of an *opera* or *oratorio*.

recorder: An *end-blown flute* with a whistle mouthpiece, most commonly found

recorde

in music of the *Middle Ages* and *Renaissance*. Modern recorders are available in four sizes, *soprano*, *alto*, *tenor* and *bass*. See pp. 322–323 for ranges.

reduction: The arrangement of a composition for a smaller number of instruments than originally intended.

reed: A thin piece of cane, metal, wood or plastic that produces a sound when air causes it to vibrate. See *single reed* and *double reed*.

reel: A lively dance in $\frac{4}{4}$ or $\frac{6}{4}$, for two or more couples, that originated in Scotland and Ireland.

refrain: A melody of a *song* that is repeated after each *stanza* (or *verse*). Also see *chorus* **3**.

regal: A small portable *organ* used from the 15th to 17th centuries.

reggae: A Jamaican popular music originating in the 1960s which was influenced by many diverse African and African-American musical styles.

register 1: A part of the range of an instrument or voice that is different from other parts. **2:** A set of pipes or reeds on an *organ* that is controlled by one *stop*.

registration: The selection of *organ stops* to be used in a composition.

relative keys: Minor and major keys that have the same *key signature*. For example C major and A minor are relative keys.

relative pitch: The ability to recognize and/or produce any pitch after having been given one note as a point of reference.

religioso (It., *reh-lee-JOH-zoh*)**:** In a religious style.

Renaissance: The historical period of music roughly from 1450 to 1600.

R

repeat: Signs that indicate a musical section should be repeated. See p. 308.

replica (It., REH-*pli-kah*): Repeat.

reprise (Fr., *re*-PREEZ): Repetition.

Requiem Mass: The Mass for the dead.

resin: See *rosin*.

resolution: The progression of notes or chords from *dissonance* to *consonance*.

resonance: The transfer of vibrations from one object to another.

resonator: Part of an instrument that reinforces its sound by *resonance*.

resonator guitar: See *dobro*.

response 1: A musical reply sung by the *choir* or congregation. **2:** The *answer* in a *fugue*.

responsorial: See *antiphonal*.

rest 1: Silence. **2:** Symbols that are used to indicate silence: whole rest: ▬, half rest: ▬, quarter rest: 𝄽, eighth rest: 𝄾, sixteenth rest: 𝄿, thirty-second rest: 𝅀. See p. 278.

retardation 1: Slowing gradually. **2:** A *suspension* that resolves upward.

retrograde: A melody performed backwards.

reverb, reverberation 1: The amount of time a sound remains in a room after the actual source has stopped. An *echo*. **2:** An electronic *effect* that simulates an echo.

rf , *rfz*: Abbreviation for *rinforzando*.

R.H.: Abbreviation for right hand.

rhapsody: A free-style composition usually in one movement, often based on folk melodies.

rhumba: See *rumba*.

rhythm: The organization of music in time using long and short note values.

rhythm & blues: A type of popular music that is the precursor of *rock 'n' roll*, characterized by repetitive *rhythms*, simple *melodies* and *harmonies*, and elements of *blues*. Abbreviated R&B.

rhythm section: In *jazz* and popular music, the instruments that sustain the rhythmic and harmonic support for the other instrumentalists, usually consisting of *drums*, *piano*, *bass* and *guitar*.

ribs: The sides that conect the back and front of *stringed intruments*.

ricercar, ricercare (It., ree-chehr-KAR, ree-chehr-KAH-reh): Instrumental compositions of the 16th and 17th centuries that use *imitation*.

ricochet: See *jeté*.

ride cymbal: The main *suspended cymbal* of a *drum kit*.

riff: A short repeated melodic pattern.

rigadoon, rigaudon (Eng., rig-a DOON; Fr., ree-goh-DOHN): A lively French dance usually in $\frac{4}{4}$ time.

rinforzando (It., reen-for-TSAHN-doh) **1:** Stressed. **2:** Suddenly loud. Abbreviated *rf* or *rfz*.

ripieno (It., ree-PYEH-noh): For the full orchestra as opposed to the soloists. See *concertino*, **2** and *concerto grosso*.

riposo (It., ree-POH-soh): Calm, tranquil.

rit.: Abbreviation for *ritardando*.

ritardando (It., ree-tar-DAHN-doh): Becoming gradually slower. Abbreviated *rit*.

ritenuto (It., ree-teh-NOO-toh): Held back. Becoming slower immediately. Abbreviated *riten*.

R

ritmo (It., REET-*moh*): Rhythm.

ritornello (It., *ree-tor*-NEL-*loh*) **1:** A conclusion that restates previously heard material. **2:** The *tutti* sections of a *concerto grosso*.

rock, rock 'n' roll: A type of popular music that grew out of *rhythm & blues* in the 1950s. Also see *punk rock*, *salsa*, *fusion*, *grunge*, *heavy metal*, *jazz-rock* and *zydeco*.

rococo (Fr., *roh-koh*-KOH, *roh*-KOH-*koh*): Highly ornamented music of the middle 18th century.

roll: A technique on *percussion instruments* that creates a rapid succession of notes which is notated: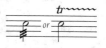

rolled chord: A chord preceded by a wavy line that indicates it is to be played as an *arpeggio* from the lowest note to the highest.

romance, romanza (Eng., *roh*-MANTS; It., *roh*-MAHN-*tsah*): A short, lyrical, instrumental or vocal composition in a romantic or sentimental mood.

Roman school: A group of composers of liturgical music that centered around Rome in the 16th century.

romantic: The historical period of music roughly from 1820 to 1910. Composers of this period include Schubert, Schumann, Chopin, Brahms, Liszt, Wagner and Bruckner among many others.

rondeau (Fr., *rohn*-DOH) **1:** A medieval French song with instrumental accompaniment. **2:** A *rondo*.

rondo (It., ROHN-*doh*): A musical form characterized by a repeated theme that alternates with other themes. With "A" representing the reoccurring theme, the following are examples of rondo forms: ABA, ABABA, ABACA and ABACABA. Also see *sonata rondo form*.

root: The *fundamental* note that gives a *chord* its name.

rosette: An ornate pattern around the *sound hole* of a *guitar*.

rosin: A substance that is applied to the hair of a *bow* to increase friction with the strings. Also called *resin*.

round: A short vocal *canon* at the unison that can be repeated indefinitely. Also see *perpetual canon*.

rounded binary: A *binary form* with a repeat of the first section: ABA.

roundelay: See *rondeau*.

row: See *tone row*.

rubato (It., *roo*-BAH-*toh*)**:** To perform with a free, flexible tempo, tastefully slowing down and speeding up at the discretion of the performer.

rudiments: Basic elements of drum techniques including the *drag*, *flam*, *paradiddle*, *ratamacue*, *roll* and *ruff*.

ruff: A drum *rudiment* that consists of a note preceded by two grace notes.

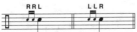

ruhig (Ger., ROO-*hig*)**:** Calm.

rumba: A *syncopated* Cuban dance whose rhythms were incorporated into *jazz* around 1930.

run: A rapid *scale* passage.

rustico (It., ROOS-*tee-koh*)**:** Rustic, pastoral.

S

S.: Abbreviation for *segno*, *senza*, *sign*, *sinistra*, *solo*, *soprano* and *subito*.

SA: Abbreviation in choral music for *soprano* and *alto*.

SAB: Abbreviation in choral music for *soprano*, *alto* and *baritone* (or *bass*).

sackbut: An early version of the *trombone*.

sacred: Religious.

Saite (*Ger.*, ZEI-*te*): String.

salsa: A Latin-American style of popular music that combines *Latin* and *rock* music.

saltato, saltando (*It.*, *sahl-TAH-toh*, *sahl-TAHN-doh*): See *sautillé*.

samba: A popular Brazilian folk dance in $\frac{2}{4}$ meter.

samisen (*Jap.*, SAH-*mee-sen*): A three-stringed Japanese *guitar* with no *frets*.

sample, sampling: A *digital* recording of a sound that is used in *synthesis*.

sampler: A device that creates a *sample*.

Sanctus (*Lat.*, SAHNK-*toos*): The fourth part of the *Ordinary* of the *Mass*.

sanft (*Ger.*, *zahnft*): Soft, gentle.

sans (*Fr.*, *sawn*): Without.

saraband: A slow, stately dance of the 17th and 18th centuries in *triple meter* with an emphasis on the second beat. In the 16th century, it was a lively, sensuous dance. Sometimes spelled saraband (*It.*), sarabande (*Fr.*, *Ger.*) or zarabanda (*Sp.*).

sarangi (Hin., *sah-RAHN-jee*): An Indian three-stringed bowed lute.

sarrusophone (*sah-ROO-soh-fohn*): A *double-reed* woodwind instrument made of brass.

SATB: Abbreviation in choral music for *soprano*, *alto*, *tenor* and *bass*.

Satz (Ger., *zots*): *Movement*.

sautillé (Fr., *soh-tee-YAY*): A staccato *bowing* style where the bow bounces off the string.

saw: See *musical saw*.

sawtooth wave: A *waveform* common in *synthesis*.

saxhorn: Valved brass instruments invented by Adolphe Sax around 1840.

saxophone: A group of *single-reed* woodwind instruments, made of brass, invented by Adolphe Sax. The different types include, from highest to lowest, the E-flat sopranino, B-flat soprano, E-flat alto, B-flat tenor, E-flat baritone, and B-flat bass. See pp. 321–322 for ranges.

tenor sax

scale: The arrangement of notes in a specific order of whole and half steps. See p. 279.

scale degrees: The names and numbers given to each note of a *scale*. They are: *tonic* (I), *supertonic* (II), *mediant* (III), *subdominant* (IV), *dominant* (V), *submediant* or *superdominant* (VI) and *subtonic* or *leading tone* (VII).

scat: A type of improvisational *jazz* singing that uses nonsense syllables rather than words.

schalmei, schalmey (*SHAL-mee*): See *shawm*.

scherzando, scherzhaft (It., *skehr-TSAHN-doh*; Ger., SHEHRTS-*hahft*): Jokingly, playful.

S

scherzo (It., SKEHR-*tsoh*) **1:** A movement of symphonies, sonatas and quartets in a quick *triple meter* that replaced the *minuet*. **2:** Light vocal music of the *baroque* period. Literally means "a joke."

schnell (Ger., *shnel*)**:** Fast.

Schneller (Ger., SHNEL-*ler*)**:** See *inverted mordent*.

schola cantorum (Lat., SKOH-*lah kahn*-TOH-*room*)**:** The papal choir and school of singing organized by St. Gregory in the late 6th century that helped promote *Gregorian chant* in other churches and monasteries.

Schottische (Ger., SHOHT-*ti-sheh*)**:** A round dance in $\frac{2}{4}$ time, similar to a slow *polka*.

scoop: To slide into a note from below, rather than attacking it cleanly.

scordatura (It., *skohr-dah*-TOO-*rah*)**:** Changing the standard tuning of one or more strings on a stringed instrument in order to play unusual chords, difficult passages or to alter the *tone color*.

score: The organized notation of all of the instrumental and/or vocal parts of a composition.

scoring 1: See *arranging*, *instrumentation* and *orchestrating*. **2:** To compose music for a film.

Scotch snap: The rhythmic figure of a *sixteenth note* followed by a *dotted eighth note*. Sometimes called a *catch*.

secco (It., SEK-*koh*)**:** Dry, simple.

secco recitative (It., SEK-*koh re-chi-tah*-TEEV)**:** A *recitative* with no expression.

second: The *interval* of two *diatonic* steps.

secondary dominant: A *dominant* chord built on the fifth above any chord other than the *tonic*.

secondo (It., *seh*-KOHN-*doh*): The second part or the second player. Also see *primo*.

secular: That which is not *sacred*.

segno (It., SAY-*nyo*): Sign. A sign used to indicate the beginning or ending of a section that is to be repeated. Usually indicated by the symbol %

segue (It., SAY-*gway*) **1:** To play the following *movement* or section without a break **2:** See *simile*.

sehr (Ger., *zehr*): Very.

semibreve: A *whole note*.

semiquaver: A *sixteenth note*.

semitone: One *half step*.

semplice (It., *sem*-PLEE-*cheh*): Simple.

sempre (It., SEM-*preh*): Always.

senza (It., SEN-*tsah*): Without.

septet 1: A composition for seven performers. **2:** A group of seven performers.

septuplet: Seven notes played in the time of four (or six) notes of the same value.

sequence 1: The repetition of a musical phrase at different pitch levels. **2:** A Roman Catholic *hymn*. **3:** The information recorded onto or played by a *sequencer*.

sequencer: A MIDI device that records and plays back musical information through a *synthesizer*. Also see *drum machine*.

serenade 1: A light vocal or instrumental composition. **2:** A *song* sung beneath a lover's window at night.

serenata (It., *seh-reh*-NAH-*tah*) **1:** A *serenade*. **2:** An 18th-century dramatic *cantata*.

sereno (It., *seh*-REH-*noh*): Serene, tranquil.

seria, serio (It., SEH-*ree*-ah, SEH-*ree*-oh): Serious.

serial music: A 20th-century compositional style where all structural and thematic material is derived from a series of notes chosen from the 12 tones of the *chromatic scale*. This term is sometimes used interchangeably with *twelve-tone* or *dodecaphonic* music.

serpent: An obsolete bass *cornett* used from the late 16th to the middle 19th centuries.

sestet, sestetto (It., *ses*-TET, *ses*-TET-*toh*): A *sextet*.

set: 1. A grouping of *pitches*. 2. Slang for a *drumset*.

seven-string guitar: A *guitar* with an added high A string.

seventh: The *interval* of seven *diatonic* steps.

seventh chord: A chord consisting of a *root*, *third*, *fifth* and *seventh* degrees. Also see *dominant seventh*.

sextet 1: A composition for six performers. **2:** A group of six performers.

sextuplet: Six notes played in the time of four notes of the same value. The first, third and fifth notes should be accented, as opposed to playing as a double *triplet*.

***sf*:** Abbreviation for *sforzando*.

sforzando (It., *sfor*-TSAHN-*doh*): A sudden, strong *accent* abbreviated ***sf*** or ***sfz***.

***sfp*:** Abbreviation for a *sforzando* followed immediately by playing *piano* (soft).

***sfz*:** Abbreviation for *sforzando*.

shake: A *trill*.

shakuhachi (Jap., *shah-koo*-HAH-*chee*): A Japanese bamboo *end-blown* *flute* with five finger holes.

Shamisen (Jap., SHAM-*i-sen*): A Japanese *lute* with three strings and a soundbox covered with a skin.

shanty: See *chantey, chanty.*

shape-note: A system of *notation* where different shapes are used to indicate different notes of the scale.

sharp 1: The symbol ♯ that indicates to raise a pitch one half step. **2:** A pitch played or sung that is slightly higher than normal. Also see *double sharp.*

shawm: A high-pitched medieval *double-reed* woodwind instrument. A forerunner of the *oboe.*

sheng: A Chinese *mouth organ* that consists of bamboo *pipes* containing free reeds that are inserted into an air chamber in the form of a circle. The Japanese version is called a *shō.*

sheng

shift, shifting: The changing of the *position* of the fingering hand of a stringed instrument.

shō: The Japanese version of the *sheng.*

shofar (*Heb.,* SHOH-*far*)**:** An ancient Jewish trumpet made from a ram's horn.

shuffle: A repetitive rhythmic style consisting of dotted eighth and *sixteenth notes* played in succession (often *swing time*) with an emphasis on the second and fourth beats in $\frac{4}{4}$ time.

si (*It., see*) **1:** In the *fixed-do* system, the note B. **2:** In the *movable-do* system, the seventh note of the scale.

side drum: A *snare drum.*

sight-reading, sight-singing: Playing, or singing a piece of music at first sight–without previous rehearsal.

signal: An electrical impulse used in *synthesis.*

signal horn: A *bugle.*

S

signal processor: An electronic device that alters an audio *signal* such as a device that produces *effects*.

signature: Signs at the beginning of a composition or *staff* that indicate the *key* or *meter*. See *key signature* and *time signature*.

sim.: Abbreviation for *simile*.

similar motion: When two or more parts move in the same direction, but the interval between them changes.

simile (It., SEE-*mee-leh*, SIM-*i-lee*): Continue to perform in the same style. Abbreviated *sim*.

simple meter: A *time signature* where each beat is divisible by two. For example, $\frac{2}{4}$, $\frac{3}{4}$ and $\frac{4}{4}$. Also see *compound meter*.

sin' (*seen*): See *sino*.

sine wave: A pure, simple *waveform* common in *synthesis*.

sinfonia (It., *seen-foh-NEE-ah*, *seen-FOH-nyah*) **1:** A *symphony*. **2:** An *overture* to an *opera*, *suite* or *cantata*. **3:** The name Bach gave to his three-part inventions. **4:** A *chamber orchestra*.

sinfonietta (It., *seen-fo-NYET-tah*): A small *symphony*, usually for a *chamber orchestra*.

singing: To make music by means of the human voice.

single reed: A single piece of cane that is attached to a *mouthpiece* by a *ligature* and creates a sound by vibrating when air is forced through. They are used on *clarinets* and *saxophones*.

Singspiel (Ger., *ZING-shpel*): A light 18th-century German *opera* that has spoken interludes.

sinistra (It., *SEEN-ees-trah*): Left.

sino (It., *SEE-noh*): Until.

sistrum: An ancient Egyptian metal rattle.

sitar: A long-necked Indian lute with 18 movable frets and two sets of strings. The upper set has three to seven strings which are used for *melody* and a *drone* accompaniment. The lower set consists of nine to thirteen *sympathetic strings*.

sitar

Six, Les: A 20th century group of six French composers who loosely followed the aesthetic ideals of Erik Satie. They were Georges Auric, Louis Durey, Arthur Honegger, Darius Milhaud, Francis Poulenc and Germaine Tailleferre.

six chord: A triad in first *inversion*, that is, with the third in the bass.

six-four chord: A triad in second *inversion*, that is, with the fifth in the bass.

sixteenth note: A note half the length of an eighth note. See p. 277.

sixteenth rest: A rest half the length of an eighth rest. See p. 278.

sixth chord 1: See *added sixth*. **2:** See *six chord*.

ska: An early form of *reggae*.

skiffle: A British style of popular music of the 1950s, influenced by *jazz* and *blues*.

skip: Melodic movement of an interval larger than a *second*.

slancio (It., ZLAHN-*choh*): Impetuosity, outburst, dash.

slave: An electronic device that is controlled by another device. See MIDI.

sleigh bells: A group of small metal bells attached to a leather strap, or a frame made of wood or steel, that is shaken.

slentando (It., *slen-TAHN-doh*): Becoming gradually slower.

slide 1: To move smoothly from one note to another. See *portamento* and *glissando*. **2:** The movable portion of brass instruments, particularly the *trombone*, that adjusts the pitch. **3:** A glass or metal tube that fits over a finger of a guitarist's fretting hand. See *bottleneck*.

slide trumpet: A trumpet that uses a *slide* rather than *valves*.

slur: A curved line notated above two or more notes that indicates they are to be played *legato*.

smear: To slide into a note from below.

smear

smorzando (It., *smor-TSAHN-doh*): Fading away.

SMPTE (SIMP-*tee*) **1:** Abbreviation for Society of Motion Picture and Television Engineers. **2:** Slang for the time code used to synchronize sound in television and motion pictures.

snare drum: A small cylindrical drum with a metal frame and two *drum heads*: the upper head is struck with *drumsticks* or *brushes*, and the bottom head has several strings (or snares) stretched across it. The snares can be removed to create the sound of a *tenor drum*.

snare drum

so: See *sol*.

soave (It., *soh-AH-veh*): Sweet, gentle.

soft pedal: The left pedal on a piano that softens the tone. Also called the *una corda* pedal.

sol (It., *sahl*): In the *fixed-do* system, the note G. **2:** In the *movable-do* system, the fifth note of the scale.

S

solfège, solfeggio (Fr., *sohl*-FEZH; It., *sohl*-FED-*joh*)**:** Vocal exercises in which syllables are assigned to notes: *do, re, me, fa, sol, la, ti*. Also see *fixed-do, movable-do,* and *solmization*.

soli, solos: To play a *solo* in unison with others.

solmization: Systems of designating syllables to the degrees of the scale. See *fixed-do, movable-do* and *solfège*.

solo (It., Lat., Sp., SOH-*loh*) **1:** A piece where a performer plays alone or with accompaniment. **2:** An indication in orchestral parts for a performer to play alone and bring out their part.

sonata (It., *soh*-NAH-*tah*)**:** A multi-movement composition for solo instrument, occasionally with piano accompaniment.

sonata allegro: See *sonata form*.

sonata da camera: Chamber sonata, see *camera*.

sonata da chiesa: Church sonata, see *chiesa*.

sonata form: A form used for the first movements of *sonatas, symphonies, chamber* works and other pieces. It consists of three main sections: *exposition, development* and *recapitulation*.

sonata rondo form: The combination of *sonata* and *rondo* forms usually with the following formula: if the complete form is ABACABA, then ABA=*exposition*, C=*development*, ABA=*recapitulation*.

sonatina (It., *soh-nah*-TEE-*nah*)**:** A short *sonata*.

song: A composition for voice with *text* or *lyrics*.

song cycle: A group of related *songs*.

song forms: A *ternary form* (ABA).

S

sonora, sonore, sonoro (It., *soh-NO-rah, soh-NO-reh, soh-NO-roh*): Sonorous.

sopra (It., *SOH-prah*): Above.

sopranino saxophone: See *saxophone.*

soprano: The highest female singing voice. See p. 336 for range.

soprano clef: The C *clef* with the middle C on the first line of the staff.

soprano saxophone: See *saxophone.*

sordini (It., *sor-DEE-nee*): The *dampers* on a piano.

sordino (It., *sor-DEE-noh*): Mute. Abbreviated *sord.*

sostenuto (It., *sohs-teh-NOO-toh*): Sustained.

sotto (It., *SOHT-toh*): Under.

sotto voce (It., *SOHT-toh VOH-cheh*): Under the voice, in soft voice.

soubrette (Fr., *soo-BRET*): A light, comic, operatic *soprano.*

soul: A style of *rhythm & blues* influenced by *gospel* music.

soundboard: A resonant piece of wood placed behind strings of various instruments in order to amplify the sound.

sound hole: An opening cut into the *belly* of a stringed instrument.

soundpost: A small piece of wood affixed inside a stringed instrument that helps distribute vibrations.

Sousaphone: A *tuba*, named after John Philip Sousa, with a circular shape for ease of carrying and forward facing bell. Used primarily for marching.

sousaphone

spacing: The arrangement of the notes in a chord.

species: A method of teaching counterpoint using five different processes: (1st) note against note, (2nd) two notes against one, (3rd) four notes against one, (4th) syncopated notes and (5th) a combination of the other species along with the use of shorter note values.

spiccato (It., *speek-KAH-toh*)**:** See *sautillé.*

spill: A technique on wind instruments where the main note is played followed by a rapid *diatonic* or *chromatic* drop.

short spill: long spill:

spinet 1: The smallest *upright piano.* **2:** An early keyboard instrument, similar to a *harpsichord.*

spirito, spiritoso (It., *SPEE-ree-toh, spee-ree-TOH-zoh*)**:** Spirit, spirited.

spiritual: American folk *hymns* most commonly associated with black slaves of the 19th century.

split keyboard: A keyboard of a *synthesizer* that can be divided into two parts with different sounds produced from each.

Sprechgesang, Sprechstimme (Ger., *SHPREKH-ge-zahng, SHPREKH-shtim-me*)**:** Speech-voice. A vocal technique halfway between singing and speaking.

square dance: A dance where several couples form a square.

square wave: A *waveform* common in *synthesis.*

SSA: Abbreviation in choral music for *soprano, soprano, alto.*

SSAA: Abbreviation in choral music for *soprano, soprano, alto, alto.*

staccatissimo (It., *stahk-kah-TEES-see-moh*)**:** As *staccato* as possible. Indicated by the mark ▾.

staccato (It., *stahk-KAH-toh*): Short, detached. Indicated by a dot over or under the note. Also see *mezzo-staccato* and *staccatissimo*.

staff, staves: The horizontal lines on and between which notes are written. Normally there are five lines, but older systems of *notation* use different numbers of lines.

standard: A song that remains popular through many generations.

stanza (It., *STAHN-tsah*, *STAN-zuh*): One poetic section of a *song*. Also see *verse*.

stationary do: See *fixed-do*.

steel: A cylindrical, solid steel device, similar to a *slide*, used to play *steel guitar* and *pedal steel guitar*.

steel drum: Caribbean percussion instrument made of an oil drum that is indented so as to create different pitches when struck in specific places.

steel guitar: An *electric guitar* that is placed horizontally, sometimes in the performers lap, and played with a *steel* or *slide*.

Steg (Ger., *shtek*): The *bridge* of a *stringed instrument*.

stem: A line that extends vertically from a *note head*.

step: The melodic movement of one or two *half steps*.

step-time mode: To enter data into a computer or *sequencer* one function at a time. As opposed to *real-time mode*.

steso (It., *STE-soh*): Slow.

stesso (It., *STES-soh*): Same.

Stil, stile (Ger., *shteel*, It., *STEE-leh*): Style, styles.

Stimme (Ger., *SHTIM-me*) **1:** Voice. **2:** Part. **3:** Organ *stop*.

stirato (It., *stee-RAH-toh*): Slowing down; dragging.

stop 1: A set of *organ* pipes. **2:** A device on an *organ* that controls which pipes are getting air. **3:** The placing of a finger on a string of a *stringed instrument*. Also see *double stop*.

stopped: Changing the pitch and tone quality of a *horn* by inserting a hand into the bell. Also see *bouché*, *gestopft* and *chiuso*.

straight eighths: Playing *eighth notes* as written, not in a *swing time* style.

strain: A section of a musical composition.

strathspey (*strath*-SPAY): A lively Scottish dance in *quadruple meter* with many *dotted* notes and a frequent use of the *Scotch snap*.

stressmark: See *tenuto*.

stretta (It., STRET-*tah*): See *stretto*, **2**.

stretto (It., STRET-*toh*) **1:** When, in a *fugue*, the *answer* begins before the *subject* is completed. It usually occurs near the end of the fugue in order to create excitement. **2:** An ending section of a piece that is in a faster tempo. Also called *stretta*.

stride: A style of *piano* playing with large *leaps* in the left hand.

string bass: See *double bass*.

stringed instruments: Instruments whose sounds are created by bowing, plucking or striking a stretched string. Also see *chordophones*.

stringendo (It., *streen*-JEN-doh): Quickening the tempo.

string quartet: An ensemble consisting of two *violins*, *viola* and *cello*, or a composition for that ensemble.

string quintet: An ensemble usually consisting of two *violins*, two *violas* and *cello*, or a composition for that ensemble. Schubert's string quintet uses the unusual ensemble of two *violins*, *viola* and two *cellos*. Occasionally composers will use two *violins*, *viola*, *cello* and *double bass*.

string trio: An ensemble usually consisting of *violin*, *viola* and *cello*, or a composition for that ensemble. Occasionally two *violins* and *cello*, or two *violins* and *viola*.

stroke 1: A motion made with a *drumstick* or *mallet*. **2:** A motion made with a *bow*.

stromento (It., *stroh-MEN-toh*): Instrument.

strophic: A *song* in which each *verse* uses the same melody.

strum: To move a *pick* or fingers rapidly across the strings of a *stringed instrument*.

Stück (Ger., *shtouk*): Piece, composition.

study score: See *miniature score*.

Sturm und Drang (Ger., *shtoorm oont drahng*): An emotional style of composition in the late 18th century characterized by the use of *minor* keys. Literally "storm and stress."

style galant: See *galant*.

subdominant: The fourth *degree* of a major or minor scale.

subito (It., *SOO-bee-toh*): Suddenly.

subject: A *melody* that forms the construction of a composition. Also see *fugue*.

submediant: The sixth *degree* of a major or minor scale.

suboctave: The *octave* below a note.

subtonic: See *leading tone*.

suite (Fr., *sweet*): An instrumental composition consisting of a number of short movements usually in dance forms such as the *allemande*, *courante*, *sarabande* and *gigue*.

sul (It., *sool*)**:** On the.

sul ponticello (It., *sool pohn-tee-*CHEL-*loh*)**:** Play on or near the *bridge*.

sul tasto (It., *sool* TAHS-*toh*)**:** Play on the *fingerboard*.

superdominant: See *submediant*.

supertonic: The second *degree* of a major or minor scale.

sur (Fr., *suer*)**:** On, over.

surf music: Popular music of the 1960s and 1970s associated with the sport of surfing.

suspension: When a *consonant* note is held over while the harmony changes, thus becoming a *dissonant* note that is then resolved.

sussurando (It., *soos-soor-*RAHN-*doh*)**:** Whispering.

sustain pedal: A pedal on a *piano* that allows the strings to vibrate by lifting the *dampers*. Also called a *damper pedal*.

swell 1: A *crescendo*. **2:** A device on an *organ* that controls the *crescendo* or *diminuendo* of sound.

swing: A style of *big band jazz* music popular in the 1930s and 1940s.

swing time: To play eighth notes as if they were a triplet consisting of a quarter note and an eighth note.

sympathetic string: On some *stringed instruments*, a string that is not bowed, plucked or struck, but vibrates along with those that are.

symphonic band: See *concert band*.

symphonic poem: An orchestral composition based on an

extramusical idea. Also see *program music*.

symphony 1: A large-scale composition for *orchestra*, usually in four movements. **2:** An *orchestra*.

syncopation: To shift the *accent* of a note or chord to a weak beat or the weak part of a beat.

synthesis: To create or manipulate sounds electronically.

synthesizer: An instrument that electronically creates and manipulates sounds.

syrinx: See *panpipes*.

system: Two or more connected staves.

T

T.: Abbreviation for *tasto, tenor, tonic* and *trill*.

TAB: Abbreviation for *tablature*.

tabla: A pair of tunable, wooden Indian drums that are played with the hands.

tabla

tablature: A system of notation where *tones* are not indicated by notes on a staff but, rather, by letters, numbers or other figures. The most common use is to show finger position for *guitar, lute* and other *stringed instruments*. See *TAB*. See p. 309.

tabor: A medieval drum played with one hand while the other hand plays an end-blown *pipe*.

tacet (Lat., TAH-*set*): Be silent. In an orchestral or vocal part, it indicates that the performer does not play or sing a movement or section.

tag: The ending of a composition. See *coda*.

talea (Lat., TAH-*lee-ah*): See *isorhythm*.

tambour (Fr., *tahm*-BOOR): Drum.

tambourine: A small, hand-held drum with *jingles* that is held in one hand and struck by the other. (See *jingles*, **2**.)

tambura (Hin., *tahm*-BOO-*rah*): An Indian long-necked *lute* with four strings that are played open as a *drone*.

tamburo (It., *tahm*-BOO-*roh*): Drum.

tam-tam: See *gong*.

tangent: See *clavichord*.

tango: A *syncopated* Argentinian dance in a slow *duple meter*, popular as an American ballroom dance in the early 20th century.

tanto (It., TAHN-*toh*): As much, so much, too much.

Tanz (Ger., *tahnts*): Dance.

tapping: A technique used on *guitar* and *electric bass* where the performer taps down on the fretted string with the index or middle finger of the pick hand. This is usually followed by a *pull-off* to sound a lower note. See p. 313.

tarantella (It., *tah*-rahn-TEL-*lah*): An Italian dance in a fast $\frac{6}{8}$ meter.

tardando (It., *tar*-DAHN-*doh*): Gradually becoming slower.

tardo, tardamente (It., TAR-*doh*, *tar-dah*-MEN-*teh*): Slow, slowly.

Taste (Ger., TAHS-*te*): A *key* on a *keyboard* instrument.

tasto (It., TAHS-*toh*) **1:** A *fingerboard* or *fretboard*. See *sul tasto*. **2:** A key on a *keyboard*. See *Taste*.

te: See *si*.

technic, technique: The physical skills involved in performing.

Te Deum (*Lat., teh* DEH-*oom*): A *hymn* of praise. Literally "we praise thee, O God."

tema (It., TEH-*mah*): Theme.

temperament: A system of tuning where intervals are altered from those that are acoustically pure. Also see *equal temperament.*

tempestoso (It., *tem-pes-*TOH-*zoh*): Stormy, passionately.

temple blocks: *Percussion instruments* made of hollow blocks of wood which are struck with a *drumstick.*

tempo (It., TEM-*poh*): The speed of a section of a *composition,* or the speed of a complete *composition.*

tempo marks: Terms, such as *allegro,* used to indicate the speed or tempo of a piece. See p. 307. Also see *M.M.*

temps (Fr., *tahm*): Beat, *tempo.*

ten.: The abbreviation for *tenor* or *tenuto.*

tenor 1: The highest natural male singing voice. See p. 336 for range. **2:** The voice, in early *polyphony,* that carries the melody or *cantus firmus.* **3:** A *viola.* **4:** A name given to instruments whose range is similar to the tenor voice.

tenor clef: The C *clef* where middle C is found on the fourth line of the staff.

tenor drum: A snareless drum, midway in size between a *snare drum* and a *bass drum.*

tenor saxophone: See *saxophone.*

tenor trombone: See *trombone.*

tenth: The interval of ten steps (an octave plus a third).

tenuto (It., *teh*-NOO-*toh*): To hold a note for its full value, indicated by a line over or under a note. Abbreviated *ten*.

ternary form: A form consisting of three sections: The first section is followed by a contrasting section and then by an exact or nearly-exact repeat of the first section (ABA). Sometimes called a *song form*.

tertian harmony: Harmony based on *thirds* or *triads*.

tessitura (It., *tes-see*-TOO-*rah*): The range of a vocal or instrumental part, whether it is high, medium or low in relation to the voice or instrument's *range*.

tetrachord (TET-*rah-kord*) **1:** A succession of four notes within a perfect fourth. **2:** In *twelve-tone* music, a set of four *pitch classes*.

text: Words that are set to music.

texture 1: The horizontal and vertical relationships of musical elements such as *monophonic*, *homophonic* and *polyphonic* textures. **2:** The instrumentation of a composition: light texture uses few instruments whereas heavy texture uses many instruments.

theme 1: The main musical idea, usually a *melody*, of a composition. **2:** A *subject*.

theme and variations: A compositional form where a *theme* is clearly stated, followed by a number of *variations*. Sometimes the *theme* is played after the variations.

theorbo (*thee*-OR-*boh*): A large *lute* used during the Renaissance.

theory: The study of the elements of musical composition.

Theremin: An electronic instrument originally played by moving the hands around an antenna.

third: The *interval* of three diatonic steps.

third-stream: Music influenced by both *classical* and *jazz* styles.

thirty-second note: A note half the length of a *sixteenth note.* See p. 277.

thirty-second rest: A rest half the length of a *sixteenth rest.* See p. 278.

thoroughbass: See *figured bass.*

three-part form: See *ternary form.*

through-composed: *S*ongs with new music composed for each *stanza.*

thumb piano: See *m'bira.*

ti (It., *tee*): See *si.*

tie: A curved line that joins two or more notes of the same pitch that last the duration of the combined note values.

timbal, timbale, timballo (Sp.,TEEM-*bahl;* Fr., *tahn*-BAHL; It., *teem*-BAHL-*loh*): Timpani.

timbales (Sp., *teem*-BAHL-*lehs*) **1:** Timpani. **2:** Cuban drums similar to *bongos* that are struck with two sticks.

timbre (Fr., TAM-*br*): Tone color or quality.

timbrel: A medieval *tambourine.*

time 1: Meter or *tempo.* **2:** The duration of a note.

time signature: A sign placed after the *clef* and *key signature* at the beginning of a piece that indicates the *meter* of the piece. It can be placed anywhere else throughout the piece if the *meter* changes.

timpani: Large, tunable drums shaped like kettles and made of copper or brass with plastic or vellum heads. They are available in various sizes (usually in pairs) and played with two mallets. Sometimes called *kettledrums*.

timpani

tin whistle: A small, high-pitched *end-blown flute* made of metal.

toccata (It., *tohk-KAH-tah*)**:** A composition for *keyboard instruments* in free form that contains *runs* and *arpeggios*. Literally means "touch."

tom-tom: Small tunable drums, played with the hands, drumsticks, mallets or brushes.

Ton (Ger., *tohn*)**:** Tone, note.

tonal: Pertaining to a *tone*, *key* or *mode*.

tonal and real: In a *fugue*, a real *answer* is an exact transposition of the *subject*; a tonal answer is not exact.

tonality: See *key*, **1**.

tone 1: A *pitch*. **2:** The interval of a second. **3:** The quality of sound of a voice or instrument. See *tone color*.

tone cluster: Several consecutive *diatonic* or *chromatic* notes played simultaneously. On a keyboard instrument a tone cluster is played with a fist or arm.

tone color: The quality of sound of a voice or instrument. Also see *timbre*.

tone poem: See *symphonic poem*.

tone row: The ordering of the twelve tones of an octave used by *serial* and *twelve tone* composers.

Tonette: A small plastic *end-blown flute* with seven finger holes and one thumb hole.

tonguing: To use the tongue to articulate on *wind instruments*.

tonic: See *keynote*.

tonicization: When harmonies outside of the tonic key are present, but no *modulation* has occurred.

tono (It., TOH-*noh*)**:** Tone, mode, key.

tosto (It., TOHS-*toh*)**:** Quick, fast.

touch: The way a *key* is depressed on a keyboard instrument.

touche (Fr., *toosh*) **1:** A *fingerboard*. **2:** The *keys* of a *piano*. **3:** A *fret*.

touch sensitivity: A feature on some *synthesizers* that measures how hard or soft a key is depressed.

tr: Abbreviation for *trill*.

track: The divisions of a recording medium that allow different musical parts or sounds to be added one, or more, at a time.

trading fours/eights: In *jazz*, when different performers alternate improvisations either four or eight measures long.

tranquillo (It., *trahn*-KWEEL-*loh*)**:** Tranquil, calm, quiet.

transcription: An *arrangement* of a composition for voices or instruments other than those for which it was originally intended.

transition 1: A section of a composition that links two substantial passages. **2:** A *modulation*.

transpose, transposition: To change a composition from one key to another.

transposing instruments: Instruments that produce a note different from the written note. For example, a B-flat *trumpet* plays a written C, but it sounds B-flat.

transverse flute: The modern *flute*, that is held horizontally, as opposed to an *end-blown flute*.

traps: Slang for a *drum set*.

tre (It., *treh*): Three.

treble: The highest part in a *choral* composition.

treble clef: The G clef on the second line of the staff.

tremolando (It., *treh-moh-LAHN-doh*): Trembling, with *tremolo*.

tremolo (It., *TREH-moh-loh*) **1:** Rapidly repeating a single note or chord. **2:** Alternating rapidly between two notes or chords.

tremolo arm: See *whammy bar*.

trepak (*treh-PAHK*): A lively Russian dance in $\frac{2}{4}$ time.

très (Fr., *treh*): Very.

triad: A three-note chord consisting of a root, third and fifth. The four kinds of triads are *major*, *minor*, *diminished* and *augmented*.

triangle: A percussion instrument made from a steel rod bent into a triangular shape that is struck with a metal beater.

triangle

triangle wave: A *waveform* common in *synthesis*.

trill: An ornament consisting of the rapid alternation

of the written note and the diatonic second above it notated as in ex. A or ex. B. A flat (ex. C) or sharp (ex. E) sign after the trill symbol indicates to trill to the flatted (ex. D) or sharped note (ex. F) above the written note. Abbreviated *tr*. See p. 304.

trio 1: A composition for three performers. **2:** An ensemble of three performers. **3:** The middle section of a *march*, *minuet* or *scherzo*.

trio sonata: A type of *baroque chamber music* with two melodic parts supported by a *figured bass*.

triple concerto: A *concerto* for *orchestra* and three soloists.

triple meter: A *time signature* with three beats to the measure.

triplet: Three notes played in the time of two notes of the same value.

triple tonguing: On a flute or brass instrument, the tonguing of rapid passages by silently pronouncing ta-ta-ka, or ta-ka-ta.

tritone: The interval of an *augmented* fourth or a *diminished* fifth.

tromba (It., TROHM-*bah*)**:** Trumpet.

tromba marina (It., TROM-*bah mah*-REE-*nah*)**:** A medieval stringed instrument with one bowed string stretched over a long wooden box that produces *natural harmonics*. Literally translated "marine trumpet."

trombone: A group of *brass instruments* with a long u-shaped *slide* used instead of valves. The different types include, from highest to lowest, the *alto trombone*, *tenor trombone* (most common) and the *bass trombone*. See pp. 327–328 for ranges.

trombone

Trommel (*Ger.*, TROM-*mel*)**:** A *drum.*

trope: The addition of words and/or music to a *Gregorian chant.*

troppo (*It.*, TROHP-*poh*)**:** Too, or too much.

troubadour: Traveling poet-musicians in France during the 12th and 13th centuries.

trumpet: A group of oval-shaped *brass instruments.* The different types include, from highest to lowest, the B-flat piccolo trumpet, A piccolo trumpet, E-flat trumpet, D trumpet, C trumpet, B-flat trumpet and bass trumpet. See pp. 325–327 for ranges.

trumpet

TTB: Abbreviation in *choral* music for *tenor, tenor* and *bass.*

TTBB: Abbreviation in *choral* music for *tenor, tenor, bass* (or *baritone*) and *bass.*

tuba: The lowest *brass instrument* commonly available in three sizes, from highest to lowest, F tuba, C tuba and B-flat tuba. It is not necessary to specify which tuba is to be used in a composition; the performer will determine which is most appropriate. See p. 328 for range.

tuba

T

tubular bells, tubular chimes: See *chimes*.

tune 1: A *melody*. **2:** To adjust the pitch of an instrument. See *tuning*.

tuned percussion: *Percussion instruments* that create a definite pitch. See *percussion instruments*.

tuning: To match the pitch of an instrument to a standard pitch of another instrument. See *tune*, **2**.

tuning fork: A two-pronged metal fork that, when struck, produces a pure pitch.

Turca, Turco (It., TOOR-*kah*, TOOR-*koh*): Turkish.

turn: An ornament ∞ usually consisting of four or five notes that embellish a main note. See p. 304.

turnaround: A chord or group of chords that takes you back to the beginning of a *progression*.

tutti (It., TOOT-*tee*): All. Usually placed at the end of an extended solo passage when the entire ensemble enters.

twelfth: The interval of twelve steps (an octave plus a fifth).

twelve-string guitar: A *guitar* with twelve strings that are tuned in pairs. The lower four pairs are tuned in octaves, and the top two are tuned at the unison.

twelve-tone scale: See *tone row*.

twelve-tone technique: See *serial music*.

two-part form: See *binary form*.

two step 1: A fast ballroom dance popular in America during the early 20th century. **2:** A fast *country & western* dance popular in the late 20th century.

tympani: The common misspelling of *timpani*.

U

ukulele: A small, fretted four-stringed Hawaiian instrument, similar to a guitar—tuned to GCEA. See p. 331 for range.

ukulele

una corda (It., *oo-nah* KOR *dah*): See *soft pedal.*

unequal voices: The mixture of men's and women's voices.

unison: Two or more performers sounding the same note or melody. See p. 300.

un peu (Fr., *uhn puh*): A little.

un poco (It., *oon* POH-*koh*): A little.

unruhig (Ger., *oon*-ROO-*eesh*): Restless.

upbeat: See *pickup.*

up bow: The symbol V that indicates the *bow* should be stroked upward from the *tip.*

upright 1: A *piano* that has its strings arranged diagonally across a vertical sound board. As opposed to a *grand piano.* **2:** Slang for a *double bass.*

upright piano

Urtext (Ger., OOR-*text*): An edition of a composition that gives, or attempts to give, the composer's original notation without editorial additions.

ut 1: See *do.* **2:** The French name for the note C.

ut supra (Lat., *oot* SOO-*prah*): As above, as before.

V

V.: Abbreviation for *verse*, *vide*, *violin*, *voice*, *voce* and *volti*.

Va.: Abbreviation for *viola*.

valse (Fr., *vahlss*): Waltz.

valve: A device on a brass instrument that allows that instrument to play chromatic notes by increasing or decreasing the length of the tubing.

valve instruments: Brass instruments with *valves*.

vamp 1: An improvised accompaniment or introduction. **2:** An accompanimental figure or introduction that is repeated until all the performers are ready to continue.

variation: To modify or develop a musical *theme* by means of harmonic, melodic or rhythmic changes.

vaudeville (Fr., VAW-*de-veel*; Eng., VAWD-*vill*) **1:** A light variety show popular in the late 19th and early 20th centuries that featured short comedies interspersed with popular songs. **2:** A late 16th-century *song* with amorous text. **3:** An early 18th-century *song* with satirical lyrics set to a popular melody.

vc.: Abbreviation for *violoncello*.

VCA: In *synthesis*, the abbreviation for "voltage-controlled amplifier," which controls the *signal* level.

VCF: In *synthesis*, the abbreviation for "voltage-controlled filter," which controls the harmonic content of a *signal*.

VCO: In *synthesis*, the abbreviation for "voltage-controlled oscillator," which controls the *frequency* of a *signal*.

velato (It., *veh-LAH-toh*): Veiled, obscured.

veloce (It., *veh-LOH-cheh*): Rapid, fast.

velocity: MIDI codes that transmit *dynamics*.

velocity sensitivity: See *touch sensitivity*.

Venetian school: A school of 16th-century Flemish and Italian composers who worked in Venice. Their innovations include an increased use of *chromaticism*, the *polychoral* style and the introduction of new instruments to ensembles. Notable composers included Adrian Willaert, Andrea and Giovanni Gabrielli, Michael Praetorius and Heinrich Schütz.

vent (Fr., *vahn*): Wind.

ventil, ventile (Ger., *fen-TEEL*; It., *ven-TEE-leh*): Valve.

Veranderungen (Ger., *fer-AN-dah-roon-gen*): Variations.

verhallend (Ger., *fehr-HAHL-lent*): Fading away.

verismo (It., *veh-REE-zmoh*): A type of late 19th-century Italian *opera* that presents realistic plots and characters. Literally means "realism."

verse 1: An introductory section of a popular *song* or *ballad*. **2:** In popular music, the section of a *song* that tells a story and changes with each repetition, which is followed by the *refrain*.

vibes, vibraharp, vibraphone: A *tuned percussion* instrument

vibraphone

similar to a *xylophone*, with metal bars, tubular metal resonators and an electronic fan in each resonator that creates a *vibrato* effect. See p. 333 for range.

See p. 333 for range.

vibraslap: A *percussion instrument* consisting of a metal handle with a wooden ball attached to one end and a wooden box filled with rivets on the other. When the wooden ball is struck with the hand, it produces a rattling sound.

vibration: The rapid movement of an object that results in creating a *tone*.

vibrato (It., *vee*-BRAH-*toh*): A rapid fluctuation of pitch slightly higher or lower than the main pitch.

vide (Fr., *veed*): Empty, open.

vielle (Fr., *vee*-EL): A *stringed instrument* of the 13th to 15th centuries with one *drone* string and four fingered strings.

Viennese school: Various composers who have worked in and around Vienna. The *classical Viennese school* includes masters of the *classical* style such as Haydn, Mozart and Beethoven. The *new Viennese school* includes the modern *twelve-tone* composer Schoenberg and his students Berg and Webern.

vigoroso (It., *vee-goh*-ROH-*soh*): Vigorous, energetic.

vihuela (Sp., *vee*-WEH-*lah*): A Spanish *lute* of the *Renaissance*.

vina (VEE-*nah*): An Indian *stringed instrument* that looks similar to a *lute* but is actually a *zither*.

viol: A family of bowed stringed instruments developed during the *Renaissance*. They appear similar to instruments of the *violin family* but have *frets*, a flat back and normally have six strings. The most common sizes are treble, tenor and bass.

viola (It., *vee*-OH-*lah*): In the *violin family*, an instrument slightly larger and tuned a fifth lower than the *violin*. See p. 329 for range.

viola

viola da braccio (It., *vee*-OH-*lah dah* BRAH-*choh*): A *stringed instrument* which is played on the arm, like a *violin* or *viola*. Literally means "*viol* for the arm."

viola da gamba (It., *vee-OH-lah dah* GAHM-*bah*)**:** The bass *viol* which was held between the knees in the same way a cellist holds a *cello*. Literally means "leg *viol*."

viola d'amore (It., *vee-OH-lah dah-MOH-reh*)**:** A fretless treble *viol* with seven bowed strings and seven *sympathetic* strings. Composers into the 20th century have written for this instrument. Literally means "*viol* of love."

violin: The *treble* member of the *violin family*. In an *orchestra* they are usually divided into groups of firsts and seconds. See p. 329 for range.

violin

violin family: A family of four-stringed, bowed instruments that includes the *violin*, *viola*, *cello* and *double bass*.

violoncello (It., *vee-oh-lohn-CHEL-loh*)**:** The tenor instrument of the *violin family*, tuned one octave below the *viola* and played between the knees. Usually abbreviated "*cello*." See p. 329 for range.

violoncello

violone (It., *vee-oh-LOH-neh*)**:** See *viola da gamba*.

virginal: A small 16th-century *harpsichord*.

virtuoso: A performer with superb technical ability.

vivace (It., *vee-VAH-cheh*)**:** Lively, quick.

vivo (It., VEE-*voh*)**:** Lively, spirited.

Vl., Vln.: Abbreviations for *violin*.

Vla.: Abbreviation for *viola*.

Vlc.: Abbreviation for *violoncello*.

vocalise (Fr., *voh-kah-LEEZ*)**:** A vocal *etude* or exercise sung to vowels.

vocalization: See *vocalise*.

vocal score: A *score* to an *opera* arranged for *piano* and voices

voce (It., VOH-cheh): *Voice.*

voice 1: The sounds produced by the human vocal cords. **2:** A *part* or *melody* line in *polyphony*.

voice leading: The logical movement of individual parts in *polyphony*.

voices: The various male and female singing ranges. Female: *soprano, mezzo soprano,* and *alto*. Male: *tenor, baritone,* and *bass*. See p. 336 for ranges.

voicing 1: How notes are arranged in a chord. **2:** To adjust *timbre* and *pitch* of the pipes in an *organ*. **3:** The adjustment of the *hammers* on a *piano* to improve tone quality.

voilé (Fr., *vwah*-LAY): Veiled, subdued.

voix (Fr., *vwah*): Voice.

Volkslied (Ger., FOHKS-*leet*): Folk song.

volta (It., VOHL-*tah*) **1:** Time, as in "prima volta" or "first time." **2:** A quick dance in *triple time* popular around 1600.

volti (It., VOHL-*tee*): Turn.

volti subito (It., VOHL-*tee* SOO-*bee-toh*): Turn quickly. In orchestral parts this indicates to turn the page quickly. Abbreviated V.S.

volume: The softness or loudness of sound.

voluntary: A composition for organ usually played before or after a church service, or as an *Offertory* piece. Sometimes a voluntary is *improvised*.

Vorspiel (Ger., FOR-*shpeel*): Prelude, overture.

vox (Lat., *vohx*): Voice.

V.S.: Abbreviation of *volti subito*.

v.v.: Abbreviation for violins.

W

Wagner tubas: *Brass instruments* that appear similar to a *baritone horn* but are actually modified *French horns* which are available as a B-flat tenor and an F bass. See p. 324 for ranges.

wah-wah pedal: A device operated by the foot of an electric guitarist or bassist, that alters the sound of their instrument by giving it a "wah" or "crying baby" sound. It removes low frequencies and accentuates high frequencies when completely depressed.

Waldhorn (*Ger.*, VAHLT-*horn*): A hunting horn, a *horn* without valves.

waltz: A dance in $\frac{3}{4}$ time that originated in the late 18th century.

Walzer (*Ger.*, VAHL-*tser*): Waltz.

washboard: A percussion instrument consisting of a metal laundry board that is played by scraping it with a stick or metal thimbles placed on the fingers.

waveform: The shape of a sound produced by an *oscillator* that determines the *timbre* of a sound. Different waveforms include *sine*, *pulse*, *sawtooth*, *square* and *triangle waves*.

wehmütig (*Ger.*, *veh*-MUE-*teeg*): Sad, melancholy.

well-tempered: See *equal temperament*.

whammy bar: A device on a *guitar* that alters the pitches of the strings by moving the *bridge*.

whistle: A small, end-blown pipe made of cane, metal, plastic or wood.

whole note: A *note* equal to the length of two *half notes*. See p. 277.

W

whole rest: A *rest* equal to the length of two *half rests*.
See p. 278.

whole step: A *whole tone*.

whole tone: Two *half steps*; the interval of a major second; a *whole step*.

whole-tone scale: A scale made up only of *whole tones*.
See p. 279.

wind chimes: A *percussion instrument* consisting of several hollow wood, bamboo or metal cylinders which are suspended from a frame and are sounded by striking or blowing wind. Also see *mark tree*.

wind instruments: Instruments whose sounds are created through an enclosed column of air including *brass* and *woodwind* instruments. Also see *aerophones*.

wind machine: A device that simulates the sound of the wind.

wind quintet: An ensemble usually consisting of *flute, oboe, clarinet, horn* and *bassoon*, or a composition for that ensemble.

wire brush: See *brushes*.

WoO: Abbreviation for "Werk ohne Opuszahl" which means work without *opus* number.

wood blocks: See *temple blocks*.

woodwind family: The family of *wind instruments* that includes *recorder, flute, oboe, clarinet, saxophone* and *bassoon*.

woodwind quintet: See *wind quintet*.

word painting: To express the meaning of the words of a *song* or other vocal piece through the music.

wuchtig (*Ger.*, VOOKH-teesh)**:** Weighty, ponderous.

würdig (*Ger.*, VUER-deesh)**:** Stately, dignified.

W

X

xota: See *jota*.

xylophone: A *percussion instrument* consisting of a set of tuned wooden bars, arranged horizontally as on a *piano keyboard*, which are struck with hard or soft *mallets*. Some have tubular *resonators* below the bars. See p. 332 for range.

xylophone

Y

yodel: A type of singing popular in the Alps of Austria and Switzerland characterized by frequent alternation of chest tones with *falsetto* tones.

X
Y

Z

zapateado (*tsah-pah-teh-AH-doh*): A syncopated Spanish dance in *triple meter* characterized by heel stamping

zarabanda: See *saraband*.

zart (*Ger., tsahrt*): Soft, tender.

zarzuela (*tsar-TSWEH-lah*): A type of Spanish *opera* where music is intermingled with spoken dialogue.

Zeitmass (*Ger., TSEIT-mahss*): *Tempo*.

ziemlich (*Ger., TSEEM-leesh*): Rather, somewhat.

Zigeunermusik (*Ger., tsee-GOY-ner-moo-zik*): Gypsy music.

zingara, zingaro (*It., tsin-GA-ra, tsin-GA-ro*): Gypsy.

zither (*Ger., TSIT-ter*) **1:** A general term for stringed instruments whose strings are stretched over the full length of the *soundboard*. **2:** A folk instrument of Bavaria and Austria consisting of a flat, wood *soundboard* with four or five melody strings which are fretted with the left hand and up to 37 accompaniment strings.

zith

zusammen (*Ger., tsoo-ZAHM-men*): Together.

zwei (*Ger., tsuei*): Two.

Zwischenspiel (*Ger., TSVISH-en-shpeel*) **1:** *Interlude*. **2:** Episode of a *fugue*.

zydeco (*ZEI-de-koh*): A popular style of music that originated in Cajun Louisiana that combines *blues*, *rhythm & blues*, *rock*, *country & western*, Caribbean and traditional Cajun music.

zymbel (*Ger., TSIM-bel*): *Cymbal*.

COMPOSERS

Names in parentheses are those not commonly used, such as a middle name.

Names in brackets are alternate spellings or name which were changed.

A

Adam, Adolphe (Charles)

BORN: July 24, 1803—Paris
DIED: May 3, 1856—Paris
HISTORICAL PERIOD: Romantic
COMPOSITIONAL MEDIA: Opera, ballet, songs.
IMPORTANT ITEMS: Notable works include the
ballet "Giselle."

Adams, John (Coolidge)

BORN: February 15, 1947—Worcester, MA
HISTORICAL PERIOD: Modern
COMPOSITIONAL MEDIA: Orchestra, opera,
chamber, keyboard, film.
IMPORTANT ITEMS: Composes in the minimalist
style. Notable works include the opera "Nixon in
China."

Addinsell, Richard (Stewart)

BORN: January 13, 1904—London
DIED: November 14, 1977—London
HISTORICAL PERIOD: Modern
COMPOSITIONAL MEDIA: Songs, film.
IMPORTANT ITEMS: Notable works include the
"Warsaw Concerto."

Adler, Richard

BORN: August 3, 1921—New York
HISTORICAL PERIOD: Modern
COMPOSITIONAL MEDIA: Musicals, songs.
IMPORTANT ITEMS: Notable musicals include
"Pajama Game" and "Damn Yankees."

Adler, Samuel (Hans)

BORN: March 4, 1928—Mannheim, Germany
HISTORICAL PERIOD: Modern
COMPOSITIONAL MEDIA: Orchestra, chamber music, keyboard, choral, opera, songs.
IMPORTANT ITEMS: Named chairman of the Eastman school of music in 1973. His compositions are inspired by Jewish liturgical music.

Albéniz, Isaac (Manuel Francesco)

BORN: May 29, 1860—Camprodón, Spain
DIED: May 18, 1909—Cambô-les-Bains, France
HISTORICAL PERIOD: Romantic
COMPOSITIONAL MEDIA: Keyboard, orchestra, choral, opera.
IMPORTANT ITEMS: Notable works include the piano suite "Iberia" which was later orchestrated by Enrique Arbós.

Alberti, Domenico

BORN: 1710—Venice
DIED: 1740—Rome
HISTORICAL PERIOD: Late Baroque/Early Classical
COMPOSITIONAL MEDIA: Keyboard, choral, opera.
IMPORTANT ITEMS: His arpeggiated style of keyboard accompaniment is known as "Alberti Bass."

Albinoni, Tomaso (Giovanni)

BORN: June 8, 1671—Venice
DIED: January 17, 1751—Venice
HISTORICAL PERIOD: Baroque
COMPOSITIONAL MEDIA: Opera, chamber music, orchestra.
IMPORTANT ITEMS: Notable works include the

"Adagio" for strings and organ and the opera "Griselda."

Anderson, Leroy

BORN: June 29, 1908—Cambridge, MA
DIED: May 18, 1975—Woodbury, CT
HISTORICAL PERIOD: Modern (Popular)
COMPOSITIONAL MEDIA: Orchestra.
IMPORTANT ITEMS: Composer of light instrumental music including "The Syncopated Clock," "Sleigh Ride" and "The Typewriter," all originally composed for the Boston Pops Orchestra.

Antheil, George [Georg] (Johann Carl)

BORN: July 8, 1900—Trenton, NJ
DIED: February 12, 1959—New York
HISTORICAL PERIOD: Modern
COMPOSITIONAL MEDIA: Orchestra, ballet, keyboard, choral, opera, film.
IMPORTANT ITEMS: Caused a furor with compositions, such as "Ballet Mécanique," which incorporates sounds of car horns, anvils and the sound of an airplane.

Arlen, Harold
[real name: Hyman Arluck]

BORN: February 15, 1905—Buffalo, NY
DIED: April 23, 1986—
HISTORICAL PERIOD: Modern (Popular)
COMPOSITIONAL MEDIA: Popular songs, film.
IMPORTANT ITEMS: Notable works include the songs "Stormy Weather" and "Over the Rainbow."

Arnold, Malcolm (Henry)

BORN: October 21, 1921—Northampton, England
HISTORICAL PERIOD: Modern
COMPOSITIONAL MEDIA: Orchestra, chamber
music, opera, ballet, songs, film.
IMPORTANT ITEMS: Prolific composer whose film
scores include "The Bridge on the River Kwai."

Auric, Georges

BORN: February 15, 1899—Lodève, Hérault, France
DIED: July 23, 1983—Paris
HISTORICAL PERIOD: Modern
COMPOSITIONAL MEDIA: Ballet, film, chamber
music, orchestra, songs.
IMPORTANT ITEMS: A member of Les Six.

B

Babbitt, Milton (Byron)

BORN: May 10, 1916—Philadelphia, PA
HISTORICAL PERIOD: Modern
COMPOSITIONAL MEDIA: Orchestra, keyboard,
songs, electronic.
IMPORTANT ITEMS: Influential serial composer.

Bach, Carl [Karl] Philipp Emanuel

BORN: March 8, 1714—Weimar, Germany
DIED: December 14, 1788—Hamburg
HISTORICAL PERIOD: Early Classical
COMPOSITIONAL MEDIA: Orchestra, chamber
music, keyboard, choral.
IMPORTANT ITEMS: Third (second surviving) son of
J.S. Bach. A prolific composer and author of a
celebrated treatise on keyboard playing.

Bach, Johann Christian

BORN: September 5, 1735—Leipzig, Germany
DIED: January 1, 1782—London
HISTORICAL PERIOD: Early Classical
COMPOSITIONAL MEDIA: Orchestra, chamber music, keyboard, choral, opera.
IMPORTANT ITEMS: Youngest son of J.S. Bach, who influenced the music of Mozart, Haydn and Beethoven.

Bach, Johann Christoph Friedrich

BORN: June 21, 1732—Leipzig, Germany
DIED: January 26, 1795—Buckeburg, Germany
HISTORICAL PERIOD: Classical
COMPOSITIONAL MEDIA: Orchestra, keyboard, choral, songs.
IMPORTANT ITEMS: Ninth son of J.S. Bach.

Bach, Johann Sebastian

BORN: March 21, 1685—Eisenach, Germany
DIED: July 28, 1750—Leipzig, Germany
HISTORICAL PERIOD: Baroque
COMPOSITIONAL MEDIA: Orchestra, chamber music, keyboard, choral.
IMPORTANT ITEMS: One of the most important and influential composers in the history of music who mastered the composition of contrapuntal music. Some notable works include the sacred cantatas, St. Matthew and St. John Passions, the B-Minor Mass, as well as keyboard works including the Well Tempered Clavier and two- and three-part inventions.

B

Bach, Wilhelm Friedemann

BORN: November 22, 1710—Weimar, Germany
DIED: July 1, 1784—Berlin
HISTORICAL PERIOD: Early Classical
COMPOSITIONAL MEDIA: Orchestra, chamber music, keyboard, choral.
IMPORTANT ITEMS: Eldest son of J.S. Bach.

Bacharach, Burt

BORN: May 12, 1928—Kansas City, MO
HISTORICAL PERIOD: Modern (Popular)
COMPOSITIONAL MEDIA: Popular songs, film.
IMPORTANT ITEMS: Notable songs include "Raindrops Keep Falling on My Head," "Do You Know the Way to San Jose" and "What the World Needs Now Is Love."

Bacon, Ernst

BORN: May 26, 1898—Chicago, IL
DIED: March 16, 1990—Orinda, CA
HISTORICAL PERIOD: Modern
COMPOSITIONAL MEDIA: Orchestra, songs, chamber music, choral, opera.
IMPORTANT ITEMS: A prolific composer of songs.

Balakirev, Mily Alexeievich

BORN: January 2, 1837—Nizhny-Novgorod
DIED: May 29, 1910—St. Petersburg
HISTORICAL PERIOD: Romantic
COMPOSITIONAL MEDIA: Orchestra, chamber music, keyboard, choral, songs.
IMPORTANT ITEMS: A Russian nationalist compose and member of the Russian Five.

Barber, Samuel

BORN: March 9, 1910—West Chester, PA
DIED: January 23, 1981—New York
HISTORICAL PERIOD: Modern
COMPOSITIONAL MEDIA: Orchestra, chamber
music, keyboard, opera, songs.
IMPORTANT ITEMS: Notable works include the
orchestral work "Adagio for Strings."

Bartók, Béla

BORN: March 25, 1881—Transylvania
DIED: September 26, 1945—New York
HISTORICAL PERIOD: Modern
COMPOSITIONAL MEDIA: Orchestra, chamber
music, ballet, keyboard, choral.
IMPORTANT ITEMS: Collector of Hungarian folk
music with Kodály. Notable works include "Concerto
for Orchestra" and "Music for Strings, Percussion
and Celesta."

Bassett, Leslie (Raymond)

BORN: January 22, 1923—Hanford, CA
HISTORICAL PERIOD: Modern
COMPOSITIONAL MEDIA: Orchestra, chamber
music, keyboard, choral, electronic.
IMPORTANT ITEMS: Awarded the Pulitzer Prize in
1966 for his "Variations for Orchestra."

Beach, Amy (Marcy)
[maiden name: Cheney]

BORN: September 5, 1867—Henniker, NH
DIED: December 27, 1944—New York
HISTORICAL PERIOD: Romantic
COMPOSITIONAL MEDIA: Songs, chamber music,

choral, orchestra, keyboard.
IMPORTANT ITEMS: One of the first important
American woman composers.

Beethoven, Ludwig van

BORN: December 16, 1770—Bonn, Germany
DIED: March 26, 1827—Vienna
HISTORICAL PERIOD: Classical
COMPOSITIONAL MEDIA: Orchestra, chamber
music, keyboard, choral, opera.
IMPORTANT ITEMS: One of the most important
composers in the history of music. Despite gradual
hearing loss and eventual complete deafness in
1819, he composed until his death. Notable works
include nine symphonies, the "Moonlight Sonata"
and "Für Elise" for piano and the "Missa Solemnis."

Bellini, Vincenzo

BORN: November 3, 1801—Catania, Sicily
DIED: September 23, 1835—Puteaux, France
HISTORICAL PERIOD: Romantic
COMPOSITIONAL MEDIA: Opera, chamber music,
choral.
IMPORTANT ITEMS: Notable works include the
opera "Norma."

Bennett, Richard Rodney

BORN: March 29, 1936—Broadstairs, Kent, England
HISTORICAL PERIOD: Modern
COMPOSITIONAL MEDIA: Opera, orchestra,
chamber music, vocal, film, TV, keyboard.
IMPORTANT ITEMS: Prolific composer who
incorporates atonality and jazz with traditional
harmony and structures.

Bennett, Robert Russell

BORN: June 15, 1894—Kansas City, MO
DIED: August 17, 1981—New York
HISTORICAL PERIOD: Modern
COMPOSITIONAL MEDIA: Orchestra, chamber music, keyboard, choral, opera, songs, film, band.
IMPORTANT ITEMS: Notable works include orchestrations of Broadway musicals including "My Fair Lady."

Berg, Alban

BORN: February 9, 1885—Vienna
DIED: December 24, 1935—Vienna
HISTORICAL PERIOD: Modern
COMPOSITIONAL MEDIA: Orchestra, chamber music, keyboard, opera, songs.
IMPORTANT ITEMS: A student of Arnold Schoenberg whose compositions incorporate twelve-tone techniques. Notable works include the opera "Wozzeck."

Berio, Luciano

BORN: October 24, 1925—Oneglia, Italy
HISTORICAL PERIOD: Modern
COMPOSITIONAL MEDIA: Orchestra, chamber music, ballet, keyboard, choral, electronic.
IMPORTANT ITEMS: Compositions incorporate graphic notation and quotes from works of other composers.

Berlin, Irving

BORN: May 11, 1888—Temun, Russia
DIED: September 22, 1989—New York
HISTORICAL PERIOD: Modern (Popular)
COMPOSITIONAL MEDIA: Popular songs.

IMPORTANT ITEMS: Notable songs include "Alexander's Ragtime Band," "White Christmas" and "God Bless America."

Berlioz, Hector

BORN: December 11, 1803—La-Cote-Saint-André, Isère
DIED: March 8, 1869—Paris
HISTORICAL PERIOD: Romantic
COMPOSITIONAL MEDIA: Orchestra, choral, opera.
IMPORTANT ITEMS: Use of the orchestra was ahead of his time, as seen in the composition "Symphonie Fantastique."

Bernstein, Elmer

BORN: April 4, 1922—New York
HISTORICAL PERIOD: Modern
COMPOSITIONAL MEDIA: Film, chamber music, musicals, orchestra, songs.
IMPORTANT ITEMS: Notable film scores include "The Ten Commandments" and "Ghostbusters."

Bernstein, Leonard

BORN: August 25, 1918—Lawrence, MA
DIED: October 14, 1990—New York
HISTORICAL PERIOD: Modern
COMPOSITIONAL MEDIA: Orchestra, chamber music, ballet, keyboard, choral, opera, musicals, film, TV.
IMPORTANT ITEMS: Popular conductor and composer whose notable works include "Candide" and "West Side Story."

Billings, William

BORN: October 7, 1746—Boston, MA
DIED: September 26, 1800—Boston, MA
HISTORICAL PERIOD: Classical
COMPOSITIONAL MEDIA: Choral.
IMPORTANT ITEMS: Best known for his hymns and anthems.

Bizet, Georges

BORN: October 25, 1838—Paris
DIED: June 3, 1875—Bougival, France
HISTORICAL PERIOD: Romantic
COMPOSITIONAL MEDIA: Opera, orchestra, keyboard, choral, songs.
IMPORTANT ITEMS: Notable works include the opera "Carmen" and the suite "L'Arlésienne."

Bliss, Sir Arthur (Edward Drummond)

BORN: August 2, 1891—London
DIED: March 27, 1975—London
HISTORICAL PERIOD: Modern
COMPOSITIONAL MEDIA: Orchestra, vocal, ballet, chamber music, opera, keyboard, films, TV.
IMPORTANT ITEMS: He was knighted in 1950 and was named Master of the Queens Music in 1953.

Bloch, Ernest

BORN: July 24, 1880—Geneva, Switzerland
DIED: July 15, 1959—Portland, OR
HISTORICAL PERIOD: Modern
COMPOSITIONAL MEDIA: Orchestra, chamber music, keyboard, opera.
IMPORTANT ITEMS: Influential teacher whose pupils included Roger Sessions, Halsey Stevens and

Randall Thompson. Many of his works are inspired by Jewish music.

Blow, John

BORN: February 23, 1649—Nottinghamshire, England
DIED: October 1, 1708—Westminster, London
HISTORICAL PERIOD: Baroque
COMPOSITIONAL MEDIA: Keyboard, choral, songs, opera.
IMPORTANT ITEMS: Organist at Westminster Abbey until succeeded by his pupil Purcell.

Boccherini, (Rudolfo) Luigi

BORN: February 19, 1743—Lucca, Italy
DIED: May 28, 1805—Madrid, Spain
HISTORICAL PERIOD: Classical
COMPOSITIONAL MEDIA: Orchestra, chamber music, choral, opera, guitar.
IMPORTANT ITEMS: A professional cellist and composer. Notable works include the minuet from the "String Quintet in E major Op. 13, No. 5."

Bolcom, William (Elden)

BORN: May 26, 1938—Seattle, WA
HISTORICAL PERIOD: Modern
COMPOSITIONAL MEDIA: Orchestra, chamber music, keyboard, opera, electronic.
IMPORTANT ITEMS: Awarded the Pulitzer Prize in 1988 for his "12 Etudes for Piano."

Bolling, Claude

BORN: April 10, 1930—Cannes, France
HISTORICAL PERIOD: Modern
COMPOSITIONAL MEDIA: Chamber music,

orchestra, film.
IMPORTANT ITEMS: Jazz pianist and band leader.
His compositions blend classical and jazz styles.

Borodin, Alexander (Porfirievich)

BORN: November 12, 1833—St. Petersburg
DIED: February 28, 1887—St. Petersburg
HISTORICAL PERIOD: Romantic
COMPOSITIONAL MEDIA: Orchestra, chamber
music, keyboard, opera, songs.
IMPORTANT ITEMS: Notable works include the
opera "Prince Igor" and the tone poem "In the
Steppes of Central Asia."

Boulanger, Nadia (Juliette)

BORN: September 16, 1887—Paris
DIED: October 22, 1979—Paris
HISTORICAL PERIOD: Modern
COMPOSITIONAL MEDIA: Orchestra, keyboard,
choral.
IMPORTANT ITEMS: Important teacher whose pupils
included Carter, Copland, Harris, Piston and other
well-known American and European composers.

Boulez, Pierre

BORN: March 26, 1925—Montbrison, France
HISTORICAL PERIOD: Modern
COMPOSITIONAL MEDIA: Orchestra, chamber
music, keyboard.
IMPORTANT ITEMS: Well respected conductor and
leader in developing and promoting serialism and
other contemporary music techniques.

B

Bowie, David
[real name: David Robert Jones]
BORN: January 8, 1947—London
HISTORICAL PERIOD: Modern (Popular)
COMPOSITIONAL MEDIA: Popular songs.
IMPORTANT ITEMS: Notable songs include "Space Oddity" and "Ziggy Stardust."

Boyce, William
BORN: September 11, 1711—London
DIED: February 7, 1779—London
HISTORICAL PERIOD: Baroque
COMPOSITIONAL MEDIA: Vocal, chamber music, orchestra, songs, keyboard, oratorios.
IMPORTANT ITEMS: Named Master of the King's Music in 1759.

Brahms, Johannes
BORN: May 7, 1833—Hamburg, Germany
DIED: April 3, 1897—Vienna
HISTORICAL PERIOD: Romantic
COMPOSITIONAL MEDIA: Orchestra, chamber music, keyboard, choral, songs.
IMPORTANT ITEMS: Notable works include four symphonies, the "Double Concerto" for violin and cello, "Liebeslieder Waltzes" for voices and piano four hands and the "Academic Festival Overture."

Britten, Benjamin
BORN: November 22, 1913—Lowestoft, England
DIED: December 4, 1976—Aldeburgh, England
HISTORICAL PERIOD: Modern
COMPOSITIONAL MEDIA: Orchestra, chamber music, choral, opera, songs, guitar.

IMPORTANT ITEMS: Notable works include "The Young Person's Guide to the Orchestra" and the opera "Peter Grimes."

Brouwer, Leo

BORN: March 1, 1939—Havana
HISTORICAL PERIOD: Modern
COMPOSITIONAL MEDIA: Guitar, keyboard, film, orchestra, chamber music.
IMPORTANT ITEMS: A concert guitarist whose guitar music incorporates Cuban rhythms.

Brown, Earle (Appleton, Jr.)

BORN: December 26, 1926—Lunenburg, MA
HISTORICAL PERIOD: Modern
COMPOSITIONAL MEDIA: Chamber music, keyboard, electronic, orchestra.
IMPORTANT ITEMS: Compositions incorporate aleatoric techniques.

Brubeck, Dave (David Warren)

BORN: December 6, 1920—Concord, CA
HISTORICAL PERIOD: Modern
COMPOSITIONAL MEDIA: Instrumental jazz, orchestra, chamber music, choral, songs.
IMPORTANT ITEMS: Notable works include "Take Five" and "Blue Rondo A La Turk"

Bruch, Max (Karl August)

BORN: January 6, 1838—Cologne, Germany
DIED: October 2, 1920—Friednau, Germany
HISTORICAL PERIOD: Romantic
COMPOSITIONAL MEDIA: Orchestra, chamber music, keyboard, choral, opera, songs.

IMPORTANT ITEMS: Notable works include "Kol Nidrei" for cello and orchestra.

Bruckner, Anton

BORN: September 4, 1824—Ansfelden, Austria
DIED: October 11, 1896—Vienna
HISTORICAL PERIOD: Late Romantic
COMPOSITIONAL MEDIA: Orchestra, chamber music, keyboard, choral.
IMPORTANT ITEMS: Outstanding organist and composer best known for his nine symphonies and "Te Deum" for choir and orchestra.

Bull, John

BORN: c. 1562—Old Radnor, Radnorshire, England
DIED: March 12, 1628—Antwerp
HISTORICAL PERIOD: Late Renaissance
COMPOSITIONAL MEDIA: Keyboard.
IMPORTANT ITEMS: Highly skilled virginalist and organist.

Burgmüller, Johann Friedrich Franz

BORN: December 4, 1806—Regensburg
DIED: February 13, 1874—Beaulieu, France
HISTORICAL PERIOD: Romantic
COMPOSITIONAL MEDIA: Ballet, keyboard, songs.
IMPORTANT ITEMS: Notable works include his piano studies which are standard in pedagogical literature.

Burke, Johnny

BORN: October 3, 1908—Antioch, CA
DIED: February 25, 1964—New York
HISTORICAL PERIOD: Modern (Popular)

COMPOSITIONAL MEDIA: Popular songs.
IMPORTANT ITEMS: Notable songs include "What's New," "Pennies from Heaven" and "Misty."

Busoni, Ferruccio (Dante Michelangiolo Benvenuto)

BORN: April 1, 1866—Empoli, Italy
DIED: July 27, 1924—Berlin, Germany
HISTORICAL PERIOD: Late Romantic
COMPOSITIONAL MEDIA: Keyboard, orchestra, chamber music, opera.
IMPORTANT ITEMS: A virtuoso pianist who wrote the influential essay "Outline for a New Aesthetics of Music."

Buxtehude, Dietrich

BORN: 1637—Oldelsloe, Holstein
DIED: May 9, 1707—Lubeck, Germany
HISTORICAL PERIOD: Baroque
COMPOSITIONAL MEDIA: Keyboard, chamber music, choral.
IMPORTANT ITEMS: Virtuoso organist who influenced J.S. Bach.

Byrd, William

BORN: 1543—Lincolnshire, England
DIED: July 4, 1623—Stondon, England
HISTORICAL PERIOD: Renaissance
COMPOSITIONAL MEDIA: Choral, songs, keyboard, chamber music.
IMPORTANT ITEMS: Keyboard works are in the Fitzwilliam Virginal Book.

C

Caccini, Giulio

BORN: October 8, 1551—Tivoli, Italy
DIED: December 10, 1618—Florence, Italy
HISTORICAL PERIOD: Renaissance
COMPOSITIONAL MEDIA: Choral, opera.
IMPORTANT ITEMS: Notable works include the opera "Euridice."

Cage, John (Milton, Jr.)

BORN: September 5, 1912—Los Angeles
DIED: August 12, 1992—New York
HISTORICAL PERIOD: Modern
COMPOSITIONAL MEDIA: Orchestra, keyboard, chamber music, choral.
IMPORTANT ITEMS: Highly experimental composer who, among other techniques, incorporated prepared piano, tape and aleatory techniques.

Caldara, Antonio

BORN: 1670—Venice
DIED: December 26, 1736—Vienna
HISTORICAL PERIOD: Baroque
COMPOSITIONAL MEDIA: Opera, oratorio, choral, chamber music, songs.
IMPORTANT ITEMS: Very prolific with over 90 operas, 43 oratorios and 30 masses.

Carissimi, Giacomo

BORN: April 18, 1605—Marino, Italy
DIED: January 12, 1674—Rome

HISTORICAL PERIOD: Baroque
COMPOSITIONAL MEDIA: Choral.
IMPORTANT ITEMS: Best remembered for his
development of the oratorio.

Carmichael, Hoagy [Hoagland] (Howard)

BORN: November 22, 1899—Bloomington, IN
DIED: December 27, 1981—Rancho Mirage, CA
HISTORICAL PERIOD: Modern (Popular)
COMPOSITIONAL MEDIA: Popular songs.
IMPORTANT ITEMS: Notable songs include
"Stardust" and "Georgia on My Mind."

Carter, Benny

BORN: August 8, 1907—New York
HISTORICAL PERIOD: Modern
COMPOSITIONAL MEDIA: Instrumental jazz, film,
TV.
IMPORTANT ITEMS: Notable works include jazz
compositions "When Lights Are Low," "Harlem
Mood" and the TV score "M Squad."

Carter, Elliott (Cook, Jr.)

BORN: December 11, 1908—New York
HISTORICAL PERIOD: Modern
COMPOSITIONAL MEDIA: Orchestra, chamber
music, ballet, keyboard, choral, opera, songs.
IMPORTANT ITEMS: His early works were neo-
classical but later turned to serial techniques.
Awarded the Pulitzer Prize in 1960 and 1973.

Casadesus, Robert

BORN: April 7, 1899—Paris
DIED: September 19, 1972—Paris

HISTORICAL PERIOD: Modern
COMPOSITIONAL MEDIA: Orchestra, chamber music, keyboard.
IMPORTANT ITEMS: Professional pianist and composer.

Casella, Alfredo

BORN: July 25, 1883—Turin, France
DIED: March 5, 1947—Rome
HISTORICAL PERIOD: Modern
COMPOSITIONAL MEDIA: Orchestra, chamber music, ballet, keyboard, choral, opera.
IMPORTANT ITEMS: Professional pianist, conductor and author. Many compositions are in the neo-classical style.

Cesti, Antonio (Pietro)

BORN: August 5, 1623—Arezzo
DIED: October 14, 1669—Florence
HISTORICAL PERIOD: Baroque
COMPOSITIONAL MEDIA: Operas, vocal, choral.
IMPORTANT ITEMS: One of the most important opera composers of his time.

Chabrier, (Alexis-) Emmanuel

BORN: January 18, 1841—Ambert, Puy de Dome, France
DIED: September 13, 1894—Paris
HISTORICAL PERIOD: Romantic
COMPOSITIONAL MEDIA: Orchestra, opera, keyboard, songs.
IMPORTANT ITEMS: Notable works include "España" for orchestra.

C

Chaminade, Cecile (Louise Stéphanie)

BORN: August 8, 1857—Paris, France
DIED: April 13, 1944—Monte Carlo, France
HISTORICAL PERIOD: Romantic
COMPOSITIONAL MEDIA: Keyboard, orchestra, chamber music, choral, songs.
IMPORTANT ITEMS: Successful concert pianist.

Chausson, (Amédée) Ernest

BORN: January 20, 1855—Paris
DIED: June 10, 1899—Limay, France
HISTORICAL PERIOD: Romantic
COMPOSITIONAL MEDIA: Opera, vocal, orchestra, chamber music, songs.
IMPORTANT ITEMS: Highly influenced by the music of Wagner and Franck.

Chavez (y Ramirez), Carlos (Antonio de Padua)

BORN: June 13, 1899—Mexico City
DIED: August 2, 1978—Mexico City
HISTORICAL PERIOD: Modern
COMPOSITIONAL MEDIA: Symphony, keyboard, ballet, choral, vocal, chamber music.
IMPORTANT ITEMS: He founded and conducted Mexico's first symphony orchestra.

Cherubini, Luigi (Carlo Zenobio Saluatore Maria)

BORN: September 14, 1760—Florence
DIED: March 13, 1842—Paris
HISTORICAL PERIOD: Classical
COMPOSITIONAL MEDIA: Orchestra, chamber music, ballet, keyboard, choral, opera.
IMPORTANT ITEMS: His music inspired Beethoven. Notable works include his "Requiem No. 2" in D minor.

C

Childs, Barney

BORN: February 13, 1926—Spokane, WA
HISTORICAL PERIOD: Modern
COMPOSITIONAL MEDIA: Orchestra, chamber music, choral.
IMPORTANT ITEMS: Compositions include aleatory techniques.

Chopin, Frédéric (-François)

BORN: February 22, 1810—Zelazowa Wola, Poland
DIED: October 17, 1849—Paris
HISTORICAL PERIOD: Romantic
COMPOSITIONAL MEDIA: Keyboard, orchestra, chamber music, songs.
IMPORTANT ITEMS: A professional pianist whose notable works include mazurkas, waltzes, polonaises and numerous other piano compositions.

Chou, Wen-chung

BORN: June 29, 1923—Chefoo, China
HISTORICAL PERIOD: Modern
COMPOSITIONAL MEDIA: Orchestra, band, chamber music, keyboard, film.
IMPORTANT ITEMS: Incorporated the principles of I Ching in some compositions.

Cimarosa, Domenico

BORN: December 17, 1749—Aversa, Italy
DIED: January 11, 1801—Venice
HISTORICAL PERIOD: Classical
COMPOSITIONAL MEDIA: Opera, chamber music, keyboard, choral, songs.
IMPORTANT ITEMS: Prolific composer of Italian opera buffa.

C

Clarke, Jeremiah

BORN: c. 1673—London
DIED: December 1, 1707—London
HISTORICAL PERIOD: Baroque
COMPOSITIONAL MEDIA: Keyboard, choral, opera,
songs, theatrical.
IMPORTANT ITEMS: Notable works include the
"Trumpet Voluntary."

Clementi, Muzlo

BORN: January 23, 1752—Rome
DIED: March 10, 1832—Evesham, England
HISTORICAL PERIOD: Classical
COMPOSITIONAL MEDIA: Orchestra, keyboard.
IMPORTANT ITEMS: Professional pianist and
conductor. Notable works include his collection of
piano studies "Gradus ad Parnassum."

Cohan, George M. [Michael]

BORN: July 3, 1878—Providence, RI
DIED: November 5, 1942—New York
HISTORICAL PERIOD: Modern (Popular)
COMPOSITIONAL MEDIA: Popular songs.
IMPORTANT ITEMS: Notable songs include "Over
There" and "Yankee Doodle Dandy."

Coleman, Cy
[real name: Seymour Kaufman]

BORN: June 14, 1929—New York
HISTORICAL PERIOD: Modern (Popular)
COMPOSITIONAL MEDIA: Popular songs, musicals,
radio, TV.
IMPORTANT ITEMS: Notable works include scores to
the Broadway musicals "Barnum," "Sweet Charity"
and the song "Hey Look Me Over."

C

Coleridge-Taylor, Samuel

BORN: August 15, 1875—London
DIED: September 1, 1912—Croydon, England
HISTORICAL PERIOD: Romantic
COMPOSITIONAL MEDIA: Orchestra, chamber
music, opera, vocal, keyboard.
IMPORTANT ITEMS: Most notable work is his "Song
of Hiawatha" trilogy.

Coleman, Ornette

BORN: March 9, 1930—Fort Worth, TX
HISTORICAL PERIOD: Modern
COMPOSITIONAL MEDIA: Instrumental jazz,
chamber music, orchestra.
IMPORTANT ITEMS: Influential jazz saxophonist and
composer. Notable works include "Lonely Woman."

Copland, Aaron

BORN: November 14, 1900—Brooklyn, NY
DIED: December 2, 1990—Westchester, NY
HISTORICAL PERIOD: Modern
COMPOSITIONAL MEDIA: Orchestra, chamber
music, ballet, keyboard, choral, songs, opera, film.
IMPORTANT ITEMS: Very popular American
composer who incorporated American folk music,
jazz, and serial techniques in his music. Notable
works include "Lincoln Portrait," "Rodeo," "Appalachian
Spring" and "Fanfare for the Common Man."

Corelli, Arcangelo

BORN: February 17, 1653—Fusignano, Italy
DIED: January 8, 1713—Rome
HISTORICAL PERIOD: Baroque
COMPOSITIONAL MEDIA: Orchestra, chamber music.

IMPORTANT ITEMS: Famous virtuoso violinist and composer who created the concerto grosso.

C

Corigliano, John (Paul)

BORN: February 16, 1938—New York
HISTORICAL PERIOD: Modern
COMPOSITIONAL MEDIA: Orchestra, chamber music, choral, electronic, theatrical.
IMPORTANT ITEMS: Notable works include the opera "The Ghosts of Versailles" and his symphony No. 1.

Costello, Elvis
[real name: Declan McManus]

BORN: August 25, 1954—London
HISTORICAL PERIOD: Modern (Popular)
COMPOSITIONAL MEDIA: Popular songs.
IMPORTANT ITEMS: Popular singer and songwriter. Notable songs include "Watching the Detectives."

Couperin, François

BORN: November 10, 1668—Paris
DIED: September 11, 1733—Paris
HISTORICAL PERIOD: Baroque
COMPOSITIONAL MEDIA: Choral, chamber music, keyboard.
IMPORTANT ITEMS: Notable works include his book on harpsichord playing, "L'art de toucher la clavecin" which is a standard of pedagogical literature

Cowell, Henry (Dixon)

BORN: March 11, 1897—Menlo Park, CA
DIED: December 1910, 1965—Shady, NY
HISTORICAL PERIOD: Modern

COMPOSITIONAL MEDIA: Orchestra, chamber
music, ballet, keyboard, choral, opera, songs.
IMPORTANT ITEMS: Innovative composer whose
compositions incorporate tone clusters, playing on
the inside of the piano and aleatory techniques.

Cramer, Johann Baptist

BORN: February 24, 1771— Mannheim
DIED: April 16, 1858—London
HISTORICAL PERIOD: Classical
COMPOSITIONAL MEDIA: Keyboard, chamber
music, orchestra.
IMPORTANT ITEMS: Best known for his piano
method.

Creston, Paul
[real name: Giuseppe Guttoveggio]

BORN: October 10, 1906—New York
DIED: August 24, 1985—San Diego, CA
HISTORICAL PERIOD: Modern
COMPOSITIONAL MEDIA: Orchestra, chamber
music, keyboard, choral.
IMPORTANT ITEMS: Prolific composer and author.

Crüger, Johann

BORN April 9, 1598—Gross Breese, Prussia
DIED: February 23, 1662—Berlin
HISTORICAL PERIOD: Baroque
COMPOSITIONAL MEDIA: Choral, orchestra.
IMPORTANT ITEMS: Notable works include the
chorale melodies "Nun danket alle Gott" and "Jesu
meine Freude" which were later used by Bach.

Crumb, George (Henry)

BORN: October 24, 1929—Charleston, WV
HISTORICAL PERIOD: Modern
COMPOSITIONAL MEDIA: Orchestra, chamber
music, keyboard, choral, songs, electronic.
IMPORTANT ITEMS: Awarded the Pulitzer Prize in
1968 for "Echoes of Time and the River." Notable
works include "Ancient Voices of Children."

Cui, César (Antonovich)

BORN: January 18, 1835—Vilna, Russia
DIED: March 26, 1918—Petrograd, Russia
HISTORICAL PERIOD: Romantic
COMPOSITIONAL MEDIA: Orchestra, chamber
music, keyboard, choral, opera, songs.
IMPORTANT ITEMS: A member of the Russian Five.

Czerny, Carl

BORN: February 20, 1791—Vienna
DIED: July 15, 1857—Vienna
HISTORICAL PERIOD: Classical
COMPOSITIONAL MEDIA: Orchestra, chamber
music, keyboard, choral.
IMPORTANT ITEMS: Notable works include keyboard
exercises which are a standard in pedagogical
literature.

D

D

Dahl, Ingolf

BORN: June 9, 1912—Hamburg, Germany
DIED: August 6, 1970—Frutigen, Switzerland
HISTORICAL PERIOD: Modern
COMPOSITIONAL MEDIA: Orchestra, chamber music, keyboard, choral.
IMPORTANT ITEMS: Teacher at the University of Southern California.

Dalcroze, Emile Jaques

BORN: July 6, 1865—Vienna
DIED: July 1, 1950—Geneva, Switzerland
HISTORICAL PERIOD: Late Romantic
COMPOSITIONAL MEDIA: Orchestra, chamber music, keyboard, choral, opera, songs, theatrical.
IMPORTANT ITEMS: Developed eurhythmics.

Dallapiccola, Luigi

BORN: February 3, 1904—Pisino, Italy
DIED: February 19, 1975—Florence, Italy
HISTORICAL PERIOD: Modern
COMPOSITIONAL MEDIA: Orchestra, chamber music, keyboard, choral, opera, songs.
IMPORTANT ITEMS: Compositions incorporate twelve-tone techniques.

Damrosch, Walter Johannes

BORN: January 30, 1862—Breslau, Germany
DIED: December 22, 1950—New York
HISTORICAL PERIOD: Late Romantic
COMPOSITIONAL MEDIA: Choral, opera, songs.

IMPORTANT ITEMS: Conductor who premiered many famous works in the United States.

Davidovsky, Mario

BORN: March 4, 1934—Buenos Aires, Argentina
HISTORICAL PERIOD: Modern
COMPOSITIONAL MEDIA: Orchestra, chamber music, keyboard, electronic.
IMPORTANT ITEMS: Awarded the Pulitzer Prize in 1971 for "Synchronisms No. 6" for piano and electronics.

Davies, Peter Maxwell

BORN: September 8, 1934—Manchester, England
HISTORICAL PERIOD: Modern
COMPOSITIONAL MEDIA: Orchestra, chamber music, keyboard, choral, opera, electronic.
IMPORTANT ITEMS: Notable works include "Eight Songs for a Mad King."

Davis, Miles (Dewy, III)

BORN: May 25, 1926—Alton, IL
DIED: September 28, 1991—Santa Monica, CA
HISTORICAL PERIOD: Modern (Jazz)
COMPOSITIONAL MEDIA: Popular instrumental.
IMPORTANT ITEMS: Influential jazz trumpeter who blended rock rhythms and jazz in his compositions.

Debussy, (Achille-) Claude

BORN: August 22, 1862—Saint Germain-en-Laye, France
DIED: March 25, 1918—Paris
HISTORICAL PERIOD: Modern
COMPOSITIONAL MEDIA: Orchestra, chamber

D

music, ballet, keyboard, choral, opera, songs.
IMPORTANT ITEMS: Important impressionist composer. Notable works include "La Mer" for orchestra, the opera "Pelléas et Mélisande" and numerous pieces for piano.

Delibes, (Clément Philibert) Léo

BORN: February 21, 1836—St. Germain-du-Val, France
DIED: January 16, 1891—Paris
HISTORICAL PERIOD: Romantic
COMPOSITIONAL MEDIA: Ballet, choral, opera, songs.
IMPORTANT ITEMS: Successful composer of operas and ballets.

Delius, (Fritz) Frederick

BORN: January 29, 1862—Bradford, England
DIED: June 10, 1934—Grez-sur-Loing, France
HISTORICAL PERIOD: Late Romantic
COMPOSITIONAL MEDIA: Orchestra, chamber music, choral, opera, songs.
IMPORTANT ITEMS: Compositions include romantic and impressionist elements.

Dello Joio, Norman

BORN: January 24, 1913—New York
HISTORICAL PERIOD: Modern
COMPOSITIONAL MEDIA: Orchestra, chamber music, keyboard, choral, opera, band.
IMPORTANT ITEMS: Notable works include the opera "The Triumph of St. Joan."

Del Tredici, David (Walter)

BORN: March 16, 1937—Cloverdale, CA
HISTORICAL PERIOD: Modern
COMPOSITIONAL MEDIA: Orchestra, chamber music, keyboard, choral, songs.
IMPORTANT ITEMS: Most famous compositions are based on "Alice in Wonderland" by Lewis Carroll.

des Prez, Josquin

BORN: c. 1440—Beaurevoir, France
DIED: August 27, 1521—Conde-sur-l'Escaut, France
HISTORICAL PERIOD: Renaissance
COMPOSITIONAL MEDIA: Choral, chamber music.
IMPORTANT ITEMS: Influential Renaissance composer of expressive choral music.

Diabelli, Anton

BORN: September 5, 1781—Mattsee, Germany
DIED: April 8, 1858—Vienna
HISTORICAL PERIOD: Classical
COMPOSITIONAL MEDIA: Chamber music, ballet, keyboard, choral, opera, songs.
IMPORTANT ITEMS: Beethoven based his "Diabelli Variations" on a waltz theme by Diabelli.

Diamond, David (Leo)

BORN: July 9, 1915—Rochester, NY
HISTORICAL PERIOD: Modern
COMPOSITIONAL MEDIA: Orchestra, chamber music, ballet, keyboard, choral, songs.
IMPORTANT ITEMS: Composer of highly contrapuntal music who adopted serial techniques in the 1950s.

Diamond, Neil (Leslie)

BORN: January 24, 1941—New York
HISTORICAL PERIOD: Modern (Popular)
COMPOSITIONAL MEDIA: Popular songs, film.
IMPORTANT ITEMS: Notable songs include "Sweet Caroline."

d'Indy, Vincent: See Indy, Vincent d'

Dittersdorf, Karl Ditters von

BORN: November 2, 1739—Vienna
DIED: October 24, 1799—Castle Rothlhotta, Bohemia
HISTORICAL PERIOD: Classical
COMPOSITIONAL MEDIA: Orchestra, chamber music, ballet, keyboard, choral, opera.
IMPORTANT ITEMS: An important member of the classical Viennese school.

Dohnanyi, Ernö (Ernst von)

BORN: July 27, 1877—Pressburg, Bratislava
DIED: February 9, 1960—New York
HISTORICAL PERIOD: Late Romantic/Modern
COMPOSITIONAL MEDIA: Orchestra, keyboard, chamber music, vocal, opera.
IMPORTANT ITEMS: His most famous work is "Variations on a Nursery Song" for piano and orchestra.

Donaldson, Walter

BORN: February 15, 1893—New York
DIED: July 15, 1947—New York
HISTORICAL PERIOD: Modern (Popular)
COMPOSITIONAL MEDIA: Popular songs.
IMPORTANT ITEMS: Notable songs include "My

Mammy," "Yes Sir, That's My Baby" and "Makin' Whoopee."

Donizetti, Gaetano

BORN: November 29, 1797—Bergamo, Italy
DIED: April 1, 1848—Bergamo, Italy
HISTORICAL PERIOD: Romantic
COMPOSITIONAL MEDIA: Opera, chamber music, keyboard, choral.
IMPORTANT ITEMS: Notable works include the operas "Lucia di Lamermoor" and "Don Pasquale."

Dowland, John

BORN: December 1562—near Dublin, England
DIED: January 21, 1626—London
HISTORICAL PERIOD: Renaissance
COMPOSITIONAL MEDIA: Songs, lute, chamber music.
IMPORTANT ITEMS: Virtuoso lutenist and singer whose works were harmonically advanced for their time.

Druckman, Jacob (Raphael)

BORN: June 26, 1928—Philadelphia, PA
DIED: May 24, 1996
HISTORICAL PERIOD: Modern
COMPOSITIONAL MEDIA: Orchestra, chamber music, choral, electronic.
IMPORTANT ITEMS:Awarded the Pulitzer Prize in 1972 for his orchestral work "Windows."

Dufay, Guillaume

BORN: c. 1400—Cambrai, France
DIED: November 27, 1474—Cambrai, France
HISTORICAL PERIOD: Late Medieval/Early Renaissance

D

COMPOSITIONAL MEDIA: Choral.
IMPORTANT ITEMS: Most famous for his cantus firmus Masses, motets and chansons.

Dukas, Paul

BORN: October 1, 1865—Paris
DIED: May 17, 1935—Paris
HISTORICAL PERIOD: Late Romantic
COMPOSITIONAL MEDIA: Orchestra, chamber music, keyboard, opera, ballet.
IMPORTANT ITEMS: Notable works include "L'Apprenti Sorcier" (The Sorcerer's Apprentice).

Duke, Vernon
[real name: Vladimir Dukelsky]

BORN: October 10, 1903—Parfianovka, Russia
DIED: January 16, 1969—Santa Monica, CA
HISTORICAL PERIOD: Modern
COMPOSITIONAL MEDIA: Orchestra, chamber music, ballet, keyboard, choral, popular songs.
IMPORTANT ITEMS: Notable popular songs include "April in Paris."

Dunstable, John

BORN: c. 1390—Dunstable, England
DIED: December 24, 1453—London
HISTORICAL PERIOD: Medieval
COMPOSITIONAL MEDIA: Choral.
IMPORTANT ITEMS: Influential composer of Masses and isorhythmic motets.

Dupre, Marcel

BORN: May 3, 1886—Rouen, France
DIED: May 30, 1971—Meudon, France
HISTORICAL PERIOD: Modern
COMPOSITIONAL MEDIA: Organ, choral.
IMPORTANT ITEMS: Award winning composer and organist.

Dussek, Jan (Johann) Ladislav

BORN: February 12, 1760—Caslav, Bohemia
DIED: March 20, 1812—St Germain-en-Laye
HISTORICAL PERIOD: Classical
COMPOSITIONAL MEDIA: Keyboard, chamber music, orchestra, choral.
IMPORTANT ITEMS: Notable works include many influential pieces for piano.

Dvořák, Antonin (Leopold)

BORN: September 8, 1841—Muhlhausen, Bohemia
DIED: May 1, 1904—Prague, Czechoslovakia
HISTORICAL PERIOD: Romantic
COMPOSITIONAL MEDIA: Orchestra, chamber music, keyboard, choral, opera, songs.
IMPORTANT ITEMS: Notable works include the symphony in E minor "From the New World."

Dylan, Bob
[real name: Robert Allen Zimmerman]

BORN: May 24, 1941—Duluth, MN
HISTORICAL PERIOD: Modern (Popular)
COMPOSITIONAL MEDIA: Popular songs.
IMPORTANT ITEMS: Notable songs include "Blowin' in the Wind," "The Times They Are A-Changin'" and "Mr. Tambourine Man."

E

E

Elgar, Sir Edward (William)

BORN: June 2, 1857—Broadheath, England
DIED: February 23, 1934—Worcester, England
HISTORICAL PERIOD: Late Romantic
COMPOSITIONAL MEDIA: Orchestra, chamber
music, opera, choral, songs, keyboard.
IMPORTANT ITEMS: Notable works include "Enigma
Variations" and his "Pomp and Circumstance"
marches.

Ellington, "Duke" (Edward Kennedy)

BORN: April 29, 1899—Washington, DC
DIED: May 24, 1974—New York
HISTORICAL PERIOD: Modern (Popular)
COMPOSITIONAL MEDIA: Instrumental jazz,
orchestra, chamber music, choral, popular songs.
IMPORTANT ITEMS: One of the most influential jazz
composers of the 20th century. Notable songs
include "Satin Doll," "Sophisticated Lady," "Take the
A Train" and "Harlem Air Shaft."

Enesco [Enescu], Georges

BORN: August 19, 1881—Liveni-Virnav, Romania
DIED: May 4, 1955—Paris
HISTORICAL PERIOD: Modern
COMPOSITIONAL MEDIA: Orchestra, chamber
music, keyboard, choral, opera.
IMPORTANT ITEMS: Many of his compositions
incorporate Romanian folk idioms.

Erb, Donald (James)

BORN: January 17, 1927—Youngstown, OH
HISTORICAL PERIOD: Modern
COMPOSITIONAL MEDIA: Orchestra, chamber
music, keyboard, choral, electronic, band.
IMPORTANT ITEMS: Incorporates many different
styles into his compositions including jazz, serial
and aleatory techniques.

F

Falla (y Matheu), Manuel (Maria) de

BORN: November 23, 1876—Cadiz, Spain
DIED: November 14, 1946—Alta Gracia, Argentina
HISTORICAL PERIOD: Modern
COMPOSITIONAL MEDIA: Orchestra, chamber
music, ballet, keyboard, opera, songs.
IMPORTANT ITEMS: Notable works include the
ballets "El amor brujo" and "The Three-Cornered
Hat."

Fauré, Gabriel (Urbain)

BORN: May 12, 1845—Pamiers, France
DIED: November 4, 1924—Paris
HISTORICAL PERIOD: Late Romantic
COMPOSITIONAL MEDIA: Chamber music,
orchestra, keyboard, choral, opera, songs.
IMPORTANT ITEMS: Important composer who used
old modes, counterpoint and free dissonance.
Notable works include his "Requiem."

F

Feldman, Morton

BORN: January 12, 1926—New York
DIED: September 3, 1987—Buffalo, NY
HISTORICAL PERIOD: Modern
COMPOSITIONAL MEDIA: Orchestra, chamber music, choral, electronic.
IMPORTANT ITEMS: Compositions incorporate graphic notation and indeterminancy.

Field, John

BORN: July 26, 1782—Dublin
DIED: January 23, 1837—Moscow
HISTORICAL PERIOD: Romantic
COMPOSITIONAL MEDIA: Keyboard, chamber music, orchestra.
IMPORTANT ITEMS: The originator of the keyboard "Nocturne."

Fillmore, (James) Henry (Jr.)

BORN: December 2, 1881—Cincinnati, OH
DIED: December 7, 1956—Miami, FL
HISTORICAL PERIOD: Modern
COMPOSITIONAL MEDIA: Band, songs.
IMPORTANT ITEMS: Notable works include the marches "American We" and "His Honor."

Finney, Ross Lee

BORN: December 23, 1906—Wells, MN
HISTORICAL PERIOD: Modern
COMPOSITIONAL MEDIA: Orchestra, chamber music, keyboard, choral, songs, electronic.
IMPORTANT ITEMS: Compositions incorporate serial techniques. Studied with Alban Berg.

F

Flowtow, Friedrich (Adolf Ferdinand) von

BORN: April 27, 1813—Teutendorf, Germany
DIED: January 24, 1883—Darmstadt, Germany
HISTORICAL PERIOD: Romantic
COMPOSITIONAL MEDIA: Opera, ballet, orchestra, chamber music, songs.
IMPORTANT ITEMS: Notable operas include "Martha" and "Alessandro Stradella."

Foss, Lukas
[real name: Lukas Fuchs]

BORN: August 15, 1922—Berlin, Germany
HISTORICAL PERIOD: Modern
COMPOSITIONAL MEDIA: Orchestra, chamber music, ballet, keyboard, choral, opera, electronic.
IMPORTANT ITEMS: Compositions include a variety of styles including American folk music and serial techniques.

Foster, Stephen Collins

BORN: July 4, 1826—Lawrenceville, PA
DIED: January 13, 1864—New York
HISTORICAL PERIOD: Romantic
COMPOSITIONAL MEDIA: Songs.
IMPORTANT ITEMS: Notable songs include "Old Folks at Home," "Oh, Susanna!" and "Camptown Races."

Françaix, Jean

BORN: May 23, 1912—Le Mans, France
HISTORICAL PERIOD: Modern
COMPOSITIONAL MEDIA: Orchestra, chamber music, keyboard, choral, songs, ballet, opera, film.
IMPORTANT ITEMS: Prolific composer and pianist.

Franck, César (-August-Jean-Guillaume-Hubert)

BORN: December 10, 1822—Liege, Belgium
DIED: November 8, 1890 Paris
HISTORICAL PERIOD: Romantic
COMPOSITIONAL MEDIA: Orchestra, chamber music, keyboard, choral, opera, songs.
IMPORTANT ITEMS: Notable works include his symphony in D minor.

Frescobaldi, Girolamo

BORN: September 9, 1583—Ferrara, Italy
DIED: March 1, 1643—Rome
HISTORICAL PERIOD: Baroque
COMPOSITIONAL MEDIA: Keyboard, chamber music, choral.
IMPORTANT ITEMS: The most famous organist of his time and a significant composer of keyboard music.

Friml, (Charles) Rudolf

BORN: December 2, 1879—Prague, Czechoslovakia
DIED: November 12, 1972—Hollywood, CA
HISTORICAL PERIOD: Modern (Popular)
COMPOSITIONAL MEDIA: Operetta, film.
IMPORTANT ITEMS: Notable works include the operettas "Rose Marie," "The Firefly" and the "Vagabond King."

Fux, Johann Joseph

BORN: 1660—Hirtenfeld, near St. Marein, Styria
DIED: February 13, 1741—Vienna
HISTORICAL PERIOD: Baroque
COMPOSITIONAL MEDIA: Opera, oratorio, choral, keyboard.

IMPORTANT ITEMS: Notable works include his treatise on counterpoint, "Gradus ad Parnassum."

G

Gabrieli, Andrea

BORN: c. 1510—Venice
DIED: 1586—Venice
HISTORICAL PERIOD: Renaissance
COMPOSITIONAL MEDIA: Choral, chamber music, keyboard.
IMPORTANT ITEMS: Versatile composer who taught his nephew Giovanni Gabrieli.

Gabrieli, Giovanni

BORN: 1554-1557—Venice
DIED: August 12, 1612—Venice
HISTORICAL PERIOD: Renaissance
COMPOSITIONAL MEDIA: Choral, chamber music, organ.
IMPORTANT ITEMS: Best known for antiphonal choral works.

Gade, Niels (Wilhelm)

BORN: February 22, 1817—Copenhagen
DIED: December 21, 1890—Copenhagen
HISTORICAL PERIOD: Romantic
COMPOSITIONAL MEDIA: Orchestra, chamber music, keyboard, choral, opera, songs, ballet.
IMPORTANT ITEMS: Prolific Danish composer influenced by the works of Mendelssohn and Schumann.

Gershwin, George

BORN: September 26, 1898—Brooklyn, NY
DIED: July 11, 1937—Beverly Hills, CA
HISTORICAL PERIOD: Modern
COMPOSITIONAL MEDIA: Orchestra, keyboard, musicals, popular songs, film.
IMPORTANT ITEMS: Compositions combined elements of classical and jazz. Notable works include "An American in Paris," "Rhapsody in Blue" and the opera "Porgy and Bess."

Gesualdo, Don Carlo, Prince of Venosa

BORN: c. 1560—Naples
DIED: September 8, 1613
HISTORICAL PERIOD: Renaissance
COMPOSITIONAL MEDIA: Choral, songs.
IMPORTANT ITEMS: Best known for his highly chromatic madrigals.

Giannini, Vittorio

BORN: October 19, 1903—Philadelphia, PA
DIED: November 28, 1966—New York
HISTORICAL PERIOD: Modern
COMPOSITIONAL MEDIA: Orchestra, chamber music, band, keyboard, choral, opera, songs.
IMPORTANT ITEMS: Prolific composer and teacher.

Gibbons, Orlando

BORN: December 25, 1583—Oxford, England
DIED: June 5, 1625—Canterbury, England
HISTORICAL PERIOD: Renaissance
COMPOSITIONAL MEDIA: Choral, chamber music.
IMPORTANT ITEMS: A master of the polyphonic style and great organist.

Ginastera, Alberto (Evaristo)

BORN: April 11, 1916—Buenos Aires, Argentina
DIED: June 25, 1983—Geneva
HISTORICAL PERIOD: Modern
COMPOSITIONAL MEDIA: Orchestra, chamber
music, ballet, keyboard, choral, songs, guitar.
IMPORTANT ITEMS: Compositions incorporate
serial, aleatoric and micro tonal techniques.

Glass, Philip

BORN: January 31, 1937—Baltimore
HISTORICAL PERIOD: Modern
COMPOSITIONAL MEDIA: Chamber music, opera,
ballet, film, orchestra.
IMPORTANT ITEMS: Compositions are in the
minimalist style.

Glazunov, Alexander (Konstantinovich)

BORN: August 10, 1865—St. Petersburg, Russia
DIED: March 21, 1936—Paris
HISTORICAL PERIOD: Romantic
COMPOSITIONAL MEDIA: Orchestra, chamber
music, ballet, keyboard, choral, songs.
IMPORTANT ITEMS: Prolific composer and teacher.
Notable works include nine symphonies and the
ballet "Raymonda."

Gliere, Reinhold (Moritzovich)

BORN: January 11, 1875—Kiev, Russia
DIED: June 23, 1956—Moscow
HISTORICAL PERIOD: Late Romantic
COMPOSITIONAL MEDIA: Orchestra, chamber
music, ballet, keyboard, opera, songs.
IMPORTANT ITEMS: Notable works include
Symphony No. 3 "Ilya Muromets."

Glinka, Mikhail (Ivanovich)

BORN: June 1, 1804—Novosspaskoye, Russia
DIED: February 15, 1857—Berlin
HISTORICAL PERIOD: Romantic
COMPOSITIONAL MEDIA: Orchestra, chamber music, ballet, keyboard, choral, opera, songs.
IMPORTANT ITEMS: Sometimes called the "Father of Russian Music." Notoble works include the opera "Russlan and Ludmilla."

Gluck, Christoph Willibald (von)

BORN: July 2, 1714—Erasbach, Austria
DIED: November 15, 1787—Vienna
HISTORICAL PERIOD: Classical
COMPOSITIONAL MEDIA: Orchestra, chamber music, ballet, choral, opera, songs.
IMPORTANT ITEMS: Highly influential composer of opera including "Orfeo ed Erudice."

Gold, Ernest

BORN: July 13, 1921—Vienna
HISTORICAL PERIOD: Modern
COMPOSITIONAL MEDIA: Orchestra, chamber music, keyboard, film.
IMPORTANT ITEMS: Notable works include the film score for "Exodus."

Gossec, François Joseph

BORN: January 17, 1734—Vergnies, Belgium
DIED: February 16, 1829—Paris
HISTORICAL PERIOD: Classical
COMPOSITIONAL MEDIA: Orchestra, chamber music, ballet, choral, opera.

IMPORTANT ITEMS: Innovator of orchestration.
Wrote a considerable amount of choral music for the
French revolution.

Gottschalk, Louis Moreau

BORN: May 8, 1829—New Orleans, LA
DIED: December 18, 1869—Rio de Janeiro, Brazil
HISTORICAL PERIOD: Romantic
COMPOSITIONAL MEDIA: Orchestra, piano, opera,
songs.
IMPORTANT ITEMS: Virtuoso pianist, most famous
for his piano compositions.

Gould, Morton

BORN: December 10, 1913—Richmond Hill NY
DIED: February 21, 1996—Orlando, FL
HISTORICAL PERIOD: Modern
COMPOSITIONAL MEDIA: Orchestra, chamber
music, ballet, keyboard, choral, film, TV, band.
IMPORTANT ITEMS: Many of his pieces have
American themes. Awarded the Pulitzer Prize in 1995
for "String Music."

Gounod, Charles (François)

BORN: June 17, 1818—Paris
DIED: October 18, 1893—Paris
HISTORICAL PERIOD: Romantic
COMPOSITIONAL MEDIA: Opera, orchestra,
chamber music, keyboard, choral, songs.
IMPORTANT ITEMS: Notable works include the
opera "Faust."

Grainger, (George) Percy (Aldridge)

BORN: July 8, 1882—Melbourne, Australia
DIED: February 20, 1961—White Plains, NY
HISTORICAL PERIOD: Modern
COMPOSITIONAL MEDIA: Orchestra, chamber music, keyboard, choral, songs, band, electronic.
IMPORTANT ITEMS: A collector of British folk songs. Notable works include "Shepherd's Hey" and "Lincolnshire Posy."

Granados (y Campiña), Enrique

BORN: July 27, 1867—Lerida, Spain
DIED: March 24, 1916—At sea
HISTORICAL PERIOD: Romantic
COMPOSITIONAL MEDIA: Opera, orchestra, vocal, chamber music, keyboard.
IMPORTANT ITEMS: Notable works include "Goyescas."

Green, Johnny
[real name: John Waldo Green]

BORN: October 10, 1908—New York
DIED: May 15, 1989—Beverly Hills, CA
HISTORICAL PERIOD: Modern (Popular)
COMPOSITIONAL MEDIA: Popular songs, film.
IMPORTANT ITEMS: Notable songs include "Body and Soul" and "I Cover the Waterfront."

Grieg, Edvard (Hagerup)

BORN: June 15, 1843—Bergen, Norway
DIED: September 4, 1907—Bergen, Norway
HISTORICAL PERIOD: Romantic
COMPOSITIONAL MEDIA: Orchestra, chamber music, keyboard, choral, songs.

IMPORTANT ITEMS: Best known for incidental music to Ibsen's "Peer Gynt" and his piano concerto.

Griffes, Charles Tomlinson

BORN: September 17, 1884—Elmira, NY
DIED: April 8, 1920—New York
HISTORICAL PERIOD: Modern
COMPOSITIONAL MEDIA: Orchestra, chamber music, keyboard, choral, songs, theatrical
IMPORTANT ITEMS: Considered the foremost American impressionist.

Grofé, Ferde [Ferdinand Rudolph van]

BORN: March 27, 1892—New York
DIED: April 3, 1972—Santa Monica, CA
HISTORICAL PERIOD: Modern
COMPOSITIONAL MEDIA: Orchestra, keyboard.
IMPORTANT ITEMS: Pianist and arranger for Paul Whiteman's band who scored Gershwin's "Rhapsody in Blue." Notable works include the orchestral composition "Grand Canyon Suite."

Guilmant, Felix Alexandre

BORN: March 12, 1837—Boulogne, France
DIED: March 29, 1911—Meudon, France
HISTORICAL PERIOD: Romantic
COMPOSITIONAL MEDIA: Orchestra, keyboard, choral.
IMPORTANT ITEMS: Virtuoso organist, composer and teacher.

Guthrie, Woody [Woodrow] (Wilson)

BORN: July 14, 1912—Okemah, OK
DIED: October 3, 1967—New York

HISTORICAL PERIOD: Modern (Popular)
COMPOSITIONAL MEDIA: Popular songs.
IMPORTANT ITEMS: Notable songs include "This Land is Your Land."

H

Hamlisch, Marvin (Frederic)

BORN: June 2, 1944—New York
HISTORICAL PERIOD: Modern (Popular)
COMPOSITIONAL MEDIA: Musicals, film.
IMPORTANT ITEMS: Notable musicals include "A Chorus Line."

Handel, George Frideric

BORN: February 23, 1685—Halle
DIED: April 14, 1759—London
HISTORICAL PERIOD: Baroque
COMPOSITIONAL MEDIA: Choral, opera, orchestra, chamber music, keyboard, songs.
IMPORTANT ITEMS: One of the most important baroque composers. Notable works include his oratorios "Messiah" and "Judas Maccabeus" and the orchestral compositions "Water Music" and "Royal Fireworks Music."

Handy, W.C. [William Christopher]

BORN: November 16, 1873—Florence, AL
DIED: March 28, 1958—New York
HISTORICAL PERIOD: Modern (Popular)
COMPOSITIONAL MEDIA: Popular songs.
IMPORTANT ITEMS: Known as "the father of the blues." Notable songs include "St. Louis Blues."

Hanon, Charles-Louis

BORN: July 2, 1819—Renescure, France
DIED: March 19, 1900—Boulogne-sur-Mer, France
HISTORICAL PERIOD: Romantic
COMPOSITIONAL MEDIA: Keyboard.
IMPORTANT ITEMS: Notable works include "60 Progressive Studies for Piano."

Hanson, Howard (Harold)

BORN: October 28, 1896—Wahoo, NE
DIED: February 26, 1981—Rochester, NY
HISTORICAL PERIOD: Modern
COMPOSITIONAL MEDIA: Orchestra, chamber music, ballet, keyboard, choral, opera, songs.
IMPORTANT ITEMS: Awarded Pulitzer Prize in 1944 for "The Requiem." Notable works include the opera "Merry Mount."

Harbison, John (Harris)

BORN: December 20, 1938—Orange, NJ
HISTORICAL PERIOD: Modern
COMPOSITIONAL MEDIA: Orchestra, chamber music, choral, opera, ballet.
IMPORTANT ITEMS: Awarded the Pulitzer Prize in 1987 for his vocal work "The Flight Into Egypt."

Harris, Roy (Leroy Ellsworth)

BORN: February 12, 1898—Chandler, OK
DIED: October 1, 1979—Santa Monica, CA
HISTORICAL PERIOD: Modern
COMPOSITIONAL MEDIA: Orchestra, chamber music, keyboard, choral, ballet, band.
IMPORTANT ITEMS: Composed in a traditional tonal style.

Harrison, George

BORN: February 25, 1943—Liverpool
HISTORICAL PERIOD: Modern (Popular)
COMPOSITIONAL MEDIA: Popular songs.
IMPORTANT ITEMS: Lead guitar player for The
Beatles. Notable songs include "Taxman,"
"Something" and "My Sweet Lord."

Harrison, Lou

BORN: May 14, 1917—Portland, OR
HISTORICAL PERIOD: Modern
COMPOSITIONAL MEDIA: Orchestra, chamber
music, ballet, choral, opera, songs, gamelan.
IMPORTANT ITEMS: Compositions incorporate
serial and aleatory techniques, Asian instruments
and unusual systems of tuning.

Hassler, Hans Leo

BORN: October 26, 1564—Nuremberg, Germany
DIED: June 8, 1612—Frankfurt, Germany
HISTORICAL PERIOD: Late Renaissance
COMPOSITIONAL MEDIA: Choral, chamber music,
keyboard.
IMPORTANT ITEMS: Notable works include his
sacred and secular choral music.

Haydn, Franz Joseph

BORN: March 31, 1732—Rohrau, Austria
DIED: May 31, 1809—Vienna
HISTORICAL PERIOD: Classical
COMPOSITIONAL MEDIA: Orchestra, chamber
music, keyboard, choral, opera, songs.
IMPORTANT ITEMS: Prolific composer, including
over 100 symphonies and numerous operas, masses,
string quartets, etc.

Haydn, (Johann) Michael

BORN: September 14, 1737—Rohrau, Austria
DIED: August 10, 1806—Salzburg, Austria
HISTORICAL PERIOD: Classical
COMPOSITIONAL MEDIA: Orchestra, chamber
music, keyboard, choral, opera, songs.
IMPORTANT ITEMS: Brother of Franz Joseph Haydn.

Hensel, Fanny: See Mendelssohn (-Bartholdy), Fanny Cäcilie [Hensel]

H

Henze, Hans Werner

BORN: July 1, 1926—Gütersloh, Germany
HISTORICAL PERIOD: Modern
COMPOSITIONAL MEDIA: Orchestra, chamber
music, ballet, keyboard, choral, opera, songs.
IMPORTANT ITEMS: Compositions incorporate
microtonal, twelve-tone and electronic techniques.

Herbert, Victor (August)

BORN: February 1, 1859—Dublin, Ireland
DIED: May 26, 1924—New York
HISTORICAL PERIOD: Late Romantic
COMPOSITIONAL MEDIA: Operettas, orchestra,
chamber music, keyboard, songs, film, opera.
IMPORTANT ITEMS: Notable works include the
operetta "Babes in Toyland."

Herrmann, Bernard

BORN: June 29, 1911—New York
DIED: December 24, 1975—Los Angeles
HISTORICAL PERIOD: Modern
COMPOSITIONAL MEDIA: Film, orchestra, chamber
music, choral.
IMPORTANT ITEMS: Notable film scores include
"Citizen Kane," "Psycho" and "Taxi Driver."

H

Hindemith, Paul

BORN: November 16, 1895—Hanau, Germany
DIED: December 28, 1963—Frankfurt, Germany
HISTORICAL PERIOD: Modern
COMPOSITIONAL MEDIA: Orchestra, chamber
music, ballet, keyboard, choral, opera, band.
IMPORTANT ITEMS: A leading advocate of
Gebrauchsmusik, he wrote numerous works to be
played by amateurs and students. Notable
compositions include "Mathis der Maler" and
"Symphonic Metamorphosis on Themes of Carl
Maria von Weber."

Holly, Buddy
[real name: Charles Harden Holley]

BORN: September 7, 1936—Lubbock, TX
DIED: February 2, 1959—Clear Lake, IA
HISTORICAL PERIOD: Modern (Popular)
COMPOSITIONAL MEDIA: Popular songs.
IMPORTANT ITEMS: Popular rock songwriter whose
notable songs include "That'll Be the Day."

Holst, Gustav Theodore

BORN: September 21, 1874—Cheltenham, England
DIED: May 25, 1934—London
HISTORICAL PERIOD: Late Romantic
COMPOSITIONAL MEDIA: Orchestra, chamber
music, ballet, keyboard, opera, songs, band.
IMPORTANT ITEMS: Professional trombonist and
organist. Notable works include the orchestral suite
"The Planets."

Honegger, Arthur (Oscar)

BORN: March 10, 1892—Le Havre, France
DIED: November 27, 1955—Paris
HISTORICAL PERIOD: Modern
COMPOSITIONAL MEDIA: Orchestra, chamber music, ballet, keyboard, choral, opera, songs, film, radio.
IMPORTANT ITEMS: A member of Les Six. Notable works include the oratorio "King David" and the orchestral composition "Pacific 231."

H

Hovhaness, Alan

BORN: March 8, 1911—Somerville, MA
HISTORICAL PERIOD: Modern
COMPOSITIONAL MEDIA: Orchestra, chamber music, keyboard, choral, opera, band, songs, electronic.
IMPORTANT ITEMS: Prolific composer whose compositions incorporate Armenian and Oriental modes and aleatoric techniques. Notable works include "And God Created Great Whales."

Hummel, Johann Nepomuk

BORN: November 14, 1778—Pressburg, Germany
DIED: October 17, 1837—Weimar, Germany
HISTORICAL PERIOD: Classical
COMPOSITIONAL MEDIA: Opera, chamber music, ballet, keyboard, orchestra, choral.
IMPORTANT ITEMS: Virtuoso pianist and composer. Although well crafted, his compositions are neglected.

Humperdinck, Engelbert

BORN: September 1, 1854—Siegburg, Germany
DIED: September 27, 1921—Neustrelitz, Germany
HISTORICAL PERIOD: Romantic
COMPOSITIONAL MEDIA: Opera, orchestra,
keyboard, choral, songs.
IMPORTANT ITEMS: Notable works include the
opera "Hansel and Gretel."

Husa, Karel

BORN: August 7, 1921—Prague
HISTORICAL PERIOD: Modern
COMPOSITIONAL MEDIA: Orchestra, chamber
music, ballet, keyboard, choral, band.
IMPORTANT ITEMS: Became an American citizen in
1959. Awarded the Pulitzer Prize in 1969 for his third
string quartet. His "Music for Prague" (1968) has had
over 7,000 performances between its band and
orchestral versions.

I

Ibert, Jacques (François Antoine)

BORN: August 15, 1890—Paris
DIED: February 5, 1962—Paris
HISTORICAL PERIOD: Modern
COMPOSITIONAL MEDIA: Orchestra, chamber
music, ballet, keyboard, choral, opera, film.
IMPORTANT ITEMS: Notable works include
"Concerto for Flute and Orchestra" and the
"Divertissement for Orchestra."

Indy, (Paul Marie Théodore) Vincent d'

BORN: March 27, 1851—Paris

DIED: December 2, 1931—Paris
HISTORICAL PERIOD: Late Romantic
COMPOSITIONAL MEDIA: Orchestra, chamber
music, keyboard, choral, songs.
IMPORTANT ITEMS: Co-founded the Schola
Cantorum of Paris. Notable works include
"Symphony on a French Mountain Air."

Ippolitov-Ivanov, Mikhail (Mikhaylovich)

BORN: November 19, 1859—Gatchina, Russia
DIED: January 28, 1935—Moscow
HISTORICAL PERIOD: Late Romantic
COMPOSITIONAL MEDIA: Orchestra, chamber
music, choral, songs.
IMPORTANT ITEMS: Notable works include the
symphonic suite "Caucasian Sketches."

Ireland, John (Nicholson)

BORN: August 13, 1879—Inglewood, England
DIED: June 12, 1962—Washington, England
HISTORICAL PERIOD: Late Romantic/Modern
COMPOSITIONAL MEDIA: Keyboard, orchestra,
chamber music, choral, songs, band.
IMPORTANT ITEMS: His finest works are those for
solo piano.

Ives, Charles (Edward)

BORN: October 20, 1874—Danbury, CT
DIED: May 19, 1954—New York
HISTORICAL PERIOD: Modern
COMPOSITIONAL MEDIA: Orchestra, chamber
music, keyboard, choral, songs.
IMPORTANT ITEMS: Compositions incorporated
complex rhythms, tone clusters, polytonality and
aleatory techniques. Awarded the Pulitzer Prize in

1947 for his third symphony. Notable works include "The Unanswered Question" and "Three Places in New England" for chamber orchestra, "Variations on America" for organ and the "Concord Sonata" for piano.

J

Jackson, Michael

BORN: August 29, 1958—Gary, IN
HISTORICAL PERIOD: Modern (Popular)
COMPOSITIONAL MEDIA: Popular songs.
IMPORTANT ITEMS: Extremely popular singer and songwriter that began his career singing with the Jackson Five. Notable songs include "Beat It" and "Thriller."

Jacob, Gordon (Percival Septimus)

BORN: July 5, 1895—London
DIED: June 8, 1984—Saffron, Walden
HISTORICAL PERIOD: Modern
COMPOSITIONAL MEDIA: Orchestra, chamber music, ballet, songs, film.
IMPORTANT ITEMS: Composer, teacher, author and conductor.

Jagger, Mick [Michael] (Philip)

BORN: July 26, 1944—Dartford, Kent, England
HISTORICAL PERIOD: Modern (Popular)
COMPOSITIONAL MEDIA: Popular songs.
IMPORTANT ITEMS: Lead singer and songwriter for the rock group The Rolling Stones.

Janáček, Leoš

BORN: July 3, 1854—Hukvaldy, Moravia
DIED: August 12, 1928—Ostrau, Czechoslovakia
HISTORICAL PERIOD: Late Romantic/Modern
COMPOSITIONAL MEDIA: Orchestra, chamber
music, keyboard, choral, opera.
IMPORTANT ITEMS: Significant and prolific
composer. Notable works include "Sinfonietta" for
orchestra.

Jaques-Dalcroze: See Dalcroze, Jaques

Joel, Billy [William] (Martin)

BORN: May 9, 1949—New York
HISTORICAL PERIOD: Modern (Popular)
COMPOSITIONAL MEDIA: Popular songs.
IMPORTANT ITEMS: Popular pianist, singer and
songwriter. Notable songs include "Piano Man."

John, Elton
[real name: Reginald Kenneth Dwight]

BORN: March 25, 1947—Middlesex, England
HISTORICAL PERIOD: Modern (Popular)
COMPOSITIONAL MEDIA: Popular songs, film.
IMPORTANT ITEMS: Highly successful pianist, singer
and songwriter. Notable works include the song
"Rocket Man" and five songs for the film "The Lion
King."

Johnson, Robert

BORN: May 8, 1911—Hazlehurst, MS
DIED: August 16, 1938—Greenwood, MS
HISTORICAL PERIOD: Modern (Popular)
COMPOSITIONAL MEDIA: Popular songs.

IMPORTANT ITEMS: Legendary blues guitarist and songwriter. Notable songs include "Cross Road Blues."

Jones, Quincy (Delight, Jr.)

BORN: March 14, 1933—Chicago, IL
HISTORICAL PERIOD: Modern (Popular)
COMPOSITIONAL MEDIA: Popular songs, instrumental jazz, film.
IMPORTANT ITEMS: Professional jazz trumpeter, composer, conductor and record producer. Notable works include the film score "The Color Purple."

Joplin, Scott

BORN: c.1868—Marshall, TX
DIED: April 1, 1917—New York
HISTORICAL PERIOD: Late Romantic (Popular)
COMPOSITIONAL MEDIA: Keyboard, opera.
IMPORTANT ITEMS: Notable works include ragtime piano pieces "Maple Leaf Rag" and "The Entertainer."

Josquin des Prez: See des Pres, Josquin

K

Kabalevsky, Dmitri (Borisovich)

BORN: December 30, 1904—St. Petersburg, Russia
DIED: February 14, 1987—Moscow
HISTORICAL PERIOD: Modern
COMPOSITIONAL MEDIA: Orchestra, chamber music, keyboard, choral, opera, songs, film.
IMPORTANT ITEMS: Notable works include the orchestral suite "The Comedians" and numerous piano pieces for children.

Kagel, Mauricio

BORN: December 24, 1931—Buenos Aires, Argentina
HISTORICAL PERIOD: Modern
COMPOSITIONAL MEDIA: Chamber music, keyboard, electronic, choral, film.
IMPORTANT ITEMS: Compositions incorporate aleatory, electronic, tape and audio-visual techniques.

Kay, Ulysses (Simpson)

BORN: January 7, 1917—Tucson, AR
DIED: May 20, 1995—Englewood, NJ
HISTORICAL PERIOD: Modern
COMPOSITIONAL MEDIA: Orchestra, chamber music, ballet, keyboard, choral, opera, songs, film, band.
IMPORTANT ITEMS: Prolific composer and teacher.

Kern, Jerome (David)

BORN: January 27, 1885—New York
DIED: November 11, 1945—New York
HISTORICAL PERIOD: Modern (Popular)
COMPOSITIONAL MEDIA: Popular songs, musicals.
IMPORTANT ITEMS: Notable works include the Broadway musical "Showboat" which includes the song "Ol' Man River."

Khachaturian, Aram (Ilich)

BORN: June 6, 1903—Tiflis, Russia
DIED: May 1, 1978—Moscow
HISTORICAL PERIOD: Modern
COMPOSITIONAL MEDIA: Orchestra, chamber music, ballet, keyboard, choral, film.
IMPORTANT ITEMS: Notable works include "Sabre Dance" from the ballet "Gayane."

K

King, Carl L. [Lawrence]

BORN: February 21, 1891—Painterville, OH
DIED: March 31, 1971—Fort Dodge, IA
HISTORICAL PERIOD: Late Romantic (Popular)
COMPOSITIONAL MEDIA: Band.
IMPORTANT ITEMS: Most popular marches include
"Barnum & Bailey's Favorite." His music inspired the
musical "The Music Man."

King, Carole [real name: Klein]

BORN: February 9, 1941—New York
HISTORICAL PERIOD: Modern (Popular)
COMPOSITIONAL MEDIA: Popular songs.
IMPORTANT ITEMS: Notable songs include "Up on
the Roof" and "Take Good Care of My Baby."

K

Kodály, Zoltán

BORN: December 16, 1882—Kecskemét, Hungary
DIED: March 6, 1967—Budapest, Hungary
HISTORICAL PERIOD: Modern
COMPOSITIONAL MEDIA: Orchestra, chamber
music, keyboard, choral, opera, songs.
IMPORTANT ITEMS: Worked with Bartok in
collecting folksongs. Notable works include the
orchestral suite "Háry János" from the opera of the
same name.

Köhler, Louis

BORN: September 5, 1820—Brunswick, Germany
DIED: February 16, 1886—Königsberg, Germany
HISTORICAL PERIOD: Romantic
COMPOSITIONAL MEDIA: Orchestra, ballet, choral,
opera.
IMPORTANT ITEMS: His methods for piano are still
used today.

Korngold, Erich Wolfgang

BORN: May 29, 1897—Brno, Austria
DIED: November 29, 1957—Hollywood, CA
HISTORICAL PERIOD: Modern
COMPOSITIONAL MEDIA: Orchestra, opera, film, chamber music, keyboard, songs.
IMPORTANT ITEMS: Prolific composer of concert music and film scores.

Kraft, William

BORN: September 6, 1923—Chicago, IL
HISTORICAL PERIOD: Modern
COMPOSITIONAL MEDIA: Orchestra, chamber music, choral, theatrical, film, radio.
IMPORTANT ITEMS: Professional percussionist, composer and conductor.

Kreisler, Fritz (Friedrich)

BORN: February 2, 1875—Vienna
DIED: January 29, 1962—New York
HISTORICAL PERIOD: Late Romantic
COMPOSITIONAL MEDIA: Chamber music, operettas, violin.
IMPORTANT ITEMS: Virtuoso violinist who composed many violin pieces, some of which he first attributed to other composers.

Krenek, Ernst

BORN: August 23, 1900—Vienna
DIED: December 22, 1991—Palm Springs, CA
HISTORICAL PERIOD: Modern
COMPOSITIONAL MEDIA: Orchestra, chamber music, ballet, keyboard, choral, opera, electronic.
IMPORTANT ITEMS: Notable works include the opera "Jonny spielt auf" which incorporates jazz.

K

Kubik, Gail (Thompson)

BORN: September 5, 1914—S. Coffeyville, OK
DIED: July 20, 1984—Covina, CA
HISTORICAL PERIOD: Modern
COMPOSITIONAL MEDIA: Orchestra, chamber
music, ballet, keyboard, choral, opera, songs, film.
IMPORTANT ITEMS: Awarded the Pulitzer Prize in
1952 for his "Symphonie Concertante" for piano,
viola, trumpet and orchestra.

Kuhlau, (Daniel) Friedrick (Rudolph)

BORN: September 11, 1786—Ülzen, Germany
DIED: March 12, 1832—Copenhagen, Denmark
HISTORICAL PERIOD: Late Classical/Early Romantic
COMPOSITIONAL MEDIA: Keyboard, chamber
music, choral, songs, theatrical.
IMPORTANT ITEMS: Notable works include
instructional piano pieces.

Kuhnau, Johann

BORN: April 6, 1660—Geising, Saxony
DIED: June 5, 1722—Leipzig, Germany
HISTORICAL PERIOD: Baroque
COMPOSITIONAL MEDIA: Keyboard, choral.
IMPORTANT ITEMS: Organist, author and composer

K

L

Lalo, Édouard (-Victor-Antoine)

BORN: January 27, 1823—Lille, France
DIED: April 22, 1892—Paris
HISTORICAL PERIOD: Romantic
COMPOSITIONAL MEDIA: Orchestra, chamber music, ballet, keyboard, choral, opera, songs.
IMPORTANT ITEMS: Notable works include "Symphonie espagnole."

Landini, Francesco

BORN: c. 1325—Florence
DIED: September 2, 1397—Florence
HISTORICAL PERIOD: Medieval
COMPOSITIONAL MEDIA: Vocal, choral.
IMPORTANT ITEMS: Became blind as a child. The Landini cadence is named after him.

Lasso, Orlando di
[other spellings: Orlandus Lassus or Roland de Lassus]

BORN: 1532—Mons, Belgium
DIED: June 14, 1594—Munich, Germany
HISTORICAL PERIOD: Renaissance
COMPOSITIONAL MEDIA: Choral, songs.
IMPORTANT ITEMS: Composed more than 2,000 works. Notable works include his Italian madrigals, Latin motets, French chansons, and German lieder.

Lauridsen, Morten (Johannes)

BORN: February 27, 1943—Colfax, WA
HISTORICAL PERIOD: Modern
COMPOSITIONAL MEDIA: Choral, songs, chamber music.
IMPORTANT ITEMS: Award winning composer and teacher. Notable works include "Lux Aeterna" as well as the song cycles "Mid-Winter Songs" and "Madrigali."

Lecuona, Ernesto

BORN: August 7, 1896—Havana, Cuba
DIED: November 29, 1963—Santa Cruz de Tenerife, Canary Islands
HISTORICAL PERIOD: Modern (Popular)
COMPOSITIONAL MEDIA: Popular songs.
IMPORTANT ITEMS: Notable songs include "Malagueña."

Lehar, Franz

BORN: April 30, 1870—Komorn, Hungary
DIED: October 24, 1948—Bad Ischl, Austria
HISTORICAL PERIOD: Modern (Popular)
COMPOSITIONAL MEDIA: Orchestra, keyboard, operettas, popular songs, film, band.
IMPORTANT ITEMS: Best remembered for the operetta "The Merry Widow."

Lennon, John (Winston Ono)

BORN: October 9, 1940—Liverpool, England
DIED: December 8, 1980—New York
HISTORICAL PERIOD: Modern (Popular)
COMPOSITIONAL MEDIA: Popular songs, film.

IMPORTANT ITEMS: Brilliant songwriter and member of the rock group The Beatles. As a member of The Beatles, he co-wrote, with Paul McCartney, such songs as "A Hard Day's Night," "Help," "In My Life," "Norwegian Wood" and "Strawberry Fields Forever." Later he wrote "Imagine," "Cold Turkey" and "(Just Like) Starting Over."

Leoncavallo, Ruggiero

BORN: April 23, 1857—Naples
DIED: August 9, 1919—Montecatini, Italy
HISTORICAL PERIOD: Romantic
COMPOSITIONAL MEDIA: Opera, orchestra, ballet, keyboard, operettas, songs.
IMPORTANT ITEMS: Notable works include the opera "Pagliacci."

Léonin [Leoninus]

BORN: c. 1135—Paris
DIED: c. 1201—Paris
HISTORICAL PERIOD: Medieval
COMPOSITIONAL MEDIA: Choral.
IMPORTANT ITEMS: Ars antiqua composer of organum for the Cathedral of Notre Dame.

Lewis, John

BORN: May 3, 1920—La Grange, IL
HISTORICAL PERIOD: Modern
COMPOSITIONAL MEDIA: Instrumental jazz, film, popular songs, ballet.
IMPORTANT ITEMS: Founded the "Modern Jazz Quartet" in 1952. Incorporates elements of classical and jazz styles in his compositions.

Ligeti, Gyorgy (Sándor)

BORN: May 28, 1923—Dicsöszentmarton, Hungary
HISTORICAL PERIOD: Modern
COMPOSITIONAL MEDIA: Orchestra, choral, keyboard, chamber music, opera.
IMPORTANT ITEMS: Frequent use of tone clusters and dense scoring. The Kyrie from his Requiem was featured in the soundtrack of "2001: A Space Odyssey."

Linn, Robert

BORN: August 11, 1925—San Francisco, CA
HISTORICAL PERIOD: Modern
COMPOSITIONAL MEDIA: Orchestra, chamber music, band, songs.
IMPORTANT ITEMS: Award winning composer and teacher. Studied with Darius Milhaud, Halsey Stevens, Roger Sessions and Ingolf Dahl.

Liszt, Franz

BORN: October 22, 1811—Raiding, Hungary
DIED: July 31, 1886—Bayreuth, Germany
HISTORICAL PERIOD: Romantic
COMPOSITIONAL MEDIA: Keyboard, orchestra, chamber music, choral, opera, songs.
IMPORTANT ITEMS: Professional pianist and composer whose notable works include "Hungarian Rhapsodies," two piano concertos, the symphonic poem "Les Préludes" and numerous piano pieces including "Liebesträume."

Lloyd Webber, Andrew

BORN: March 22, 1948—London
HISTORICAL PERIOD: Modern (Popular)

L

COMPOSITIONAL MEDIA: Musicals, orchestra, choral, film.
IMPORTANT ITEMS: Tremendously popular musicals including "Jesus Christ Superstar," "Evita," "Cats" and "Phantom of the Opera."

Loesser, Frank (Henry)

BORN: June 29, 1910—New York
DIED: July 28, 1969—New York
HISTORICAL PERIOD: Modern (Popular)
COMPOSITIONAL MEDIA: Musicals, popular songs.
IMPORTANT ITEMS: Notable works include the Broadway musicals "Guys and Dolls" and "How to Succeed in Business Without Really Trying."

Loewe, Frederich

BORN: June 10, 1901—Vienna
DIED: February 14, 1988—Palm Springs, CA
HISTORICAL PERIOD: Modern (Popular)
COMPOSITIONAL MEDIA: Musicals, popular songs.
IMPORTANT ITEMS: Notable works include the Broadway musicals "My Fair Lady," "Brigadoon" and "Camelot."

Luening, Otto (Clarence)

BORN: June 15, 1900—Milwaukee, WI
HISTORICAL PERIOD: Modern
COMPOSITIONAL MEDIA: Orchestra, chamber music, ballet, keyboard, choral, opera, songs, electronic.
IMPORTANT ITEMS: Compositions incorporate tape and electronic techniques. Collaborated with Vladimir Ussachevsky.

Lully, Jean-Baptiste

BORN: November 28, 1632—Florence, Italy
DIED: March 22, 1687—Paris
HISTORICAL PERIOD: Baroque
COMPOSITIONAL MEDIA: Opera, chamber music, ballet, choral, songs, theatrical.
IMPORTANT ITEMS: Developed the French overture. Notable works include the opera "Le Bourgeois Gentilhomme."

Lutoslawski, Witold

BORN: January 25, 1913—Warsaw
DIED: February 7, 1994—Warsaw
HISTORICAL PERIOD: Modern
COMPOSITIONAL MEDIA: Orchestra, chamber music, keyboard, choral, songs, theatrical, film, radio.
IMPORTANT ITEMS: Award winning composer of well-crafted music. Texture is an important element of his compositions.

M

MacDowell, Edward (Alexander)

BORN: December 18, 1860—New York
DIED: January 23, 1908—New York
HISTORICAL PERIOD: Romantic
COMPOSITIONAL MEDIA: Keyboard, orchestra, choral, songs.
IMPORTANT ITEMS: Prolific composer whose notable works include the piano piece "To a Wild Rose" from "Woodland Sketches."

L

Machaut, Guillaume de

BORN: c.1300—Machaut, Champagne, France
DIED: April 1377—Rheims, France
HISTORICAL PERIOD: Medieval
COMPOSITIONAL MEDIA: Choral.
IMPORTANT ITEMS: One of the most important ars nova composers. His "Messe de Notre Dame" for four voices is one of the earliest complete polyphonic settings of the Mass.

Mahler, Gustav

BORN: July 7, 1860—Kalischt, Bohemia
DIED: May 18, 1911—Vienna
HISTORICAL PERIOD: Late Romantic
COMPOSITIONAL MEDIA: Orchestra, choral, songs, keyboard, chamber music.
IMPORTANT ITEMS: Notable works include ten large-scale symphonies and the song cycle "Kindertotenlieder."

Mancini, Henry

BORN: April 16, 1924 —Cleveland, OH
DIED: June 14, 1994—Beverly Hills, CA
HISTORICAL PERIOD: Modern (Popular)
COMPOSITIONAL MEDIA: Popular songs, film, TV.
IMPORTANT ITEMS: Notable works include the film scores "Breakfast at Tiffany's" and "The Pink Panther."

Marenzio, Luca

BORN: c.1553—Coccaglio, Bresica, Italy
DIED: August 22, 1599—Rome
HISTORICAL PERIOD: Renaissance
COMPOSITIONAL MEDIA: Choral.
IMPORTANT ITEMS: Best known as a composer of madrigals.

Martin, Frank

> BORN: September 15, 1890—Geneva, Switzerland
> DIED: November 21, 1974—Naarden, the Netherlands
> HISTORICAL PERIOD: Modern
> COMPOSITIONAL MEDIA: Orchestra, chamber music, ballet, keyboard, choral, opera, songs.
> IMPORTANT ITEMS: Compositions incorporate folk song materials and twelve-tone techniques.

Martino, Donald (James)

> BORN: May 16, 1931—Plainfield, NJ
> HISTORICAL PERIOD: Modern
> COMPOSITIONAL MEDIA: Chamber music, orchestra, choral, keyboard, songs, electronic.
> IMPORTANT ITEMS: Awarded the Pulitzer Prize in 1974 for his chamber piece, "Notturno."

M

Martinů, Bohuslav

> BORN: December 8, 1890—Polička, Czech
> DIED: August 28, 1959—Basel, Switzerland
> HISTORICAL PERIOD: Modern
> COMPOSITIONAL MEDIA: Orchestra, opera, ballet, chamber music, choral.
> IMPORTANT ITEMS: Influenced by Bohemian folk music, neoclassicism and impressionism.

Mascagni, Pietro

> BORN: December 7, 1863—Livorno, Italy
> DIED: August 2, 1945—Rome
> HISTORICAL PERIOD: Late Romantic/Modern
> COMPOSITIONAL MEDIA: Opera, chamber music, choral, songs, keyboard.
> IMPORTANT ITEMS: Notable works include the opera "Cavalleria rusticana."

Massenet, Jules (-Émile-Frédéric)

BORN: May 12, 1842—Montaud, France
DIED: August 13, 1912—Paris
HISTORICAL PERIOD: Romantic
COMPOSITIONAL MEDIA: Opera, orchestra, choral, chamber music, ballet, keyboard, songs.
IMPORTANT ITEMS: Notable works include the opera "Manon."

Mayuzumi, Toshiro

BORN: February 20, 1929—Yokohama, Japan
HISTORICAL PERIOD: Modern
COMPOSITIONAL MEDIA: Orchestra, chamber music, ballet, choral, opera, electronic, film.
IMPORTANT ITEMS: Compositions incorporate traditional Japanese music, electronic sounds and serial techniques.

McCartney, (James) Paul

BORN: June 18, 1942—Liverpool, England
HISTORICAL PERIOD: Modern (Popular)
COMPOSITIONAL MEDIA: Popular songs, film, choral.
IMPORTANT ITEMS: Popular songwriter and member of the rock group The Beatles. As a member of the Beatles, he co-wrote, with John Lennon, such songs as "Michelle," "Eleanor Rigby" and "Yesterday." In 1991 he premiered his "Liverpool Oratorio."

Mendelssohn (-Bartholdy), Fanny Cäecilie [married name: Hensel]

BORN: November 14, 1805—Hamburg
DIED: May 14, 1847—Berlin
HISTORICAL PERIOD: Romantic

COMPOSITIONAL MEDIA: Songs, chamber music, choral, keyboard.
IMPORTANT ITEMS: Talented pianist and composer; sister of Felix Mendelssohn.

Mendelssohn (-Bartholdy), Felix

BORN: February 3, 1809—Hamburg, Germany
DIED: November 4, 1847—Leipzig, Germany
HISTORICAL PERIOD: Romantic
COMPOSITIONAL MEDIA: Orchestra, chamber music, keyboard, choral, opera, songs, theatrical.
IMPORTANT ITEMS: A prolific composer whose notable works include incidental music to Shakespeare's "A Midsummer Night's Dream," the oratorio "Elijah," the "Hebrides" overture and violin concerto.

M

Mennin, Peter (real name: Peter Mennini)

BORN: May 17, 1923—Erie, PA
DIED: June 17, 1983—New York
HISTORICAL PERIOD: Modern
COMPOSITIONAL MEDIA: Orchestra, chamber music, keyboard, choral, songs.
IMPORTANT ITEMS: Award winning composer and president of the Juilliard School.

Menotti, Gian Carlo

BORN: July 7, 1911—Cadegliano, Italy
HISTORICAL PERIOD: Modern
COMPOSITIONAL MEDIA: Opera, orchestra, ballet, keyboard, songs, film, radio, TV.
IMPORTANT ITEMS: Awarded the Pulitzer Prize for "The Consul." Notable works include the opera "Amahl and the Night Visitors."

Messiaen, Olivier (Eugéne Prosper Charles)

BORN: December 10, 1908—Avignon, France
DIED: April 28, 1992—Clichy, Hauts-de Seine, France
HISTORICAL PERIOD: Modern
COMPOSITIONAL MEDIA: Orchestra, chamber music, keyboard, opera, songs.
IMPORTANT ITEMS: Highly influential composer and teacher. Pupils included Boulez, Stockhausen and Xenakis. Compositions incorporate extra musical sources (such as bird songs), Gregorian chant and oriental rhythms. Notable works include "Quatuor pour la fin du temps" and "Turàngalîla-Symphonie."

Meyerbeer, Giacomo
[real name: Jakob Liebmann Beer]

BORN: September 5, 1791—Berlin, Germany
DIED: May 2, 1864—Paris
HISTORICAL PERIOD: Romantic
COMPOSITIONAL MEDIA: Opera, chamber music, choral, orchestra, songs.
IMPORTANT ITEMS: Notable works include the opera "Les Huguenots."

Milhaud, Darius

BORN: September 4, 1892—Aix-en-Provence, France
DIED: June 22, 1974—Geneva, Switzerland
HISTORICAL PERIOD: Modern
COMPOSITIONAL MEDIA: Orchestra, chamber music, ballet, keyboard, choral, opera, songs, theatrical, film.
IMPORTANT ITEMS: Many of his compositions use polytonality. Notable works include the ballet "La Création du monde" which incorporates blues and jazz. A member of Les Six.

Mingus, Charles

BORN: April 22, 1922—Nogales, AZ
DIED: January 8, 1979—Cuernavaca, Mexico
HISTORICAL PERIOD: Modern (Jazz)
COMPOSITIONAL MEDIA: Songs, instrumental jazz, film.
IMPORTANT ITEMS: Professional jazz bassist whose notable works include "Epitaph" for 30 instruments.

Monk, Thelonious

BORN: October 10, 1918—Rock Mountain, NC
DIED: February 17, 1982—Weehawken, NJ
HISTORICAL PERIOD: Modern (Jazz)
COMPOSITIONAL MEDIA: Instrumental jazz.
IMPORTANT ITEMS: Professional jazz pianist whose notable works include "Round Midnight."

M

Monteverdi, Claudio (Giovanni Antonio)

BORN: May 15, 1567—Cremona, Italy
DIED: November 29, 1643—Venice
HISTORICAL PERIOD: Late Renaissance
COMPOSITIONAL MEDIA: Opera, ballet, choral, songs.
IMPORTANT ITEMS: The first important composer of operas. Notable works include "Ariadne's Lament" from the opera "L'Arianna," and the operas "Orfeo" and "L'Incaronazione di Poppea."

Moore, Douglas (Stuart)

BORN: August 10, 1893—Cutchogue, NY
DIED: July 25, 1969—Greenport, NY
HISTORICAL PERIOD: Modern
COMPOSITIONAL MEDIA: Opera, orchrestra, chamber music, choral, songs.

IMPORTANT ITEMS: Notable works include the opera "Ballad of Baby Doe."

Morley, Thomas

BORN: c. 1557—Norwich, England
DIED: October, 1602—London
HISTORICAL PERIOD: Renaissance
COMPOSITIONAL MEDIA: Choral, songs, chamber music.
IMPORTANT ITEMS: Notable works include his numerous madrigals and lute music.

Morton, Ferdinand "Jelly Roll"

BORN: October 20, 1890—New Orleans
DIED: July 10, 1941—Los Angeles
HISTORICAL PERIOD: Modern (Jazz)
COMPOSITIONAL MEDIA: Popular instrumental jazz.
IMPORTANT ITEMS: An early pioneer of jazz arranging. Notable works include "Jelly Roll Blues."

Mouret, Jean-Joseph

BORN: April 11, 1682—Avignon, France
DIED: December 20, 1738—Charenton, France
HISTORICAL PERIOD: Baroque
COMPOSITIONAL MEDIA: Opera, ballet, choral, orchestra.
IMPORTANT ITEMS: Notable works include his "Rondeau" which is used as the theme of the TV program "Masterpiece Theatre."

Mozart, (Johann Georg) Leopold

BORN: November 14, 1719—Augsburg, Austria
DIED: May 28, 1787—Salzburg, Austria
HISTORICAL PERIOD: Early Classical

M

COMPOSITIONAL MEDIA: Chamber music, keyboard, choral, opera, songs.
IMPORTANT ITEMS: Father of W.A. Mozart whose most popular work is his "Toy Symphony."

Mozart, Wolfgang Amadeus

BORN: January 27, 1756—Salzburg, Austria
DIED: December 5, 1791—Vienna
HISTORICAL PERIOD: Classical
COMPOSITIONAL MEDIA: Orchestra, chamber music, keyboard, choral, opera, ballet, songs.
IMPORTANT ITEMS: One of the most important composers of the classical period. A very prolific composer who wrote over 600 pieces during his short lifetime. Notable works include 41 symphonies, 27 piano concertos, the "Requiem" in D minor, "Eine Kleine Nachtmusik" for strings, and the operas "Don Giovanni" and "The Magic Flute."

Mussorgsky, Modest (Petrovich)

BORN: March 21, 1839—Karevo, Russia
DIED: March 28, 1881—St. Petersburg, Russia
HISTORICAL PERIOD: Romantic
COMPOSITIONAL MEDIA: Opera, orchestra, keyboard, choral, songs.
IMPORTANT ITEMS: Notable works include the orchestral composition "Night on Bald Mountain," the piano piece "Pictures at an Exhibition" (which is best known in the version orchestrated by Ravel) and the opera "Boris Godunov."

N

Nelhybel, Vaclav

BORN: September 24, 1919—Polanka, Czechoslovakia
DIED: March 22, 1996—Scranton, PA
HISTORICAL PERIOD: Modern
COMPOSITIONAL MEDIA: Orchestra, chamber music, choral, ballet, keyboard, opera, band.
IMPORTANT ITEMS: Notable works include his numerous works for symphonic band.

Newman, Alfred

BORN: March 17, 1900—New Haven, CT
DIED: February 17, 1970—Los Angeles
HISTORICAL PERIOD: Modern
COMPOSITIONAL MEDIA: Film.
IMPORTANT ITEMS: Award winning film composer. Notable scores include "The Hunchback of Notre Dame" (1939) and "Wuthering Heights."

Nicolai, (Carl) Otto (Ehrenfried)

BORN: June 9, 1810—Königsberg, Germany
DIED: May 11, 1849—Berlin, Germany
HISTORICAL PERIOD: Romantic
COMPOSITIONAL MEDIA: Orchestra, opera, chamber music, keyboard, choral, songs.
IMPORTANT ITEMS: Notable works include the opera "The Merry Wives of Windsor."

Nielsen, Carl (August)

BORN: June 9, 1865—Nøre-Lyndelse, Denmark
DIED: October 3, 1931—Copenhagen, Denmark

HISTORICAL PERIOD: Late Romantic
COMPOSITIONAL MEDIA: Orchestra, choral,
chamber music, keyboard, opera, songs, theatrical.
IMPORTANT ITEMS: Notable works include six
symphonies.

Nilsson, Bo

BORN: May 1, 1937—Skelleftehamn, Sweden
HISTORICAL PERIOD: Modern
COMPOSITIONAL MEDIA: Chamber music,
orchestra, keyboard, electronic.
IMPORTANT ITEMS: Compositions incorporate
serial and electronic techniques.

Nono, Luigi

BORN: January 29, 1924—Venice
DIED: May 8, 1990—Venice
HISTORICAL PERIOD: Modern
COMPOSITIONAL MEDIA: Orchestra, chamber
music, ballet, keyboard, choral, opera, songs,
electronic.
IMPORTANT ITEMS: Compositions incorporate tape,
electronic and serial techniques.

Nordoff, Paul

BORN: June 4, 1900—Philadelphia, PA
DIED: January 18, 1977—Herdecke, Germany
HISTORICAL PERIOD: Modern
COMPOSITIONAL MEDIA: Orchestra, chamber
music, ballet, opera.
IMPORTANT ITEMS: Specialized in music therapy of
handicapped children.

O

Obrecht, Jacob

BORN: November 22, 1450—Bergen-op-Zoom, Netherlands
DIED: c. 1505—Ferrara, Italy
HISTORICAL PERIOD: Renaissance
COMPOSITIONAL MEDIA: Choral, songs.
IMPORTANT ITEMS: A master of the Flemish school best remembered for religious motets and Masses.

Ockeghem, Johannes

BORN: c. 1410
DIED: February 6, 1497—Tours, France
HISTORICAL PERIOD: Early Renaissance
COMPOSITIONAL MEDIA: Choral, songs.
IMPORTANT ITEMS: Composed numerous Masses. His Requiem is the earliest surviving polyphonic example of this form.

Offenbach, Jacques

BORN: June 20, 1819—Cologne, Germany
DIED: October 5, 1880—Paris
HISTORICAL PERIOD: Romantic
COMPOSITIONAL MEDIA: Operettas, opera, ballet, chamber music.
IMPORTANT ITEMS: Notable works include the opera "The Tales of Hoffmann," and the cancan from from the operetta "Orpheus in the Underworld."

Orff, Carl

BORN: July 10, 1895—Munich, Germany
DIED: March 29, 1982—Munich, Germany
HISTORICAL PERIOD: Modern
COMPOSITIONAL MEDIA: Orchestra, choral, opera, chamber music.
IMPORTANT ITEMS: Notable works include the oratorio "Carmina burana." Was active in teaching music to young children throughout his life.

P

Pachelbel, Johann

BORN: September 1, 1653—Nuremberg, Germany
DIED: March 3, 1706—Nuremberg, Germany
HISTORICAL PERIOD: Baroque
COMPOSITIONAL MEDIA: Keyboard, chamber music, choral.
IMPORTANT ITEMS: Notable works include the "Canon and Gigue" in D.

Paderewski, Ignace (Jan)

BORN: November 18, 1860—Kurylowka, Russia
DIED: June 29, 1941—New York
HISTORICAL PERIOD: Romantic
COMPOSITIONAL MEDIA: Keyboard, orchestra, opera, songs.
IMPORTANT ITEMS: World-famous pianist and composer.

Paganini, Niccolò

BORN: October 27, 1782—Genoa, Italy
DIED: May 27, 1840—Nice, France

HISTORICAL PERIOD: Romantic
COMPOSITIONAL MEDIA: Violin, chamber music, orchestra.
IMPORTANT ITEMS: Virtuoso violinist whose notable works include "24 Caprices" for solo violin and six violin concertos.

Palestrina, Giovanni Pierluigi da

BORN: c. 1525—Palestrina, Italy
DIED: February 2, 1594—Rome
HISTORICAL PERIOD: Renaissance
COMPOSITIONAL MEDIA: Choral, songs.
IMPORTANT ITEMS: Notable works include Masses, motets and other polyphonic sacred music.

Palmer, Willard A. [Aldrich] Jr.

BORN: January 31, 1917—McComb, MS
DIED: April 30, 1996—Houston, TX
HISTORICAL PERIOD: Modern
COMPOSITIONAL MEDIA: Accordion, keyboard.
IMPORTANT ITEMS: Substantial contributor to supberb accordion and piano methods and highly respected editor of piano repertoire.

P

Parker, Horatio (William)

BORN: September 15, 1863—Auburndale, MA
DIED: December 18, 1919—Cedarhurst, NY
HISTORICAL PERIOD: Romantic
COMPOSITIONAL MEDIA: Choral, orchestra, chamber music, keyboard, opera, songs.
IMPORTANT ITEMS: Award winning composer and teacher of Charles Ives.

Partch, Harry

BORN: June 24, 1901—Oakland, CA
DIED: September 3, 1974—San Diego, CA
HISTORICAL PERIOD: Modern
COMPOSITIONAL MEDIA: Chamber music,
theatrical, choral, film.
IMPORTANT ITEMS: Developed numerous musical
instruments, some of which use a scale consisting of
43 tones to the octave.

Peeters, Flor

BORN: July 4, 1903—Thielen, Belgium
DIED: July 4, 1986—Antwerp, Belgium
HISTORICAL PERIOD: Modern
COMPOSITIONAL MEDIA: Keyboard, choral, songs.
IMPORTANT ITEMS: Professional organist and
composer best known for his numerous works for
organ.

Penderecki, Krzysztof

BORN: November 23, 1933—Debica, Poland
HISTORICAL PERIOD: Modern
COMPOSITIONAL MEDIA: Orchestra, chamber
music, choral, opera, songs.
IMPORTANT ITEMS: Compositions incorporate
graphic notation. Notable works include "Threnody
to the Victims of Hiroshima" for string orchestra.

Pergolesi, Giovanni Battista

BORN: January 4, 1710—Jesi, Italy
DIED: March 16, 1736—Pozzuoli, Italy
HISTORICAL PERIOD: Baroque
COMPOSITIONAL MEDIA: Opera, chamber music,
keyboard, choral.

IMPORTANT ITEMS: Notable works include the intermezzo "La Serva padrona."

Peri, Jacopo

BORN: August 20, 1561—Rome
DIED: August 12, 1633—Florence
HISTORICAL PERIOD: Baroque
COMPOSITIONAL GENRE(S): Opera, choral, ballet, songs.
IMPORTANT ITEMS: Notable for what is considered the first opera, "Dafne."

Perle, George

BORN: May 6, 1915—Bayonne, NJ
HISTORICAL PERIOD: Modern
COMPOSITIONAL MEDIA: Orchestra, chamber music, keyboard, choral.
IMPORTANT ITEMS: Compositions incorporate twelve-tone techniques. Awarded the Pulitzer Prize for his "Wind Quintet No. 4."

Perotin [Perotinus]

BORN: c. 1155-1160
DIED: c. 1200-1205
HISTORICAL PERIOD: Medieval
COMPOSITIONAL MEDIA: Choral.
IMPORTANT ITEMS: French ars antiqua composer of sacred music for the Cathedral of Notre Dame.

Persichetti, Vincent (Ludwig)

BORN: June 6, 1915—Philadelphia, PA
DIED: August 13, 1987—Philadelphia, PA
HISTORICAL PERIOD: Modern
COMPOSITIONAL MEDIA: Orchestra, chamber music, keyboard, choral, songs, band.

IMPORTANT ITEMS: Prolific composer, conductor and teacher.

Pezel [Petzel], Johann Christoph

BORN: December 5, 1639—Glatz, Germany
DIED: October 13, 1694—Bautzen, Germany
HISTORICAL PERIOD: Baroque
COMPOSITIONAL MEDIA: Chamber music, choral.
IMPORTANT ITEMS: A prolific composer of music for wind instruments.

Piccinni, Niccolo

BORN: January 16, 1728—Bari, Italy
DIED: May 7, 1800—Passy, France
HISTORICAL PERIOD: Classical
COMPOSITIONAL MEDIA: Opera.
IMPORTANT ITEMS: Prolific composer of opera who was a rival, yet still an admirer, of Gluck.

Pinkham, Daniel (Rogers, Jr.)

BORN: June 5, 1923—Lynn, MA
HISTORICAL PERIOD: Modern
COMPOSITIONAL MEDIA: Choral, orchestra, chamber music, keyboard, opera, electronic.
IMPORTANT ITEMS: Compositions are neo-classical as well as incorporating tape and electronic techniques.

Piston, Walter (Hamor, Jr.)

BORN: January 20, 1894—Rockland, ME
DIED: November 12, 1976—Belmont, MA
HISTORICAL PERIOD: Modern
COMPOSITIONAL MEDIA: Orchestra, chamber music, keyboard, choral, ballet.

P

IMPORTANT ITEMS: Award winning composer and teacher. Pupils included Adler, Bernstein and Carter. Awarded the Pulizter Prize twice for "Symphony No. 3" and "Symphony No. 7."

Ponchielli, Amilcare

BORN: August 31, 1834—Paderno, Italy
DIED: January 15, 1886—Milan
HISTORICAL PERIOD: Romantic
COMPOSITIONAL MEDIA: Opera, orchestra, band, chamber music, choral, keyboard.
IMPORTANT ITEMS: Notable works include "Dance of the Hours" from the opera "La Gioconda."

Porter, Cole (Albert)

BORN: June 9, 1891—Peru, IN
DIED: October 15, 1964—Santa Monica, CA
HISTORICAL PERIOD: Modern (Popular)
COMPOSITIONAL MEDIA: Popular songs, musicals, film.
IMPORTANT ITEMS: Notable works include the Broadway musical "Kiss Me Kate" and the songs "Begin the Beguine" and "Let's Do It."

P

Poulenc, Francis (Jean Marcel)

BORN: January 7, 1899—Paris
DIED: January 30, 1963—Paris
HISTORICAL PERIOD: Modern
COMPOSITIONAL MEDIA: Orchestra, choral, chamber music, ballet, keyboard, opera, songs, guitar, film.
IMPORTANT ITEMS: A member of Les Six. Notable works include the sacred choral works "Stabat Mater" and "Gloria," and the opera "Les Dialogues des Carmélites."

Powell, Mel
[real name: Melvin Epstein]

BORN: February 12, 1923—New York
DIED: April 24, 1998—Sherman Oaks, CA
HISTORICAL PERIOD: Modern
COMPOSITIONAL MEDIA: Chamber music, orchestra, keyboard, choral, electronic.
IMPORTANT ITEMS: Professional jazz pianist who later turned to serious composition. Awarded the Pulitzer Prize in 1990 for "Duplicates," a concerto for two pianos and orchestra.

Praetorius, Michael

BORN: February 15, 1571—Kreuzberg, Germany
DIED: February 15, 1621—Wolfenbüttel, Germany
HISTORICAL PERIOD: Renaissance
COMPOSITIONAL MEDIA: Choral, chamber music.
IMPORTANT ITEMS: Prolific composer best known for his sacred choral music.

Prokofiev, Sergei Sergeievich

BORN: April 27, 1891—Sontzovka, Russia
DIED: March 5, 1953—Moscow
HISTORICAL PERIOD: Modern
COMPOSITIONAL MEDIA: Orchestra, chamber music, opera, ballet, keyboard, choral, film.
IMPORTANT ITEMS: Highly prolific composer. Notable works include the opera "Love of Three Oranges," the cantata "Alexander Nevsky," the ballet "Romeo and Juliet," and the orchestral pieces "Classical Symphony," "Suite from Lieutenant Kije," "Scythian Suite" and "Peter and the Wolf."

Puccini, Giacomo

BORN: December 22, 1858—Lucca, Italy
DIED: November 29, 1924—Brussels, Belgium
HISTORICAL PERIOD: Late Romantic
COMPOSITIONAL MEDIA: Opera, orchestra,
chamber music, organ, choral, songs.
IMPORTANT ITEMS: Notable works include the
operas "Madama Butterfly," "La Boheme" and
"Tosca "

Purcell, Henry

BORN: 1659—London
DIED: November 21, 1695—Dean's Yard,
Westminster, England
HISTORICAL PERIOD: Baroque
COMPOSITIONAL MEDIA: Choral, orchestra,
chamber music, keyboard, opera, songs, theatrical.
IMPORTANT ITEMS: Notable works include the
opera "Dido and Aeneas."

Q

Q

Quantz, Johann Joachim

BORN: January 30, 1697—Oberscheden, Germany
DIED: July 12, 1773—Potsdam, Germany
HISTORICAL PERIOD: Late Baroque
COMPOSITIONAL MEDIA: Chamber music, choral,
songs.
IMPORTANT ITEMS: Professional flutist, composer
and author. Notable works include numerous
compositions for flute.

R

Rachmaninov, Sergei Vassilievich

BORN: April 1, 1873—Semyonouo, Russia
DIED: March 28, 1943—Beverly Hills, CA
HISTORICAL PERIOD: Late Romantic
COMPOSITIONAL GENRE(S) Keyboard, orchestra, chamber music, choral, opera, songs.
IMPORTANT ITEMS: Professional pianist, conductor and composer who settled in the United States in 1939. Notable works include the "Piano Concerto No. 2," "Isle of the Dead" for orchestra, "Rhapsody on a Theme of Paganini" for piano and orchestra and the "Prelude in C sharp minor" for solo piano.

Rameau, Jean-Philippe

BORN: September 25, 1683—Dijon, France
DIED: September 12, 1764—Paris
HISTORICAL PERIOD: Baroque
COMPOSITIONAL MEDIA: Ballet, opera, chamber music, keyboard, choral.
IMPORTANT ITEMS: Organist, composer and music theorist best known for his text book on harmony "Traité de l'harmonie."

Raposo, Joseph G.

BORN: February 8, 1937—Fall River, MA
DIED: February 5, 1989—Bronxville, NY
HISTORICAL PERIOD: Modern (Popular)
COMPOSITIONAL GENRE(S) Popular songs, TV.
IMPORTANT ITEM(S) Notable songs include those written for children's TV programs including "The Electric Company," "The Muppet Show" and "Sesame Street."

Ravel, (Joseph) Maurice

BORN: March 7, 1875—Ciboure, France
DIED: December 28, 1937—Paris
HISTORICAL PERIOD: Modern
COMPOSITIONAL MEDIA: Chamber music,
orchestra, ballet, keyboard, choral, opera.
IMPORTANT ITEMS: Important impressionist
composer. Notable works include "Pavane pour une
Infante défunte," "Rhapsodie espagnole," "Ma Mère
L'Oye," "La Valse" and "Bolero."

Read, Gardner

BORN: January 2, 1913—Evanston, IL
HISTORICAL PERIOD: Modern
COMPOSITIONAL MEDIA: Orchestra, chamber
music, keyboard, choral, opera, songs.
IMPORTANT ITEMS: Award-winning composer and
author.

Reed, Lou [Louis] (Allen)

BORN: March 2, 1942—New York
HISTORICAL PERIOD: Modern (Popular)
COMPOSITIONAL MEDIA: Popular songs.
IMPORTANT ITEMS: Guitarist, singer and songwriter
whose notable songs include "Walk on the Wild Side."

Reger, (Johann Baptist Joseph) Max [Maximillian]

BORN: March 19, 1873—Brand, Bavaria
DIED: May 11, 1916—Leipzig, Germany
HISTORICAL PERIOD: Late Romantic
COMPOSITIONAL MEDIA: Orchestra, chamber
music, keyboard, choral.
IMPORTANT ITEMS: Notable works include
"Variations and Fugue on a Theme By Mozart."

Reich, Steve [Stephan] (Michael)

BORN: October 3, 1936—New York
HISTORICAL PERIOD: Modern
COMPOSITIONAL MEDIA: Chamber music, electronic, orchestra.
IMPORTANT ITEMS: Compositions are in the minimalist style.

Reicha, Antoine [Antonin or Anton] (-Joseph)

BORN: February 26, 1770—Prague
DIED: May 28, 1836—Paris
HISTORICAL PERIOD: Classical
COMPOSITIONAL MEDIA: Chamber music, orchestra.

IMPORTANT ITEMS: Notable works include numerous chamber music compositions for wind instruments.

Reinecke, Carl (Heinrich Carsten)

BORN: June 23, 1824—Altona, Germany
DIED: March 10, 1910—Leipzig, Germany
HISTORICAL PERIOD: Romantic
COMPOSITIONAL MEDIA: Chamber music, orchestra, keyboard, choral, opera, songs.
IMPORTANT ITEMS: Professional pianist, conductor, teacher and prolific composer.

Respighi, Ottorino

BORN: July 9, 1879—Bologna, Italy
DIED: April 18, 1936—Rome
HISTORICAL PERIOD: Late Romantic/Modern
COMPOSITIONAL MEDIA: Orchestra, chamber music, opera, ballet, keyboard, choral, songs.

R

IMPORTANT ITEMS: Notable works include the symphonic poems "The Pines of Rome" and "The Fountains of Rome."

Reynolds, Roger (Lee)

BORN: July 18, 1934—Detroit, MI
HISTORICAL PERIOD: Modern
COMPOSITIONAL MEDIA: Orchestra, chamber music, theater, keyboard, choral, electronic.
IMPORTANT ITEMS: Awarded the Pulitzer Prize in 1989 for "Whispers Out of Time."

Reynolds, Verne (Becker)

BORN: July 18, 1926—Lyons, KS
HISTORICAL PERIOD: Modern
COMPOSITIONAL MEDIA: Chamber music, orchestra, choral, songs, band.
IMPORTANT ITEMS: Professional horn player and composer.

Richard, Keith
[real name: Keith Richards]

BORN: December 18, 1943—Dartford, Kent, England
HISTORICAL PERIOD: Modern (Popular).
COMPOSITIONAL MEDIA: Popular songs.
IMPORTANT ITEMS: Lead guitar player of the rock group The Rolling Stones. Notable songs include "(I Can't Get No) Satisfaction" and "Get Off of My Cloud."

R

Riegger, Wallingford (Constantin)

BORN: April 29, 1885—Albany, GA
DIED: April 2, 1961—New York
HISTORICAL PERIOD: Modern

COMPOSITIONAL MEDIA: Orchestra, chamber music, ballet, keyboard, choral, songs.
IMPORTANT ITEMS: Prolific composer and teacher whose compositions incorporate twelve-tone techniques.

Rimsky-Korsakov, Nikolai (Andreievich)

BORN: March 18, 1844—Tikhvin, Russia
DIED: June 21, 1908—Liubensk, Russia
HISTORICAL PERIOD: Romantic
COMPOSITIONAL MEDIA: Orchestra, chamber music, opera, keyboard, choral, songs, band.
IMPORTANT ITEMS: Notable works include the symphonic poems "Scheherazade," "Capriccio espagnol" and "Russian Easter Overture."

Rochberg, George

BORN: July 5, 1918—Paterson, NJ
HISTORICAL PERIOD: Modern
COMPOSITIONAL MEDIA: Chamber music, orchestra, keyboard, choral, songs, opera, band.
IMPORTANT ITEMS: Compositions incorporate twelve-tone techniques and quotations of other composers works.

R

Rodgers, Richard (Charles)

BORN: June 28, 1902—Long Island, NY
DIED: December 30, 1979—New York
HISTORICAL PERIOD: Modern (Popular)
COMPOSITIONAL MEDIA: Popular songs, musicals.
IMPORTANT ITEMS: Notable works include the Broadway musicals "Oklahoma" (awarded the Pulitzer Prize in 1944), "Carousel," "South Pacific" (awarded the Pulitzer Prize in 1950), "The King and I," "Flower Drum Song" and "The Sound of Music."

Rodrigo, Joaquín

BORN: November 22, 1901—Sagunto, Valencia, Spain
HISTORICAL PERIOD: Modern
COMPOSITIONAL MEDIA: Orchestra, chamber music, ballet, keyboard, guitar.
IMPORTANT ITEMS: Became blind as a child. Notable works include "Concierto de Aranjuez" for guitar and orchestra.

Rorem, Ned

BORN: October 23, 1923—Richmond, IN
HISTORICAL PERIOD: Modern
COMPOSITIONAL MEDIA: Orchestra, songs, chamber music, keyboard, choral, opera.
IMPORTANT ITEMS: Awarded the Pulitzer Prize in 1976 for "Air Music." He is considered the foremost American composer of songs.

Rossini, Gioacchino (Antonio)

BORN: February 29, 1792—Pesaro, Italy
DIED: November 13, 1868—Paris
HISTORICAL PERIOD: Late Classical
COMPOSITIONAL MEDIA: Opera, orchestra, chamber music, keyboard, choral, songs.
IMPORTANT ITEMS: Notable works include the operas "William Tell," "La Cenerentola" and "Il Barbiere de Siviglia" (The Barber of Seville).

R

Rota (Rinaldi), Nino

BORN: December 3, 1911—Milan
DIED: April 10, 1979—Rome
HISTORICAL PERIOD: Modern
COMPOSITIONAL MEDIA: Film, opera, orchestra,

ballet, choral, chamber music, keyboard.
IMPORTANT ITEMS: Notable works include the
soundtracks to the films "Fellini's 8½" and "The
Godfather" parts 1 & 2.

Roussel, Albert (Charles Paul Marie)

BORN: April 5, 1869—Tourcoing, France
DIED: August 23, 1937—Royan, France
HISTORICAL PERIOD: Late Romantic/Modern
COMPOSITIONAL MEDIA: Orchestra, chamber
music, opera, ballet, keyboard, songs.
IMPORTANT ITEMS: Compositions are in a neo-
classical style. Notable works include the ballet
"Bacchus et Ariane."

Rózsa, Miklós

BORN: April 18, 1907—Budapest
DIED: July 27, 1995—Los Angeles
HISTORICAL PERIOD: Modern
COMPOSITIONAL MEDIA: Film, orchestra, chamber
music, choral, songs.
IMPORTANT ITEMS: Notable works include the score
for the film "Ben-Hur."

Rubinstein, Anton (Grigorievich)

BORN: November 28, 1829—Vykhvatinetz, Russia
DIED: November 20, 1894—Peterhof, Russia
HISTORICAL PERIOD: Romantic
COMPOSITIONAL MEDIA: Keyboard, opera,
orchestra, chamber music, choral, songs.
IMPORTANT ITEMS: Professional pianist and prolific
composer.

R

Ruggles, Carl (Charles Sprague)

BORN: March 11, 1876—Marion, MA
DIED: October 24, 1971—Bennington, VT
HISTORICAL PERIOD: Modern
COMPOSITIONAL MEDIA: Orchestra, choral,
chamber music, keyboard, songs.
IMPORTANT ITEMS: Professional violinist,
composer, teacher and painter. Compositions are
dissonant and atonal.

S

Saint-Saëns, (Charles-) Camille

BORN: October 9, 1835—Paris
DIED: December 16, 1921—Algiers
HISTORICAL PERIOD: Romantic
COMPOSITIONAL MEDIA: Orchestra, chamber
music, ballet, keyboard, choral, opera, songs.
IMPORTANT ITEMS: Prolific composer whose
notable works include "Carnival of the Animals" and
the opera "Samson et Dalila."

Salieri, Antonio

BORN: August 18, 1750—Verona, Italy
DIED: May 7, 1825—Vienna
HISTORICAL PERIOD: Classical
COMPOSITIONAL MEDIA: Opera, orchestra,
chamber music, keyboard, choral.
IMPORTANT ITEMS: Prolific composer, conductor
and teacher whose students included Beethoven,
Schubert and Liszt.

S

Salonen, Esa-Pekka

BORN: June 30, 1958—Helsinki
HISTORICAL PERIOD: Modern
COMPOSITIONAL MEDIA: Orchestra, chamber music, keyboard.
IMPORTANT ITEMS: In addition to composing, he was appointed music director of the Los Angeles Philharmonic in 1992.

Salzédo, (Leon) Carlos

BORN: April 6, 1885—Arcachon, France
DIED: August 17, 1961—Waterville, ME
HISTORICAL PERIOD: Modern
COMPOSITIONAL MEDIA: Orchestra, chamber music
IMPORTANT ITEMS: Professional harpist, composer, author and teacher. All compositions include the harp. Introduced special effects for the harp.

Sammartini, Giovanni Battista

BORN: c. 1700—Milan
DIED: January 15, 1775—Milan
HISTORICAL PERIOD: Early Classical
COMPOSITIONAL MEDIA: Symphony, chamber music, opera, choral.
IMPORTANT ITEMS: Very prolific composer and teacher of Gluck.

Satie, Erik (Alfred-Leslie)

BORN: May 17, 1866—Honfleur, France
DIED: July 1, 1925—Paris
HISTORICAL PERIOD: Modern
COMPOSITIONAL MEDIA: Keyboard, orchestra, ballet, choral, theatrical.
IMPORTANT ITEMS: Influential composer whose

S

most notable works include the "Gymnopédie" for solo piano.

Scarlatti, (Pietro) Alessandro (Gaspare)

BORN: May 2, 1660—Palermo, Italy
DIED: October 22, 1725—Naples, Italy
HISTORICAL PERIOD: Baroque
COMPOSITIONAL MEDIA: Opera, choral, chamber music, keyboard.
IMPORTANT ITEMS: Founder of the Neopolitan school and prolific composer who helped develop the opera. Father of Domenico Scarlatti.

Scarlatti, (Giuseppe) Domenico

BORN: October 26, 1685—Naples, Italy
DIED: July 23, 1757—Madrid
HISTORICAL PERIOD: Late Baroque
COMPOSITIONAL GENRE(S): Keyboard, choral, opera.
IMPORTANT ITEMS: Prolific and important composer of keyboard (especially harpsichord) music. Son of Alesandro Scarlatti.

Scheidt, Samuel

BORN: November 3, 1587—Halle, Germany
DIED: March 24, 1654—Halle, Germany
HISTORICAL PERIOD: Early Baroque
COMPOSITIONAL MEDIA: Keyboard, choral, chamber music.
IMPORTANT ITEMS: Professional organist, teacher and composer best known for his organ and choral music.

S

Schein, Johann Hermann

BORN: January 20, 1586—Grünhain, Saxony
DIED: November 19, 1630—Leipzig, Germany
HISTORICAL PERIOD: Baroque
COMPOSITIONAL MEDIA: Choral, chamber music.
IMPORTANT ITEMS: Prolific composer who brought an Italian influence to German music. Notable works include numerous choral compositions.

Schnabel, Artur

BORN: April 17, 1882—Lipnik, Austria
DIED: August 15, 1951—Axenstein, Switzerland
HISTORICAL PERIOD: Modern
COMPOSITIONAL GENRE(S): Orchestra, chamber music, keyboard, songs.
IMPORTANT ITEMS: Professional pianist and composer whose works are dissonant and atonal.

Schoenberg, Arnold (Franz Walter)

BORN: September 13, 1874—Vienna
DIED: July 13, 1951—Los Angeles
HISTORICAL PERIOD: Modern
COMPOSITIONAL MEDIA: Orchestra, chamber music, keyboard, choral, opera, songs, band.
IMPORTANT ITEMS: Influential composer and teacher who originated the twelve-tone technique. Pupils include Berg and Webern. Notable works include "Verklärte Nacht" for strings, "Five Piano Pieces" Op.23 and "Pierrot lunaire" for voice and instruments.

S

Schubert, Franz (Peter)

BORN: January 31, 1797—Vienna
DIED: November 19, 1828—Vienna
HISTORICAL PERIOD: Early Romantic
COMPOSITIONAL MEDIA: Songs, orchestra,
chamber music, keyboard, choral, opera.
IMPORTANT ITEMS: Highly prolific and important
composer. Notable works include the "Unfinished"
and "Great C Major" symphonies, six Masses,
numerous chamber and piano pieces, and a large
number of brilliant songs including "Gretchen am
Spinnrade," "Erlkönig" and the song cycles "Die
schöne Müllerin" and "Die Winterreise."

Schuller, Gunther (Alexander)

BORN: November 22, 1925—New York
HISTORICAL PERIOD: Modern
COMPOSITIONAL MEDIA: Orchestra, chamber
music, ballet, keyboard, choral, opera, songs, band,
film, TV.
IMPORTANT ITEMS: Compositions incorporate jazz
and serial techniques.

Schuman, William

BORN: August 4, 1910—New York
DIED: February 15, 1992—New York
HISTORICAL PERIOD: Modern
COMPOSITIONAL MEDIA: Orchestra, chamber
music, keyboard, choral, opera, songs, band.
IMPORTANT ITEMS: Awarded the Pulitzer Prize in
1943 for "A Free Song" and again in 1985.
Compositions are melodic and contain elements of
jazz.

S

Schumann, Clara Josephine
[maiden name: Wieck]

BORN: September 13, 1819—Leipzig, Germany
DIED: May 20, 1896—Frankfurt, Germany
HISTORICAL PERIOD: Romantic
COMPOSITIONAL MEDIA: Keyboard, chamber
music, orchestra, songs.
IMPORTANT ITEMS: Professional pianist, teacher
and talented composer. Wife of Robert Schumann.

Schumann, Robert (Alexander)

BORN: June 8, 1810—Zwickau, Saxony
DIED: July 29, 1856—Endenich, Germany
HISTORICAL PERIOD: Romantic
COMPOSITIONAL MEDIA: Orchestra, chamber
music, keyboard, choral, songs, opera.
IMPORTANT ITEMS: Professional pianist, author and
prolific composer. Notable works include four
symphonies, a piano concerto, chamber music and
numerous pieces for solo piano including
"Papillons" and "Kinderscenen" (Scenes from
Childhood).

Schütz, Heinrich

BORN: October 8, 1585—Köstritz, Germany
DIED: November 6, 1672—Dresden
HISTORICAL PERIOD: Baroque
COMPOSITIONAL MEDIA: Choral, chamber music,
opera, songs.
IMPORTANT ITEMS: Significant composer who
adapted Italian styles to German music. He
composed the first German opera "Dafne" (which is
now lost) and numerous sacred choral works.

S

Scriabin, Alexander (Nikolaievich)

BORN: January 6, 1872—Moscow
DIED: April 27, 1915—Moscow
HISTORICAL PERIOD: Late Romantic/Modern
COMPOSITIONAL MEDIA: Keyboard, orchestra, chamber music.
IMPORTANT ITEMS: Virtuoso pianist and composer whose compositions are harmonically daring.

Sessions, Roger (Huntington)

BORN: December 28, 1896—Brooklyn, NY
DIED: March 16, 1985—Princeton, NJ
HISTORICAL PERIOD: Modern
COMPOSITIONAL MEDIA: Orchestra, chamber music, keyboard, choral, opera, songs.
IMPORTANT ITEMS: Influential composer and teacher. Compositions are usually atonal and later works incorporated serial techniques.

Shostakovich, Dmitri (Dmitrievich)

BORN: September 25, 1906—St. Petersburg
DIED: August 9, 1975—Moscow
HISTORICAL PERIOD: Modern
COMPOSITIONAL MEDIA: Orchestra, choral, chamber music, ballet, keyboard, opera, songs, film.
IMPORTANT ITEMS: Notable works include 15 symphonies, the operas "The Nose" and "The Lady Macbeth of the Mtsensk" and the ballet "The Age of Gold."

S

Sibelius, Jean [Johan Julius Christian]

BORN: December 8, 1865—Hämeenlinna, Finland
DIED: September 20, 1957—Järvenpää, Finland
HISTORICAL PERIOD: Romantic

COMPOSITIONAL MEDIA: Orchestra, chamber music, keyboard, choral, opera, songs.
IMPORTANT ITEMS: Composed nationalistic Finnish music. Notable works include the orchestral works "The Swan of Tuonela" and "Finlandia."

Siegmeister, Elie

BORN: January 15, 1909—New York
DIED: March 10, 1991—Manhasset, NY
HISTORICAL PERIOD: Modern
COMPOSITIONAL MEDIA: Orchestra, choral, chamber music, keyboard, opera, songs.
IMPORTANT ITEMS: Prolific composer, conductor, pianist and teacher.

Simon, Paul

BORN: October 13, 1941—Newark, NJ
HISTORICAL PERIOD: Modern (Popular).
COMPOSITIONAL MEDIA: Popular songs.
IMPORTANT ITEMS: After a successful partnership with Art Garfunkel (Simon and Garfunkel) he continued with a successful solo career. Notable works include "The Sound of Silence" and "Graceland."

S

Slonimsky, Nicolas [Nikolai] (Leonidovich)

BORN: April 27, 1894—St. Petersburg
DIED: December 25, 1995—Los Angeles
HISTORICAL PERIOD: Modern
COMPOSITIONAL MEDIA: Orchestra, chamber music, keyboard, songs.
IMPORTANT ITEMS: Compositions incorporate polytonality, atonality and quarter-tone techniques. Known as a well-respected author and lecturer.

Smetana, Bedřich

BORN: March 2, 1824—Leitomischl, Bohemia
DIED: May 12, 1884—Prague
HISTORICAL PERIOD: Romantic
COMPOSITIONAL MEDIA: Orchestra, chamber music, keyboard, choral, opera, songs.
IMPORTANT ITEMS: Notable works include the opera "The Bartered Bride," the symphonic poem "Ma Vlast" and the string quartet "From My Life."

Smith, Hale

BORN: June 29, 1925—Cleveland, OH
HISTORICAL PERIOD: Modern
COMPOSITIONAL MEDIA: Orchestra, chamber music, keyboard, choral, songs, band.
IMPORTANT ITEMS: Compositions incorporate serial techniques and jazz.

Soler, Antonio

BORN: December 3, 1729—Olot, Spain
DIED: December 20, 1783—El Escorial, Spain
HISTORICAL PERIOD: Late Baroque
COMPOSITIONAL MEDIA: Choral, chamber music, keyboard.
IMPORTANT ITEMS: Notable works include "Fandango" for keyboard.

S

Sondheim, Stephen (Joshua)

BORN: March 22, 1930—New York
HISTORICAL PERIOD: Modern (Popular)
COMPOSITIONAL MEDIA: Popular songs, musicals.
IMPORTANT ITEMS: Composer and lyricist whose notable works include the Broadway musicals "Company," "A Little Night Music" and "Sunday in the Park With George."

Sor [Sors], Fernando

BORN: February 13, 1778—Barcelona
DIED: July 10, 1839—Paris
HISTORICAL PERIOD: Classical
COMPOSITIONAL MEDIA: Guitar, ballet, chamber music, opera, orchestra.
IMPORTANT ITEMS: Notable for his method and works for guitar.

Sousa, John Philip

BORN: November 6, 1854—Washington, DC
DIED: March 6, 1932—Reading, PA
HISTORICAL PERIOD: Late Romantic (Popular)
COMPOSITIONAL MEDIA: Band, opera, orchestra, chamber music, songs, choral.
IMPORTANT ITEMS: Considered "The March King." Notable marches include "The Stars and Stripes Forever," "El Capitan," "The Liberty Bell," "Nobles of the Mystic Shrine," "The Washington Post" and "Semper Fidelis."

Sowerby, Leo

BORN: May 1, 1895—Grand Rapids, MI
DIED: July 7, 1968—Port Clinton, OH
HISTORICAL PERIOD: Modern
COMPOSITIONAL MEDIA: Orchestra, chamber music, keyboard, choral, songs.
IMPORTANT ITEMS: Awarded the Pulitzer Prize in 1946 for "Canticle of the Sun."

Spohr, Ludwig [Ludewig]

BORN: April 5, 1784—Braunschweig, Germany
DIED: October 22, 1859—Kassel, Germany
HISTORICAL PERIOD: Early Romantic

COMPOSITIONAL MEDIA: Orchestra, chamber music, opera, keyboard, choral, songs.
IMPORTANT ITEMS: Professional violinist and composer.

Stamitz, Johann Wenzel Anton

BORN: June 19, 1717—Deutsch-Brod, Bohemia
DIED: March 27, 1757—Mannheim, Germany
HISTORICAL PERIOD: Late Baroque/Early Classical
COMPOSITIONAL MEDIA: Orchestra, chamber music.
IMPORTANT ITEMS: Professional violinist and prolific composer who influenced Haydn and Mozart. Father of Carl Philipp Stamitz.

Stamitz, Carl Philipp

BORN: May 7, 1745—Mannheim, Germany
DIED: November 9, 1801—Jena, Germany
HISTORICAL PERIOD: Classical
COMPOSITIONAL MEDIA: Orchestra, chamber music, choral, opera.
IMPORTANT ITEMS: Professional violinist and prolific composer.

Starer, Robert

BORN: January 8, 1924—Vienna
DIED: April 22, 2001—New York
HISTORICAL PERIOD: Modern
COMPOSITIONAL MEDIA: Orchestra, chamber music, ballet, opera, keyboard, choral, songs.
IMPORTANT ITEMS: Award-winning composer, teacher and author. Became a citizen of the United States in 1957.

S

Steiner, Max [Maximilian Raoul Walter]

BORN: May 10, 1888—Vienna
DIED: December 28, 1971—Beverly Hills, CA
HISTORICAL PERIOD: Modern
COMPOSITIONAL MEDIA: Songs, operetta, ballet, musicals, film.
IMPORTANT ITEMS: Notable film scores include "King Kong," "Gone With the Wind," "Casablanca" and many others.

Stevens, Halsey

BORN: December 3, 1908—Scott, NY
DIED: January 20, 1989—Long Beach, CA
HISTORICAL PERIOD: Modern
COMPOSITIONAL MEDIA: Orchestra, chamber music, keyboard, songs.
IMPORTANT ITEMS: Prolific composer and teacher. Chairman of the music department at the University of Southern California from 1948–1976.

Still, William Grant

BORN: May 11, 1895—Woodville, MS
DIED: December 3, 1978—Los Angeles
HISTORICAL PERIOD: Modern
COMPOSITIONAL MEDIA: Orchestra, chamber music, ballet, keyboard, choral, opera, songs, band.
IMPORTANT ITEMS: Compositions incorporate American folk songs. Notable works include the "Afro-American Symphony."

Stockhausen, Karlheinz

BORN: August 22, 1928—Mödrath, Germany
HISTORICAL PERIOD: Modern

S

COMPOSITIONAL MEDIA: Orchestra, chamber music, keyboard, choral, electronic.
IMPORTANT ITEMS: Compositions incorporate graphic notation and serial, aleatory, spatial and electronic techniques.

Stradella, Alessandro

BORN: c. 1639—Nepi, Italy
DIED: February 25, 1682—Genoa, Italy
HISTORICAL PERIOD: Baroque
COMPOSITIONAL MEDIA: Opera, chamber music, choral.
IMPORTANT ITEMS: Numerous operas were written about his life and murder.

Strauss, Jr., Johann

BORN: October 25, 1825—Vienna
DIED: June 3, 1899—Vienna
HISTORICAL PERIOD: Romantic
COMPOSITIONAL MEDIA: Orchestra, operetta.
IMPORTANT ITEMS: Considered "The Waltz King." Notable works include the waltzes "The Blue Danube," "Wine Women and Song" and "Tales from the Vienna Woods," and the operetta "Die Fledermaus." Son of Johann Strauss, Sr.

Strauss, Sr., Johann

BORN: March 14, 1804—Vienna
DIED: September 25, 1849—Vienna
HISTORICAL PERIOD: Romantic
COMPOSITIONAL MEDIA: Orchestra.
IMPORTANT ITEMS: Composer of numerous waltzes and other dances. The father of Johann Strauss, Jr.

S

Strauss, Richard (Georg)

BORN: June 11, 1864—Munich, Germany
DIED: September 8, 1949—Garmisch-Partenkirchen, Germany
HISTORICAL PERIOD: Late Romantic
COMPOSITIONAL MEDIA: Orchestra, opera, chamber music, ballet, keyboard, choral, songs.
IMPORTANT ITEMS: Prolific composer and conductor. Notable works include the tone poems "Till Eulenspiegel's Merry Pranks," "Also Sprach Zarathustra" and "Don Juan" and the operas "Salome," "Der Rosenkavalier" and "Elektra."

Stravinsky, Igor (Feodorovich)

BORN: June 17, 1882—Oranienbaum, Russia
DIED: April 6, 1971—New York
HISTORICAL PERIOD: Modern
COMPOSITIONAL MEDIA: Orchestra, ballet, chamber music, keyboard, choral, opera, songs.
IMPORTANT ITEMS: One of the most important composers of the 20th century. He settled in the U.S. in 1939. Compositions incorporate many techniques including extreme dissonance, jazz, bitonality and serial techniques. Notable works include the "Symphony of Psalms" and the ballets "The Firebird" "Petrushka," and "The Rite of Spring."

Strayhorn, Billy

BORN: November 29, 1915—Dayton, OH
DIED: May 31, 1967—New York
HISTORICAL PERIOD: Modern (Popular)
COMPOSITIONAL MEDIA: Popular songs, jazz.
IMPORTANT ITEMS: Professional jazz pianist, arranger and composer. Co-wrote many of Duke Ellington's works including "Take the A Train."

Styne, Jule

BORN: December 31, 1905—London
HISTORICAL PERIOD: Modern (Popular)
COMPOSITIONAL GENRE(S): Popular songs, musicals, film.
IMPORTANT ITEMS: Notable works include the Broadway musicals "Gentlemen Prefer Blondes," "Gypsy" and "Funny Girl."

Subotnick, Morton

BORN: April 14, 1933—Los Angeles
HISTORICAL PERIOD: Modern
COMPOSITIONAL MEDIA: Orchestra, chamber music, electronic.
IMPORTANT ITEMS: Compositions incorporate electronic, mixed media and tape techniques.

Suk, Josef

BORN: January 4, 1874—Křečovice
DIED: May 29, 1935—Benešov, near Prague
HISTORICAL PERIOD: Late Romantic
COMPOSITIONAL GENRE(S): Orchestra, chamber music, keyboard, choral.
IMPORTANT ITEMS: Early compositions influenced by Dvořák but later works were harmonically daring, almost atonal.

Sullivan, Sir Arthur (Seymour)

BORN: May 13, 1842—London
DIED: November 22, 1900—London
HISTORICAL PERIOD: Romantic
COMPOSITIONAL MEDIA: Operettas, orchestra, chamber music, ballet, choral, songs.
IMPORTANT ITEMS: Notable works include the popular operettas "H.M.S. Pinafore," "The Pirates of Penzance" and "The Mikado."

Suppe, Franz von

> BORN: April 18, 1819—Spalato, Dalmatia
> DIED: May 21, 1895—Vienna
> HISTORICAL PERIOD: Romantic
> COMPOSITIONAL MEDIA: Operettas, orchestra, chamber music, choral, opera, songs.
> IMPORTANT ITEMS: Notable works include the "Poet and Peasant" overture.

Süssmayr, Franz Xaver

> BORN: 1766—Schwanenstadt, Austria
> DIED: September 17, 1803—Vienna
> HISTORICAL PERIOD: Classical
> COMPOSITIONAL MEDIA: Opera, orchestra, chamber music, choral.
> IMPORTANT ITEMS: Best known for completing Mozart's unfinished Requiem.

Sweelinck, Jan Pieterszoon

> BORN: 1562—Deventer, Netherlands
> DIED: October 16, 1621—Amsterdam
> HISTORICAL PERIOD: Renaissance
> COMPOSITIONAL MEDIA: Keyboard, choral.
> IMPORTANT ITEMS: The first composer to use the pedals of the organ as an independent part in a fugue.

S

T

Tailleferre [Taillefesse], (Marcelle) Germaine

> BORN: April 19, 1892—Parc-Saint-Maur, France
> DIED: November 7, 1983—Paris
> HISTORICAL PERIOD: Modern

COMPOSITIONAL MEDIA: Orchestra, chamber music, ballet, keyboard, choral, opera, songs, theatrical, film.
IMPORTANT ITEMS: The only female member of Les Six.

Takemitsu, Toru

BORN: October 8, 1930—Tokyo
DIED: February 20, 1996—Tokyo
HISTORICAL PERIOD: Modern
COMPOSITIONAL MEDIA: Orchestral, choral, chamber music, electronic, keyboard.
IMPORTANT ITEMS: Combined Eastern and Western compositional styles and philosophies.

Tallis, Thomas

BORN: c. 1505
DIED: November 23, 1585—Greenwich, England
HISTORICAL PERIOD: Renaissance
COMPOSITIONAL GENRE(S): Choral, keyboard, chamber music.
IMPORTANT ITEMS: One of the finest composers of his time. Notable works include the 40-part motet "Spem in alium."

Tartini, Giuseppe

BORN: April 8, 1692—Pirano, Istria
DIED: February 26, 1770—Padua, Italy
HISTORICAL PERIOD: Baroque
COMPOSITIONAL MEDIA: Orchestra, chamber music, choral.
IMPORTANT ITEMS: Professional violinist and prolific composer best known for his violin music. Notable works include the "Devil's Trill" sonata for violin.

T

Tchaikovsky, Piotr Ilyich

BORN: May 7, 1840—Votkinsk, Russia
DIED: November 6, 1893—St. Petersburg
HISTORICAL PERIOD: Romantic
COMPOSITIONAL MEDIA: Orchestra, chamber
music, opera, ballet, keyboard, choral, songs.
IMPORTANT ITEMS: Notable works include
"Symphony No. 6" (Pathetique), the ballets "Swan
Lake" and the "Nutcracker," and the orchestral works
"Romeo and Juliet," "1812 Overture" and "Capriccio
Italien."

Tcherepnin, Alexander (Nikolaievich)

BORN: January 20, 1899—St. Petersburg
DIED: September 29, 1977—Paris
HISTORICAL PERIOD: Modern
COMPOSITIONAL MEDIA: Orchestra, chamber
music, ballet, keyboard, opera, choral, songs.
IMPORTANT ITEMS: Professional pianist, conductor
and composer whose music explores European and
oriental folk music.

Telemann, Georg Philipp

BORN: March 14, 1681—Magdeburg, Germany
DIED: June 25, 1767—Hamburg, Germany
HISTORICAL PERIOD: Late Baroque/Early Classical
COMPOSITIONAL MEDIA: Opera, choral, chamber
music, orchestra, keyboard.
IMPORTANT ITEMS: Professional organist and
prolific composer who composed in the gallant
style.

T

Thompson, Randall

BORN: April 21, 1899—New York
DIED: July 9, 1984—Boston, MA
HISTORICAL PERIOD: Modern
COMPOSITIONAL MEDIA: Choral, orchestra, chamber music, keyboard, opera, songs.
IMPORTANT ITEMS: Award-winning composer and teacher. Notable works include numerous choral works and the successful "2nd Symphony."

Thomson, Virgil (Garnett)

BORN: November 25, 1896—Kansas City, MO
DIED: September 30, 1989—New York
HISTORICAL PERIOD: Modern
COMPOSITIONAL MEDIA: Orchestra, chamber music, film, ballet, keyboard, choral, opera, songs.
IMPORTANT ITEMS: Awarded the Pulitzer Prize in 1948 for the film score "Louisiana Story." Notable works include the opera "Four Saints in Three Acts" and the film score "The Plough That Broke the Plains."

Tippett, Sir Michael (Kemp)

BORN: January 2, 1905—London
DIED: January 8, 1998—London
HISTORICAL PERIOD: Modern
COMPOSITIONAL MEDIA: Orchestra, choral, chamber music, opera, keyboard, songs.
IMPORTANT ITEMS: Notable works include the opera "King Priam."

T

Toch, Ernst

BORN: December 7, 1887—Vienna
DIED: October 1, 1964—Los Angeles
HISTORICAL PERIOD: Modern
COMPOSITIONAL MEDIA: Orchestra, chamber
music, choral, keyboard, opera, songs, film.
IMPORTANT ITEMS: Award-winning composer and
author who settled in the United States in 1934.
Awarded the Pulitzer Prize in 1956 for his "Third
Symphony."

Torelli, Giuseppe

BORN: April 22, 1658—Verona, Italy
DIED: February 8, 1709—Bologna, Italy
HISTORICAL PERIOD: Baroque
COMPOSITIONAL MEDIA: Orchestra, chamber
music, choral.
IMPORTANT ITEMS: Professional violinist and one
of the first composers of the concerto grosso.

Townshend, Pete [Peter] (Dennis Blandford)

BORN: May 19, 1945—Chiswick, England
HISTORICAL PERIOD: Modern (Popular).
COMPOSITIONAL MEDIA: Popular songs.
IMPORTANT ITEMS: Singer, guitarist and songwriter
for the group The Who. Notable works include the
song "My Generation" and the rock opera "Tommy."

Torke, Michael

BORN: September 22, 1961—Milwaukee, WI
HISTORICAL PERIOD: Modern
COMPOSITIONAL MEDIA: Orchestra, chamber
music, keyboard, choral, opera, ballet.
IMPORTANT ITEMS: Award winning composer and
pianist. Compositions incorporate rock, jazz and
classical styles.

Tudor, David (Eugene)

BORN: January 20, 1926—Philadelphia, PA
HISTORICAL PERIOD: Modern
COMPOSITIONAL MEDIA: Chamber music, ballet, electronic.
IMPORTANT ITEMS: Pioneer in electronic music techniques.

Türk, Daniel Gottlob

BORN: August 10, 1750—Clausnitz, Saxony
DIED: August 26, 1813—Halle, Germany
HISTORICAL PERIOD: Classical
COMPOSITIONAL MEDIA: Choral, keyboard, orchestra, opera, songs.
IMPORTANT ITEMS: Notable works include keyboard and choral compositions.

U

Ussachevsky, Vladimir (Alexis)

BORN: November 3, 1911—Hailar, Manchuria
DIED: January 2, 1990—New York
HISTORICAL PERIOD: Modern
COMPOSITIONAL MEDIA: Electronic, chamber music, orchestra, keyboard, choral, film, radio, TV.
IMPORTANT ITEMS: Settled in the United States in 1930. Compositions incorporate electronic and tape techniques. Collaborated with Otto Luening.

V

Van Heusen, Jimmy
[real name: Edward Chester Babcock]

BORN: January 26, 1913—Syracuse, NY
HISTORICAL PERIOD: Modern (Popular)
COMPOSITIONAL MEDIA: Popular songs, film, TV.
IMPORTANT ITEMS: Notable songs include "High Hopes," "Swingin' on a Star" and "Love and Marriage."

Varèse, Edgard (Victor Achille Charles)

BORN: December 22, 1883—Paris
DIED: November 6, 1965—New York
HISTORICAL PERIOD: Modern
COMPOSITIONAL MEDIA: Orchestra, chamber music, choral, electronic.
IMPORTANT ITEMS: Settled in New York in 1915. Notable works include "Ionisation" for percussion orchestra.

Vaughan Williams, Ralph

BORN: October 12, 1872—Down Ampney, England
DIED: August 26, 1958—London
HISTORICAL PERIOD: Late Romantic/Modern
COMPOSITIONAL MEDIA: Orchestra, chamber music, ballet, keyboard, choral, opera, songs, theatrical, film, band.
IMPORTANT ITEMS: Prolific composer of melodic music. Notable works include "3 Norfolk Rhapsodies" and "Fantasia on a Theme by Thomas Tallis."

Verdi, Giuseppe (Fortunino Francesco)

BORN: October 9, 1813—Le Roncole, Italy
DIED: January 27, 1901—Milan, Italy
HISTORICAL PERIOD: Romantic
COMPOSITIONAL MEDIA: Opera, choral, chamber music, songs, keyboard.
IMPORTANT ITEMS: One of the greatest opera composers of all time. Notable works include the "Requiem" and the operas "Rigoletto," "Il Trovatore," "La forza del destino," "La Traviata," "Aida" and "Otello."

Victoria (Vittoria), Tomas Luis de

BORN: c. 1548—Avila, Spain
DIED: August 20, 1611—Madrid
HISTORICAL PERIOD: Late Renaissance
COMPOSITIONAL MEDIA: Choral.
IMPORTANT ITEMS: One of the most important composers of sacred choral music of the late Renaissance.

Villa-Lobos, Heitor

BORN: March 5, 1887—Rio de Janeiro, Brazil
DIED: November 17, 1959—Rio de Janeiro, Brazil
HISTORICAL PERIOD: Modern
COMPOSITIONAL MEDIA: Orchestra, chamber music, keyboard, choral, opera, ballet, songs.
IMPORTANT ITEMS: Prolific composer whose compositions incorporate Brazilian folk music. Notable works include "Bachianas brasileiras No. 5" for soprano voice and eight cellos.

V

Viotti, Giovanni Battista

BORN: May 12, 1755—Fontanetto da Po, Italy
DIED: March 3, 1824—London

HISTORICAL PERIOD: Classical
COMPOSITIONAL MEDIA: Orchestra, chamber music, keyboard.
IMPORTANT ITEMS: Professional violinist and composer.

Vivaldi, Antonio (Lucio)

BORN: March 4, 1678—Venice
DIED: July 28, 1741—Vienna
HISTORICAL PERIOD: Late Baroque
COMPOSITIONAL MEDIA: Orchestra, opera, chamber music, choral.
IMPORTANT ITEMS: Prolific composer best remembered for "The Four Seasons" for solo violin and strings.

W

Wagner, (Wilhelm) Richard

BORN: May 22, 1813—Leipzig, Germany
DIED: February 13, 1883—Venice
HISTORICAL PERIOD: Late Romantic
COMPOSITIONAL MEDIA: Opera, orchestra, chamber music, keyboard, choral, opera, songs.
IMPORTANT ITEMS: One of the most influential composers of opera who believed that story and music should have equal importance. He called his operas "Music Dramas." Notable operas include "Der fliegende Holländer," "Tannhäuser," "Lohengrin," "Der Ring des Nibelungen," "Tristan und Isolde" and "Die Meistersinger von Nürnberg."

W

Waldteufel (Lévy), Emil

BORN: December 9, 1837—Strasbourg, France
DIED: February 12, 1915—Paris
HISTORICAL PERIOD: Romantic
COMPOSITIONAL MEDIA: Orchestral.
IMPORTANT ITEMS: Composer of numerous waltzes and other dances.

Waller, (Thomas Wright) "Fats"

BORN: May 21, 1904—New York
DIED: December 15, 1943—Kansas City, MO
HISTORICAL PERIOD: Modern (Popular)
COMPOSITIONAL MEDIA: Musicals, popular songs, jazz.
IMPORTANT ITEMS: Significant jazz pianist and composer. Notable songs include "Ain't Misbehavin'."

Walton, Sir William (Turner)

BORN: March 29, 1902—Oldham, England
DIED: March 8, 1983—Ischia, Italy
HISTORICAL PERIOD: Modern
COMPOSITIONAL MEDIA: Orchestra, chamber music, ballet, keyboard, choral, opera, songs, film.
IMPORTANT ITEMS: Notable works include the chamber piece "Facade" for reciter and 6 instruments, and the oratorio "Belshazzar's Feast."

Ward, Robert

BORN: September 13, 1917—Cleveland, OH
HISTORICAL PERIOD: Modern
COMPOSITIONAL MEDIA: Orchestra, choral, chamber music, keyboard, opera, songs.
IMPORTANT ITEMS: Awarded the Pulitzer Prize in 1962 for his opera "The Crucible."

Webber, Andrew Lloyd   See Lloyd Webber, Andrew.

Weber, Carl Maria (Friedrich Ernst) von

> BORN: November 18, 1786—Eutin, Germany
> DIED: June 5, 1826—London
> HISTORICAL PERIOD: Late Classical/Early Romantic
> COMPOSITIONAL MEDIA: Orchestra, opera, chamber music, keyboard, choral, songs, theatrical.
> IMPORTANT ITEMS: Notable works include the operas "Der Freischütz" and "Oberon."

Webern, Anton (Freidrich Wilhelm von)

> BORN: December 3, 1883—Vienna
> DIED: September 15, 1945—Mittersill, Germany
> HISTORICAL PERIOD: Modern
> COMPOSITIONAL MEDIA: Songs, choral, orchestra, chamber music, keyboard.
> IMPORTANT ITEMS: Compositions incorporate twelve-tone techniques and emphasize tone color. Notable works include "Five Pieces" for orchestra.

Weill, Kurt (Julian)

> BORN: March 2, 1900—Dessau, Germany
> DIED: April 3, 1950—New York
> HISTORICAL PERIOD: Modern
> COMPOSITIONAL MEDIA: Songs, musicals, orchestra, chamber music, keyboard, choral, opera, film.
> IMPORTANT ITEMS: Settled in the United States in 1935. Compositions incorporate jazz, atonal, polyrhythmic and polytonal elements. Notable works include the "Threepenny Opera" which includes the song "Mack the Knife" and the musical play "Lady in the Dark."

Weinberger, Jaromir

BORN: January 8, 1896—Prague
DIED: August 8, 1967—St. Petersburg, FL
HISTORICAL PERIOD: Late Romantic/Modern
COMPOSITIONAL MEDIA: Orchestra, chamber
music, keyboard, choral, opera, songs, band.
IMPORTANT ITEMS: Settled in the United States in
1939. Notable works include the polka and fugue
from the opera "Schwanda the Bagpiper."

Weisgall, Hugo (David)

BORN: October 13, 1912—Eibenschütz, Moravia
HISTORICAL PERIOD: Modern
COMPOSITIONAL MEDIA: Chamber music, ballet,
choral, opera, songs.
IMPORTANT ITEMS: Award winning composer and
teacher.

Widor, Charles-Marie

BORN: February 21, 1844—Lyons, France
DIED: March 12, 1937—Paris
HISTORICAL PERIOD: Late Romantic
COMPOSITIONAL MEDIA: Keyboard, opera, ballet,
orchestra, choral, chamber music.
IMPORTANT ITEMS: Notable works include 10 organ
symphonies.

Willan, Healey

BORN: October 12, 1880—Balham, England
DIED: February 16, 1968—Toronto, Canada
HISTORICAL PERIOD: Modern
COMPOSITIONAL MEDIA: Orchestra, chamber
music, keyboard, choral, opera, band, songs, radio.
IMPORTANT ITEMS: Organist, teacher and prolific
composer.

Williams Sr., Hank (Hiram)

BORN: September 17, 1923—Georgiana, AL
DIED: January 1, 1953—Oak Hill, VA
HISTORICAL PERIOD: Modern (Popular)
COMPOSITIONAL MEDIA: Popular songs.
IMPORTANT ITEMS: Popular singer, guitarist and
songwriter of country music. Notable songs include
"Hey, Good Lookin'" and "Move It On Over."

Williams, John (Towner)

BORN: February 8, 1932—New York
HISTORICAL PERIOD: Modern
COMPOSITIONAL MEDIA: Film, orchestra, chamber
music.
IMPORTANT ITEMS: Notable film scores include
"Jaws," "Star Wars," "ET (The Extraterrestrial)," "Close
Encounters of the Third Kind," "Jurassic Park" and
"Schindler's List."

Wilson, Brian (Douglas)

BORN: June 20, 1942—Hawthorne, CA
HISTORICAL PERIOD: Modern (Popular)
COMPOSITIONAL MEDIA: Popular Songs.
IMPORTANT ITEMS: A member of the surf-music
rock group The Beach Boys. Notable songs include
"Surfin' USA" and "Help Me Rhonda."

Wolf, Hugo (Filipp Jakob)

BORN: March 13, 1860—Windischgraz, Austria
DIED: February 22, 1903—Vienna
HISTORICAL PERIOD: Late Romantic
COMPOSITIONAL MEDIA: Keyboard, songs, choral,
orchestra, chamber music, opera.
IMPORTANT ITEMS: Notable works include the
"Italian Serenade" and numerous lieder.

W

Wonder, Stevie
[real name: Steveland Judkins Hardaway]

BORN: May 13, 1951—Saginaw, MI
HISTORICAL PERIOD: Modern (Popular)
COMPOSITIONAL MEDIA: Popular songs, film.
IMPORTANT ITEMS: A significant composer of
popular songs. Notable songs include "You Are the
Sunshine of My Life," and "I Just Called to Say I Love
You."

Wuorinen, Charles

BORN: June 9, 1938—New York
HISTORICAL PERIOD: Modern
COMPOSITIONAL MEDIA: Chamber music,
orchestra, keyboard, choral, electronic.
IMPORTANT ITEMS: Compositions incorporate
electronic, tape and serial techniques. Awarded the
Pulitzer Prize in 1970 for "Time's Encomium" for
synthesized sound.

X

Xenakis, Yannis

BORN: May 29, 1922—Braila, Rumania
DIED: February 4, 2001—Paris
HISTORICAL PERIOD: Modern
COMPOSITIONAL MEDIA: Chamber music,
orchestra, keyboard, ballet, electronic.
IMPORTANT ITEMS: Compositions incorporate
aleatory, computer and mathematical techniques.

Y, Z

Young, La Monte (Thornton)

BORN: October 14, 1935—Bern, ID
HISTORICAL PERIOD: Modern
COMPOSITIONAL MEDIA: Chamber music, electronic, keyboard.
IMPORTANT ITEMS: Highly experimental composer

Zappa, Frank

BORN: December 21, 1940—Baltimore, MD
DIED: December 4, 1993—Los Angeles
HISTORICAL PERIOD: Modern (Popular)
COMPOSITIONAL MEDIA: Popular songs, film, orchestra, choral.
IMPORTANT ITEMS: Best known for popular songs that combined classical and jazz elements.

Zemlinsky, Alexander (Von)

BORN: October 14, 1871—Vienna
DIED: March 15, 1942—Larchmont, NY
HISTORICAL PERIOD: Late Romantic
COMPOSITIONAL MEDIA: Opera, chamber music, orchestra, choral, songs.
IMPORTANT ITEMS: Teacher of Arnold Schoenberg

Zwilich, Ellen Taaffe

BORN: April 30, 1939—Miami, FL
HISTORICAL PERIOD: Modern
COMPOSITIONAL MEDIA: Orchestra, chamber music, ballet, vocal.
IMPORTANT ITEMS: Awarded the Pulitzer Prize in 1983 for her "Symphony No. 1."

THEORY

NOTES

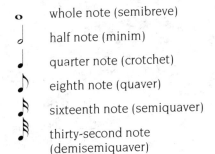

- whole note (semibreve)
- half note (minim)
- quarter note (crotchet)
- eighth note (quaver)
- sixteenth note (semiquaver)
- thirty-second note (demisemiquaver)

Terms in parentheses are those used in the United Kingdom and other countries.

NOTE RELATIONSHIPS

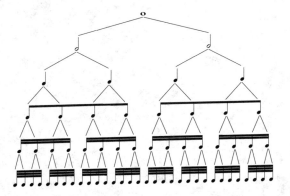

RESTS

▬	whole rest (semibreve rest)
▬	half rest (minim rest)
𝄽	quarter rest (crotchet rest)
𝄾	eighth rest (quaver rest)
𝄿	sixteenth rest (seniquaver rest)
𝅀	thirty-second rest (demisemiquaver rest)

Terms in parentheses are those used in the United Kingdom and other countries.

REST RELATIONSHIPS

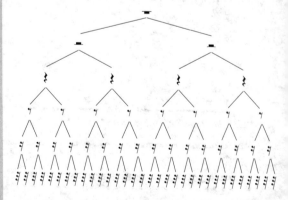

SCALE TYPES

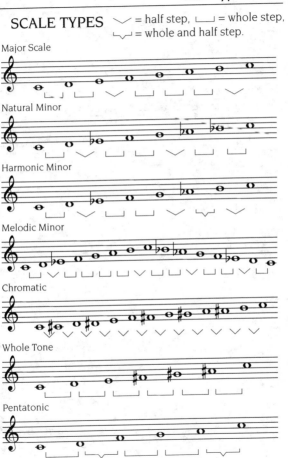

MAJOR SCALES

A♭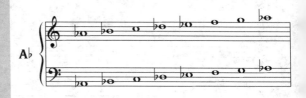

A

B♭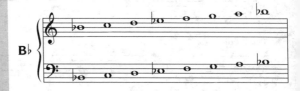

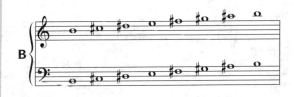

B

C♭

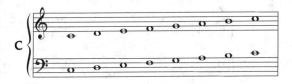

C

C♯

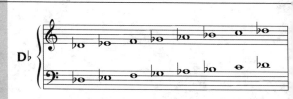

D♭

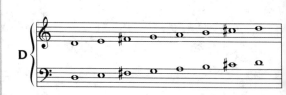

D

E♭

E

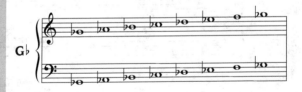

NATURAL MINOR SCALES

A♭
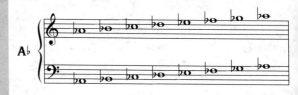

A
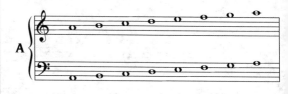

A♯
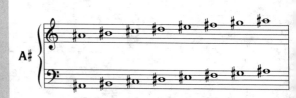

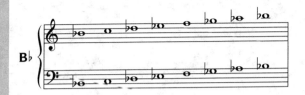

D

D♯
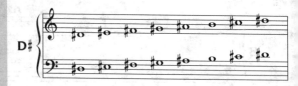

E♭
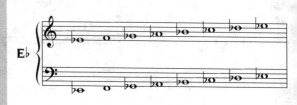

E
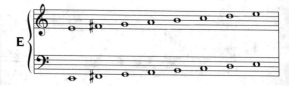

F

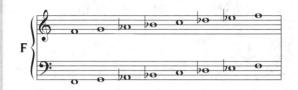

F#

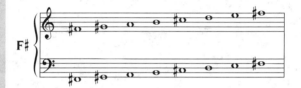

G

G#

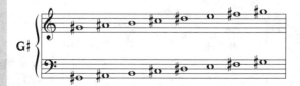

HARMONIC MINOR SCALES

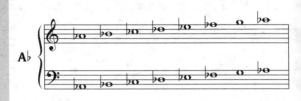

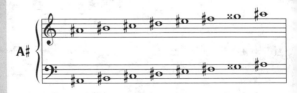

B♭

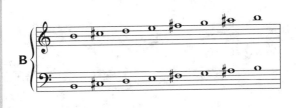

B

C

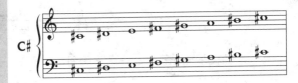

C♯

D

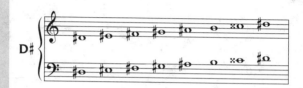

D#

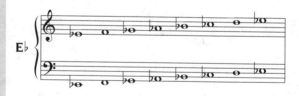

E♭

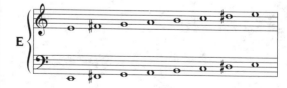

E

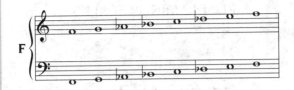

F

F♯

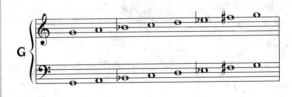

G

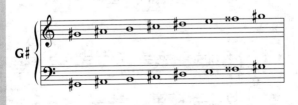

G♯

MELODIC MINOR SCALES

Ab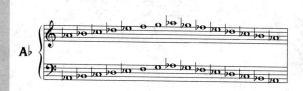

A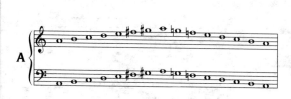

A#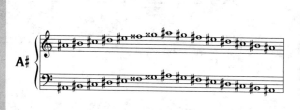

Bb

B

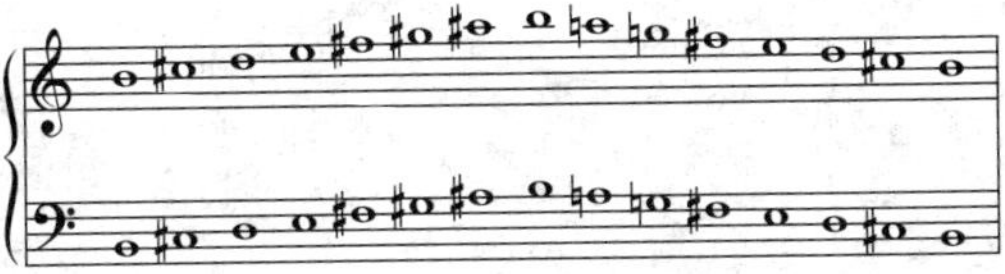

C

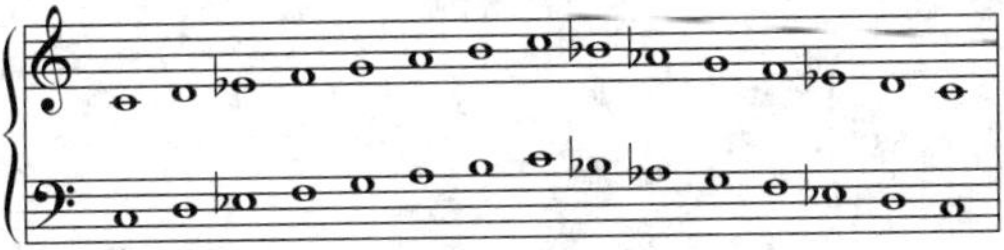

C♯

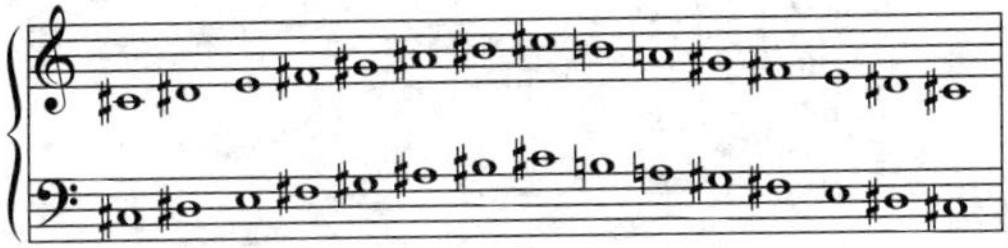

D

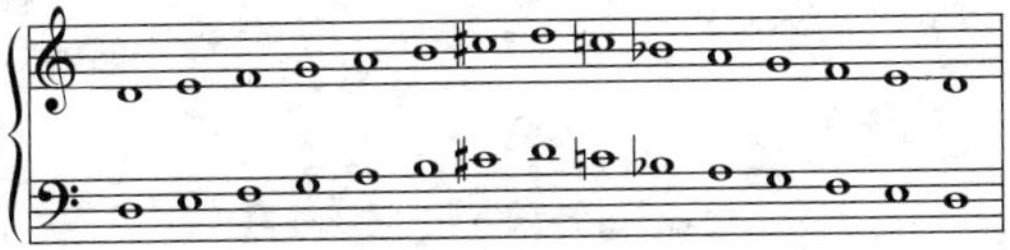

D♯

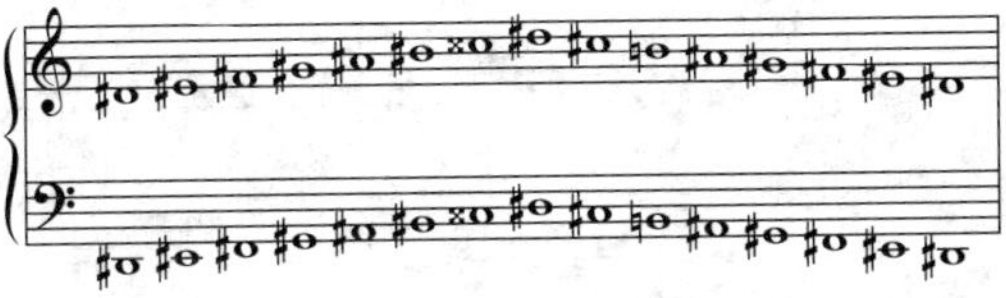

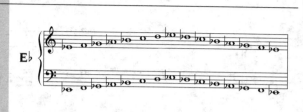

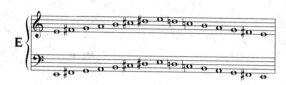

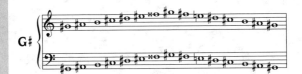

G♯

MODES

On the white keys
of a keyboard: Starting on C:

Ionian (identical to major scale)

Dorian

Phrygian

On the white keys
of a keyboard:　　　Starting on C:

Lydian

Mixolydian

Aeolian (identical to the natural minor scale)

Locrian

CIRCLE OF FIFTHS

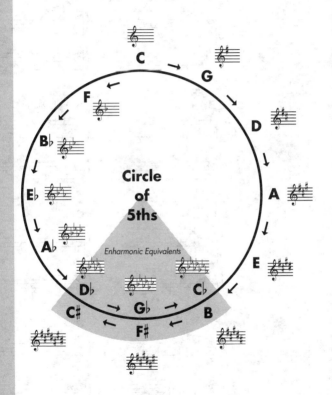

KEY SIGNATURES

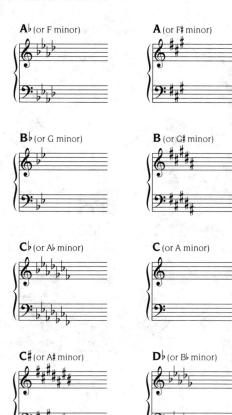

INTERVALS

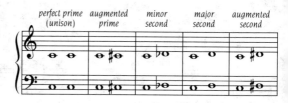

CHORD TYPES

Major
(root, major third,
perfect fifth)

Minor
(root, minor third,
perfect fifth)

Diminished
(root, minor third,
diminished fifth)

Augmented
(root, major third,
augmented fifth)

Dominant Seventh
(root, major third, perfect
fifth, minor seventh)

Major Seventh
(root, major third, perfect
fifth, major seventh)

CHORD CHART

Major
Minor
Diminished
Augmented
Dominant Seventh
D♭
D
E♭
E
F
F♯
G♭
G

ORNAMENTS

DYNAMIC MARKS

pianississimo	*ppp*	Very, very soft.
pianissimo	*pp*	Very soft.
piano	*p*	Soft.
mezzo piano	*mp*	Moderately soft.
mezzo forte	*mf*	Moderatly loud.
forte	*f*	Loud.
fortissimo	*ff*	Very loud.
fortississimo	*fff*	Very, very loud.
crescendo	<	Gradually get louder (Abbr.—*cresc.*).
decrescendo	>	Gradually get softer (Abbr.—*decresc.*).
diminuendo	*dim.*	Gradually get softer.

MUSIC SYMBOLS

Flat	♭	
Sharp	♯	
Natural	♮	
Double Flat	♭♭	
Double Sharp	×	
Fermata (Pause)*	⌒	Hold the note longer than its normal value.
Marcato	∧	Accented, stressed.
Accent	>	Play the note a little louder.
Staccato	.	Play the note short.

*"Pause" is the term used in the United Kingdom and other countries.

Staccatissimo	▾	Play the note as short as possible.
Tenuto	_	Hold the note for its full value.
Mezzo Staccato	⨪	Play the note short, but not as short as staccato.
Breath Mark	,	
Down Bow	⊓	
Up Bow	V	
Caesura	//	
a due	a2	
quindicesima	*15ma*	Play the note(s) two octaves higher.
all'ottava	*8va*	Play the note(s) one octave higher.
ottava bassa	*8va bassa* [or *8va* placed below the note(s)]	Play the note(s) one octave lower.

TEMPO MARKS

Largo	Very slow and broad.
Larghetto	Slightly faster than largo.
Adagio	Faster than largo but slower than andante.
Lento	Slow.
Andante	A moderate graceful tempo.
Andantino	Slightly faster than andante.
Moderato	A moderate tempo.
Allegretto	Slightly slower than allegro.
Allegro	Fast.
Presto	Very fast.
Prestissimo	Extremely fast.
ritardando	Becoming gradually slower (abbr.—*rit.*).
accelerando	Becoming gradually faster (abbr.—*accel.*).

REPEAT SIGNS

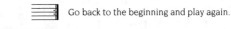

Go back to the beginning and play again.

Go back to the repeat sign and play again.

First time only   Second time only

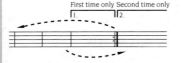

Play 1st ending first time repeat to the beginning, then skip 1st ending and play 2nd ending.

D.C. al Fine   Go back to the beginning and end at *Fine.*

D.C. al Coda   Go back to the beginning and play to the coda sign (⊕), then skip to the **Coda** to end the piece.

D.S. al Fine   Go back to the sign (𝄋) and end at *Fine.*

D.S. al Coda   Go back to the sign (𝄋) and play to the coda sign (⊕), then skip to the **Coda** to end the piece.

Repeat the previous measure.

Repeat the previous two measures.

GUITAR TABLATURE & NOTATION

Tablature is a system of notation that graphically represents the strings and frets of the guitar fingerboard. Each note is indicated by placing a number, which indicates the fret or finger position to be picked, on the appropriate string. For example:

4th String, 5th Fret

1st String, 10th Fret
2nd String, 10th Fret ⎤ Played together

An open G chord

Arpeggio

Strike the notes of the chord shown from the bottom to the top. Quickly release each note after striking.

Bends

One- or Two-Note Up Bend: Pick the first note, then bend the string to sound up either one or two frets.

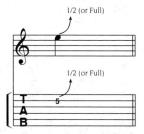

Pick Bend and Release: Pick the first note, bend the string up one or two frets to sound the higher (second) note, then straighten the string to sound the original (first) note again. Pick only the first note.

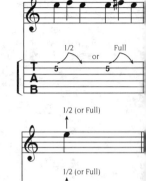

Bend and Then Pick: Bend the first note up one or two frets before picking it. This is usually followed by a down bend.

Harmonics

Natural Harmonics: The fret finger lightly touches the string over the fret, and then the string is picked. A chimelike sound is produced.

Artificial Harmonics:
After the note is fretted
normally, the pick hand
lightly touches the
string at the fret (in
parentheses) with one
finger while plucking
with another.

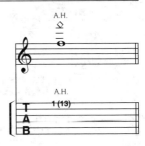

Mutes

Muffled Strings: A
percussive sound is
produced by laying the
fret hand across the
strings without
depressing them to the
fretboard, and then
striking the strings with
the pick hand.

Palm Mute (P.M.): The
note is partially muted
by the pick hand by
lightly touching the
string or strings just
before the bridge.

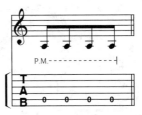

Slides

Slide: Pick the lower (first) note, then slide the fret finger up to sound the higher (second) note. The higher note is not picked again.

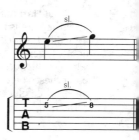

Long Slide: Strike the note during the slide up to the desired note.

Pick Slide: The edge of the pick slides down the entire string. A scratchy, downward sound is produced.

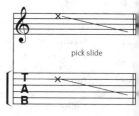

Tapping

Hammer-on: Pick the lower (first) note, then hammer-on (tap down) the higher (second) note with another finger. Pick only the first note. These notes are always played on the same string.

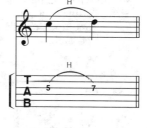

Pull-off: Place both fret fingers on the two notes to be played. Pick the higher (first) note, then pull-off (raise up) the finger of the higher note while keeping the lower note fretted. Pick only the first note.

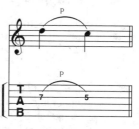

Tapping: Tap down on the fretted string with the index or middle finger of the pick hand. This is usually followed by a pull-off to sound the lower note.

Tremolos

Tremolo Picking: The string is picked down-and-up as rapidly as possible.

Vibrato

Pick the string as the fret finger or a tremolo bar rapidly rolls back and forth or bends up and down, making the note sound slightly higher and lower. An exaggerated vibrato can be achieved by rolling the fret finger a greater distance.

INSTRUMENT
& VOCAL
RANGES

Notes in parentheses are those which may be included on some instruments, but not all.

WOODWINDS

Piccolo (in C)

written: sounds one octave
                                  higher:

Flute

(sounds as written)

Alto Flute in G

written: sounds a perfect
                                  fourth lower:

Bass Flute

written: sounds one octave
lower:

Oboe

(sounds as written)

English Horn (in F)

written: sounds a perfect
fifth lower:

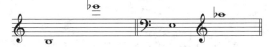

Heckelphone (in C) (infrequently used)

written: sounds one octave
lower:

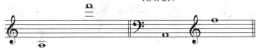

Bassoon

(sounds as written)

Contrabassoon

written: sounds one octave
                                     lower:

E♭ Clarinet

written: sounds a minor
                                     third higher:

B♭ Clarinet

written: sounds a major
                                     second lower:

A Clarinet

written: sounds a minor
                            third lower:

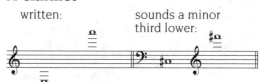

E♭ Alto Clarinet

written: sounds a major
                            sixth lower:

B♭ Bass Clarinet

written: sounds a major
                            ninth lower:

E♭ Contra Alto Clarinet

written: sounds one octave
                            plus a major sixth
                            lower:

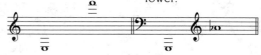

B♭ Contrabass Clarinet

written:

sounds one octave
plus a major ninth
lower:

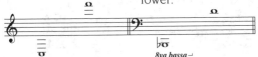

8va bassa

E♭ Sopranino Saxophone (infrequently used)

written:

sounds a minor
third higher:

B♭ Soprano Saxophone

written:

sounds a major
second lower:

E♭ Alto Saxophone

written:

sounds a major
sixth lower:

B♭ Tenor Saxophone

written: sounds a major
ninth lower:

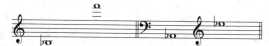

E♭ Baritone Saxophone

written: sounds one octave
plus a major sixth
lower:

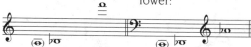

B♭ Bass Saxophone (infrequently used)

written: sounds one octave
plus a major ninth
lower:

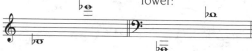

Soprano Recorder

written: sounds one octave
higher:

Alto Recorder

(sounds as written)

Tenor Recorder

(sounds as written)

Bass Recorder

written: sounds one octave
                            lower:

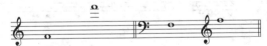

Bagpipes

written: sounds a minor
                            second higher:

BRASS

French Horn (in F)

written: sounds a perfect
                            fifth lower:

Note: In many older compositions, horn parts written
in bass clef sound a perfect fourth higher.

B♭ Tenor Wagner Tuba

written: sounds a major
                            second lower:

F Bass Wagner Tuba

written: sounds a perfect
                            fifth lower:

Piccolo Trumpet in B♭ (infrequently used)

written: sounds a minor
                                  seventh higher:

Piccolo Trumpet in A

written: sounds a major
                                  sixth higher:

Trumpet in E♭

written: sounds a minor
                                  third higher:

Trumpet in D (infrequently used)

written: sounds a major
                                  second higher:

Trumpet in C
(sounds as written)

Trumpet in B♭ (Cornet)

written: sounds a major
                            second lower:

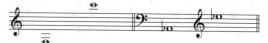

Bass Trumpet in E♭ (infrequently used)

written: sounds a major
                            sixth lower:

Bass Trumpet in C (infrequently used)

written: sounds one octave
                            lower:

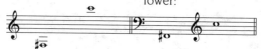

Bass Trumpet in B♭ (infrequently used)

written: sounds a major
                            ninth lower:

Flugelhorn (in B♭)

written: sounds a major
                            second lower:

Alto Trombone (infrequently used)
(sounds as written)

Tenor Trombone
(sounds as written)

Bass Trombone
(sounds as written)

Baritone Horn (Euphonium) Treble Clef

written: sounds a major
                                      ninth lower:

Baritone Horn (Euphonium) Bass Clef

(sounds as written)

Tuba
(sounds as written)

8va bassa⌐

STRINGED INSTRUMENTS

Violin (sounds as written)

open strings: range:

Viola (sounds as written)

open strings: range:

Violoncello (Cello) (sounds as written)

open strings: range:

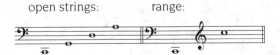

Double Bass (sounds one octave lower)

open strings: written range:

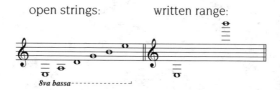

Guitar (sounds one octave lower)

open strings: written range:

Mandolin (sounds as written)

open strings: range:

Ukulele (sounds as written)

open strings: range:

Banjo (Five String)
(sounds one octave lower)

standard tuning
open strings: written range:

Banjo (Four-String Tenor)
(sounds one octave lower)

open strings: written range:

PERCUSSION

Timpani (sounds as written)

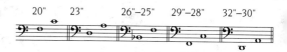

20"   23"   26"–25"   29"–28"   32"–30"

Glockenspiel (orchestra bells)

written: sounds two octaves
                            higher:

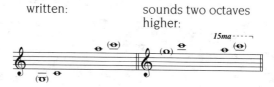

Xylophone

written: sounds one octave
                            higher:

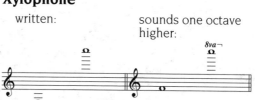

Vibraphone

(sounds as written)

Chimes (tubular bells)

(sounds as written)*

* Because of complex overtones, some hear chimes as sounding an octave lower than written.

Marimba

(sounds as written)

OTHER INSTRUMENTS

Accordion (sounds as written)

keyboard: bass   chords:

patterns:

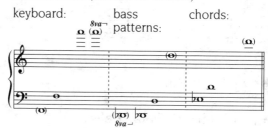

Celesta

written: sounds one
octave higher:

Piano (sounds as written)

Harp (sounds as written)

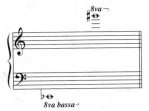

Harpsichord (sounds as written)

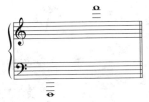

Harmonica—12-hole chromatic
(sounds as written)

Harmonica—10-hole diatonic in C
(sounds as written)

VOICES (with the exception of tenor,
all sound as written)

Soprano

Alto

Tenor*

written: sounds one octave
lower:

*Tenor parts are sometimes written
in bass clef and sound as written.

Baritone

Bass